A YANK BACK TO ENGLAND

A YANK BACK TO

THE PRODIGAL
TOURIST RETURNS

DENIS LIPMAN

Boston

A Yank Back to England: The Prodigal Tourist Returns

First published by GemmaMedia in 2010.

GemmaMedia
230 Commercial Street
Boston MA 02109 USA
617 938 9833
www.gemmamedia.com

Printed in the United States of America

Cover design by Night & Day Design

12 11 10 09 08 12345

ISBN: 978-1-934848-24-1

Library of Congress Preassigned Control Number (PCN) applied for

For Frances

Contents

Year Four: A Carriage House on the Saxon Shore   163

Year Five: A Coastguard's House on a Pebble Beach   215

Year Six: A Regency Cottage on a Bridle Path   269

Introduction

CLINGING TO THE FAR EASTERN EDGE of Greater London, where the land is flat and low, is a place called Dagenham. Not Dagenham as in Birmingham, Alabama, but Dagenham as in "Dag-nem," Essex, sounding as foreshortened and blandly functional as the place looks. Entering Dagenham from the East End of London, detached houses become virtually nonexistent. Even semi-detached houses grow scarce until you reach the undefined edges of the town, and then they disappear entirely. The vast majority of homes are joined together in endless rows, covered in sand-blasted stucco the color of long-congealed blood. In front are porches and small yards about ten feet square contained within green and mustard yellow privet hedges, veined with dust, snapped into shape once a year by council-employed hedge trimmers. There are no trees lining the streets.

"Dagenham. You can't possibly come from Dagenham," a flamboyant acquaintance in the West End of London once told me. "You simply must tell people you come from 'Darn-em,' and you must place your hand over your mouth as you say it, just in case."

Just in case? In case of what? I felt an urge to defend the place, but then thought better of it.

The Becontree Housing Estate in Dagenham, where I grew up, was once the largest rent-controlled housing project in the world. This is not the bucolic, picturesque part of the Thames that gently meanders down from the honey-hued Chiltern Hills. This is the carbolic, industrial end of it. Where Dagenham banks against the Thames, it's more estuary than river, more barges than badgers, more mud than mole, more Fart in the Reeds than Wind in the Willows.

The Dagenham marshes once stretched for miles, snaking along the edge of the river as it made its way towards the English Channel. The marshes were filled with bright, creamy pea soup bogs and stagnant rivulets like so many varicose veins that discolored the landscape. This was close to the marshland Dickens described in *Great Expectations*, the place where Magwitch scared the daylights out of Pip. It scared me. No convicts now, but when I was a boy there was still a vast undeveloped tract of marshland. Now, of course, it would be called wetlands, a bird sanctuary, a *cause celebre* for a pristine environment. Back then, fleets of rotating cement mixers were itching to fill it all in.

Henry Ford purchased the neglected marsh of Dagenham very cleverly, and very cheaply, in the early part of the twentieth century. He drained the marsh, covered it in concrete, tarmac, and railway track. He then built one of the biggest car plants in Europe. He also built a large jetty on the river and so gained access to the trading routes of the world. Around his factory, the housing estates of Dagenham grew as the village shrank. What green bogs of marsh remained now reflected the rainbow colors of oil spillage and industrial pollution. The fish were no more and the birds had flown, but people migrated here in flocks. The Ford Motor Company offered employment to thousands of Cockneys from East and South London, and from farther afield. The lure of steady work also attracted Irish and Scottish immigrants. Some came from Wales and went home at the weekend. But the vast majority of the Ford workforce lived in Dagenham, in very small two-bedroom, terraced houses. Concrete, tarmac, and no trees.

Interestingly, none of the homes were built with garages. Workers at the Ford plant were never expected to own the cars they helped to build. But decades later the streets, like the marshes before, were all filled in, not with concrete this time but with cars. Parked on sidewalks. Parked on both sides of narrow streets. Parked on street corners. And some of these cars were even made by Ford.

Dagenham. "Call it Daggers," said another wag. Well, I called it home. I had returned every year for ten years, to see my parents and spend time with friends in Central London. But this time would be different. I was returning with my American wife, who was happy to visit family and see friends but also wanted to tour the country. The country? She had been to England before. What more could she possibly want to see? Hadn't she seen enough?

I had.

A Tiny Home on a Large Estate

CHAPTER 1

Dagenham

I PARKED OUR RENTED CAR on the sidewalk by a dusty privet hedge. I looked down the street—there was nowhere else to park. And there were still no trees. The front porch that was shared with the house next door was now enclosed with a mock Tudor façade, and glass doors were crisscrossed with black plastic leading. With Frances by my side, I entered the shared vestibule and knocked on the door of my parents' home.

"Hello, Dad! Mum, hello, old love."

Smiles. Hugs. Old eyes glinting with emotion. I pointed to Frances, nervous, almost casual.

"Smashing, isn't she, Mum?"

"I can see that!" More hugs.

"Sit yourself down, then." Mum beamed. Silence for a moment, then suddenly everyone was very busy. Lew sorted out teacups. Mum started reorganizing cake slices on a plate. A quiet happiness permeated the air.

"Come here, let me look at you then." Mum shuffled towards me and smiled approvingly. "My big son, how did you get so big?" I patted her hand. She grabbed mine suddenly, squeezed and shook it as if to make sure I was really there. "Still a toe-rag then, aren't you?"

I smiled, enjoying being called a toe-rag or cheeky kid, a smile away from trouble. It's almost a compliment. I stood up, stretched my fingertips, scratched the ceiling.

"Look, Mum, we've got to get this stuff upstairs. And we need to, you know—"

Lew stood up straight, chest out. "Now steady the buffs. Before you go upstairs and do your business—"

"Yes, Dad." I sighed.

"Now you listen, son, I gotta tell you straight. You too, gel," he said, wagging a finger at Frances. "The wedding. I know you wanted us both there. I know that. And I would've given my eyeteeth to be there but, at our age, son—"

"Dad, it's okay," I said, trying to sound reassuring.

"A few years ago, would've been different." Lew lowered his voice to a gruff whisper. "But now, your mother's got her legs—"

"It's okay, we understand. It's a long flight, even for us," said Frances.

"Well, you're both here now anyway, aren't you?" said Jessie, moving on.

"And we're bleedin' glad of it! And you, son, you must be busting!"

"I am, I certainly am!" I said, as I sprinted up the stairs to the loo.

"Your mother and me, we 'went' earlier, so you can take your time. Go on, up you go then! You know where everything is."

I knew where everything was. The house had one toilet. And everything lay in close proximity to everything else. Growing up, we seemed to live in even greater proximity to one another. Not that nearness led to closeness. Far from it. Our house was a tiny shoe box of a place, a two-bedroom, utilitarian, cold water council house, devoid of charm, with a living room and kitchen downstairs and two bedrooms and one bathroom upstairs, all connected by a very narrow passageway and a twisting staircase.

I came back downstairs and started maneuvering the large suitcase around the curve in the stairs. Propping it on the banisters, I slid it around and onto the straight part of the stairs. Using my knee, I propelled the suitcase up and forward. Frances grabbed it and tugged it onto the landing.

Across the tiny landing was my equally tiny bedroom, about eight feet wide by ten feet long. I had shared it with my older brother Tony, or he had reluctantly shared it with me. Two small beds, with a gap between them that could only be negotiated by walking sideways. But something had changed. The tiny beds had been replaced by one twin. A small piece of red carpet now covered part of the floor and, beyond this, the mottled green, black, and yellow lino looked as it always had, like camouflage. Most of the other fixtures remained the same, including the small dark wood wardrobe, a tiny dresser, and a bookcase custom-made by a neighbor to fit over a defunct gas fire. In the ceiling, a clear bulb with a daddy long legs filament hung below a pleated plastic lampshade. The damp stain that always looked to me like the silhouette of Mister Punch was still up there. Oatmeal and gold-colored curtains hung on either side of the window, and the brown-red flowered wallpaper, although faded, still clung tenaciously to the walls. We looked around the dimly lit room, trying to figure out where and how to open our suitcase.

So little had changed. The boy scout sticker for Buckmore Park was still on the window, and a sticker for the movie *Zulu* remained on the library case, now devoid of books except for a few World War Two novels my dad re-read time and again. There was nothing more. Except what could not be seen but was always felt. The cold. The freezing, head-numbing cold.

For most of the year, this bedroom was so glacial my brother and I called it the sepulcher. Only the dead would find comfort in this chamber. I remember ranting and raving about it, and Lew growling at us but doing nothing to alleviate our discomfort. He imagined us to be young, spoiled wimps in need of toughening up. "Just get out of bed and get dressed quickly." That was his only advice. As a kid, I would wake in the morning, my nose and chin frozen, my head aching with cold. And there I would lay, watching my breath turn to mist. Perhaps it was how the room was situated, but if there was a wind anywhere in the vicinity, our room would somehow catch it, like a giant sail. Years later a space heater was installed, a useless lump of wrought iron. It was advertised as a "heat saver," and save heat it did, for it never gave out any heat at all. Mum bought it hoping to save money, and I supposed she did, because no one ever used it. This economical "heat saving" heater took hours to warm up, and all it succeeded in warming were the iron feet it stood on.

～

"Still bloody cold! Like brass monkeys up there, is it?" Lew chuckled good-naturedly.

"Yes! Just a bit." I shouted back down to him. "Hard to believe this is spring!"

He trundled upstairs with another room heater, then plugged it in.

"Don't forget to turn it off when you come out. You'll feel the benefit of it in a minute."

We thanked him profusely. This was an electric bar fire that glared a dangerous orange and managed to heat approximately nothing unless you got very, very close to it. Oh, well, better than nothing. I turned to my bed and there, on the pillow, was my old Teddy, whom I had since I was born. I gasped in horror. My parents had safety-pinned a welcome home note to his much-hugged, almost furless chest. I quickly removed the pin and tried to smooth a few strands of fur over the wound.

"Poor old chap."

"I think he'll survive," Frances said, humoring me.

I gave old Ted another hug and determined to take him with me back to the States. A boy and his bear. My wife smiled.

"I need to go to the bathroom now." Frances started for the door. I moved quickly to get ahead of her.

"Follow me," I said. "I'll explain how it works."

"Explain?" Frances raised her eyebrows a little. I tried to reassure her as best I could. The bathroom consisted of a huge toilet that looked like a well, above which was a big black cistern with a ball and chain attached to it, containing enough water to drown a sackful of cats. I explained rather apologetically that, after your toilet is completed, you must grip the ball attached to the chain, very hard. Then you step away from the bowl and pull down sharply.

"Whatever you do, do not remain seated when you flush, or remain in close proximity to the seat, and try not to attempt this procedure in a state of semi-undress. Here's why."

To demonstrate, I jerked the chain. Sound of clanking metal, thump of pipe, then suddenly a tidal wave of water gushed into the toilet bowl with the force of the Red Sea closing over the Egyptians. The water splashed downwards then spiraled upwards, splashing the seat and the immediate vicinity. Then, just as quickly as it had appeared, the water was sucked away, emitting an echoing burp followed by the sound of what can only be described as a giant gargling mouthwash. Then the cistern started to refill, making a steady shushing sound rounded off with a metallic clank.

"Spectacular, isn't it?" I could see Frances was impressed. "I'll leave you to it, then. Good luck, darling."

A couple of minutes passed.

"Where do I wash my hands?" asked Frances with growing concern in her voice. As there was no sink in the bathroom, I conceded that was a good question.

"Use the bath," I said.

Several inches from the toilet was a long narrow bathtub, under a heating cistern that resembled a megaton bomb. Such an object should have been located in an attic or stairwell, but here, the enormous canister was suspended ominously over the bath.

"Just put a stopper in and run some water in it, from the cistern." I added quickly, "And don't forget to mix!"

Mix! In the States, where cold and hot water come gently together, mixing is not required. In my parents' house, the hot water faucet spat liquid that could produce third degree burns on contact. By contrast, the cold faucet pumped out ice water that could congeal a slashed artery in a matter of seconds. The only way to survive the plumbing was to mix. Only when faucets were shut off was it safe to swirl the water and so create a bearable temperature in which hands could be washed. Probably another reason why the English are innately patient at supermarket checkouts, long suffering when waiting for hospital appointments, and very good at waiting for buses. Our Job-like forbearance is tested from the moment we wake up. The English who do not possess this kind of fortitude, like me, tend to emigrate.

I was starting to feel embarrassed, ashamed. This was my wife's first trip to Dagenham. I should have done a better job of preparing her. Why was I subjecting her to all the discomfort I had once endured? I should have taken her to a hotel, visited my parents and not stayed with them. Was I so cheap? Was I just not thinking? I had assumed that she would quickly adapt to the little inconveniences, minor annoyances, and eccentricities of living with my family. I assumed she would find them quirky, quaint, cute. But, why? I never did. I tried to apologize, explain, but it all came out sounding like someone who was feeling sorry for himself, which it was, but that just made it worse.

"It's okay. It really is okay. That's why it's called a family visit." She smiled. "And you owe me." Frances nailed it on the head. I hurried downstairs in pursuit of a large plastic bowl.

When I was a kid, daily ablutions took place in the kitchen, simply because this was the warmest room in the house. Everyone in my house washed, one after the other, in an unwritten pecking order, with Lew acting as bathhouse attendant. And because we had no running hot water, Lew would boil endless kettles of water and pour them into plastic bowls so that hands, faces, necks, and scuffed knees could be washed. On scout nights, when I had to wear my green-rimmed socks, I was obliged to wash my feet and remove days' worth of accumulated toe jam.

Friday night was bath night, and this was a ritual in itself. Bathing was a full frontal experience and took place in the freezing bathroom upstairs, far away from the bright warmth of the kitchen below. This procedure meant clambering into the steep, narrow, iron-clad tub. Bathing held special challenges, and not just because electricity was so expensive, but also because it all took so much time, a labor-intensive activity that required the patience of the bather and the willing assistance of the bath attendant.

Strangely enough, these weekly ablutions all began in the kitchen. Underneath the sink was a metal box my parents called "the copper." This was a huge, enameled, tub-like water heater that looked like a washing machine. Lew would rig a pump to it and, after a couple of hours, when the water was boiling hot, he would crank the pump back and forth and, gradually, in fits and starts, the water would be drawn up an ancient pipe and into the bath above. Like a runner at the start of a race, I would be positioned at the top of the stairs near the bathroom. A shallow amount of cold water would already be in the bath, freezing and waiting. Minutes would pass, and then it would happen. The water pipe would suddenly shudder and gurgle as the heated liquid ascended. Meanwhile, the spout in the bath would begin to waggle and meander around the top of the bath like a drunken snake, and eventually water would gush forth. Sounding like vomit, the boiling hot water would come out in spurts and erratic spasms, depending on how rigorously Lew cranked the lever below. A few steaming torrents later, the steady clonk-clonk of distant cranking would cease.

"That's it. That'll do for you!" Lew would shout up from below, and the water flow would cease.

"More!" I would yell down from the darkened landing. "The water's still freezing. Dad!"

"What you want up there, a swimming pool? Go on, get on with it!" was Lew's raspy reply, signifying that my ration of hot water had been issued and I would get no more. Arguing was pointless. Time was not on my side. The race was on. As quickly as I could, I would dart back to my room, take off my clothes, run back, and jump into the bath. I could not get undressed in the bathroom—there was no room, nowhere to hang clothes except over the toilet bowl. And the floor on bath night was always sodden wet. So, I would leap from room to room and bathe very quickly, before the water froze over like the North Atlantic in November. Afterwards, watery footprints froze on the cold oilcloth flooring as I sprinted back across the landing into my sepulcher. Here, I would rapidly finish drying myself, then throw on clothes I had previously laid out, saving precious seconds and saving myself from pneumonia, frostbite, a head cold, or a combination of all three. Seconds later I would be cleaning the bath for the next victim. Mercifully all this only happened once a week.

~

Although hot water pipes had since been installed, my parents still upheld many of the old cleansing and bathing rituals. Hands were still washed in cold water. A kettle of hot water cleaned faces and necks as well as cups and plates. And the extravagance of bathing was still reserved for Friday night.

"You alright in there?" I asked Frances tentatively. So much to explain.

Moments later Frances emerged ahead of the sound of rushing water. She drifted into the bedroom, lay down on the bed, and passed out. Jetlag had yet to catch up with me, so I covered my wife with an extra blanket and took the opportunity to go out for a walk with Lew.

We went "up the top," which meant walking up to the shops that cluster around the local railway station, a ten-minute stroll. He bought what he always did—a loaf of bread and a newspaper. The walk home took us past my old doctor's office, my infant school and my junior school, and the place where I went to boy scouts. I could see the church where I was christened. It was strange to walk through my old neighborhood; so little had changed. Dog poop still dotted the sidewalks, dust and dirt still banked against the edge of the pavement. The faces still looked sour, pinched, and old before their time. Even the clothing seemed the same. The quilted blue anoraks, the sweaty collars, the unwashed blue denim, the black and red striped track suits, the plastic baseball shoes, the rough felt zipper jackets—it was all as I remembered from years earlier. The lifestyle was being handed down from one generation to another, like an industrial Brigadoon. Only this village never disappeared. Not even for me. As I stood there in a quiet moment of panic, nothing seemed to have changed at all. My successes, my achievements faded away. I was a kid again, trying to escape the assembly line, trying to be a magician. Only then did I realize what I was really escaping from was not my past but what might have been my future. We walked on quickly. Jet lag crept up on me reassuringly and I smiled, eager to get back and to sleep.

~

"Come on, it's time for your tea," Lew yelled up to us in the bedroom.

"Tea" meant dinner in the working class world I grew up in. Frances and I made our way to the front room.

"It's coming to a good bit now. You should watch this, Den, you should." She waved her paw at the TV screen. She was watching the *EastEnders*, a soap opera beloved in England and championed by PBS viewers in the States. Daytime drivel, but the English accents gave it the patina of quality American soaps apparently lack.

"This is real life, this is, and I should know."

"Yes, Mum, you should know, and what you should know is that all those earthy Cockneys are a bunch of BBC actors, and the closest they've ever gotten to the East End is when they've had to shoot on location. If ever!"

My pearly words of knowingness went over her head. She flustered up.

"They're real Cockneys, they are. I know, I can tell!"

Lew entered the room, threatening to do the unforgivable.

"Come on now, Jessie, come and have your food. I'm turning it off!"

"I'll bloody well turn you off, I will! Hell next!" Mum cast a withering look at Lew, then flashed me a winning smile. "See what I have to put up with?"

Mum watched the end of her show, and then we ate dinner, now mostly cold. Roast lamb, mint sauce, roast potatoes, Yorkshire pudding, and Brussels sprouts. I complimented Mum, even though I knew Lew had done the cooking. Or most of it. He grunted in reply. This was normal. Evening meals in our house were always eaten in silence. The only sound above the clatter of cutlery was the radio broadcasting the six o'clock news. If anyone spoke during the news, all hell would break loose. Old habits die hard. Even now we ate as if we were mismatched Trappists. Frances, unaware of this mealtime vow of silence, thought someone was upset, so she tried to jolly us all up with cheery comments.

"Can't get lamb like this at home. The meat's almost white, like veal. It's really good," she said brightly.

Silence.

"The gravy is delicious," Frances went on.

"Granules." Mum was very matter-of-fact.

"Granules?"

"In a jar, the gravy comes in a jar, like the coffee," Mum explained.

After dinner, she showed Frances what the gravy product looked like, and she was right. It looked like instant coffee; hot water was added and gravy appeared.

"I made it, the gravy. And picked out the lamb. English. Lovely bit of English lamb. Tried to palm me off with a fatty bit, but I wasn't having it. Fatty. Not this. I bought this special." Mum did everything with the lamb except cook it.

After the table was cleared, Frances raided our bags and produced wedding photos and two sizable portions of cake we had frozen and brought over. One was chocolate, homemade, the other was a chunk of wedding cake we had kept for this occasion. While Frances sliced up the cake, my parents perused the pictures.

"Was it a church wedding?" Mum inquired.

"No, Mum, we're not religious, and Frances is Jewish, so—"

"Is she Jewish?"

"Yes, Mum."

"On both sides?" Mum looked directly at Frances.

"Yes. How about some cake?" asked Frances. "Chocolate or fruit cake, or both?"

Mum seemed reluctant to try either one. "I'm alright with my Benny. That's all I want." She smiled and turned red and cheerful, indicating the glass of Benedictine in her hand. "This'll do me alright, this will." She stared at the green-gold liquid, then drank half the glass.

"You don't know what you're missing, you don't. This is lovely, this cake is. I could get used to this." Lew's hollow cheeks filled out happily. He devoured the cake on his plate, gray sunken eyes staring at the rest of it with furtive interest.

"It will make you fat. You'll get fat," Mum admonished.

"Eeercha! Not in a month of Sundays!" Lew was thin, always had been, childhood malnutrition had played its part and his thinness was exacerbated by his height. He was just over six feet tall, broad-chested, with shoulders like a pair of draughtsman's tee squares. As the years chipped away at him, he had gotten a little smaller and a lot thinner. He tried to speak with his chops ballooned with cake, but couldn't manage it. Instead, he smiled and nodded in Frances' direction, pointing enthusiastically.

"Alright," Mum reluctantly pointed to the chocolate cake. "Give me a bit of brown." Although jealous of Frances' baking ability, her interest was piqued by all the fuss the cake was generating. So Frances cut her a slice of "brown." Mum ate about half before passing judgment.

"Different. Nice to have something different. For a change."

It was the closest she got to complimenting someone else's cooking.

After tea, the ladies went up to bed, and I shared a glass of Jack Daniels with Lew.

"I don't know what gets into her, I really don't. She can't bake, she never baked. Didn't do much in the way of cooking. But it was better than I had growing up. Cor, was it ever—"

"Long time ago, Dad."

"Bloody long time ago."

"All ready for tomorrow, then? I told you, Frances wants to do a bit of touring."

"Touring?" He sounded surprised.

"You know, sightseeing. I've no idea what she wants to see. Not that keen myself, but—"

"Whatever you want to do, son, we'll go along with it," Lew said reassuringly.

The jet lag started kicking in, helped along by my nightcap. I said goodnight and crept upstairs to the bedroom. Whereas most people undress before getting into bed, I re-dressed. A sweater, scarf, socks, along with tee shirt and sweat pants were definitely advisable. The damp in my old bedroom seemed to cling to the wallpaper like an extra layer of skin. Thankfully, we had a hot water bottle made of heavy glazed pottery, like a large stone whiskey flask with a bulbous, knob-like handle at one end and a spout in the center. Not as cuddly as a rubber hot water bottle shaped like a plush-toy bear, nevertheless, it did possess wonderful advantages: it never leaked, it retained heat and, best of all, you could take the chill out of the bed by standing it up between the sheets prior to retiring for the night. Admittedly, with the bottle so positioned, it looked as if the bed had a huge erection, but it did the job, and, apart from the faintly odious smell of the rubber washer, the stone hot water bottle was a lifesaver.

Even with the "electric" on and the hot water bottle standing upright in the bed, it was still bitterly cold in the room. Frances was wearing a woolly hat and wagging Teddy's paw at me from beneath the covers. She looked slightly mad, eccentric at best, but she fit in perfectly with the surroundings and with the person she had married.

Then a forceful wind hit the window like a giant flat hand, rattled the panes noisily. I jumped into bed. The howls of the night subsided and all three of us managed to sleep very well.

~

Morning came, and light poured into the bedroom like shards of ice piercing the exposed parts of our faces. I exhaled and saw my breath. Not a pretty sight. I felt the hot water bottle, now stone cold at my feet, and then I heard someone knocking on the door.

"It's nine o'clock." Lew made it sound as if we had done something wrong, but it was just his way of speaking. "You both ready for some tea?"

My parents drank tea the color of dark rust. Even with milk, it still looked as dark as caramel. It was strong enough to stain the inside of a cup on contact and cause those unaccustomed to such a beverage instant headache, indigestion, or both. A few minutes later Lew was back, knocking on my bedroom door, the aroma of strong tea wafting through. Just as I remembered. When Lew would come off the night shift at Ford's, dog tired, he would stay up long enough to serve us all tea in bed. Then he would make porridge or poached eggs on toast, or my favorite, bacon and baked beans—my cowboy breakfast! Mum would still be in bed glancing at the newspaper, picking out the horses she would back that day. And before he went to bed, he would go up to the local turf accountant and place her bet. On the weeks Lew worked the day shift, he would be long gone before I got up. Even so, tea would be brewing, a newspaper would be waiting for my mum, and our dog, Rex, would have been fed. Nothing much had changed in the intervening years.

"Okay! Come in," I said.

Lew shuffled in with a large tray that held two big mugs of steaming hot tea.

"Well done, Dad, and you know, about Frances—"

"Yes, I know, I know, no milk in her tea. I remembered!"

"And not too strong." I added.

"Don't worry your arse, this tea's as weak as—"

"Thanks, Dad!"

CHAPTER 2

In the footfalls of Becket, Merlin, and Darwin

WHEN FRANCES AND I got downstairs with our empty teacups, Mum was all dressed up in a bright red knitted hat and pink raincoat, with a thick red sweater. Lew looked reasonably dapper in green slacks, a collar and tie; he also wore the waistcoat I had bought him years before from Dunn's, a very proper and traditional men's outfitters. My parents ushered us into the kitchen, where breakfast was waiting. We gobbled down buttered toast and marmalade and more tea. Physically, my parents were an odd-shaped couple. Lew was very tall and thin, sallow-faced with sad gray eyes, whereas Mum was short, ruddy-faced, bright blue eyes open to a smile. As the years passed, Lew became more angular, Mum more rounded, which only exaggerated their physical differences. Only on the dance floor did they seem a pair well matched. They danced well, emulating their heroes, Fred and Adele. They had seen the Astaires in a show in London, in the nineteen twenties, just before the brother-sister act went separate ways with different partners. Not so with Lew and Jessie. They had stayed together, never sitting out a dance but always fighting each other for the lead.

"Where we going again?" asked Mum.

"Canterbury, Mum, Canterbury. Frances wants to have a look around. Might be interesting, it's very old," I conceded. "Can't remember going there, myself."

"All that way—a cathedral. Hmmm."

"Well, if you want to go to Canterbury, we have to make an early start of it," said Lew.

"It's only just after nine, Dad. Come on, relax a bit. We're on holiday."

"Canterbury's a long way. And the traffic!" Lew shook his head ominously, as if he knew, which he didn't. "Well, the traffic, I wouldn't like to say."

The day was sunny, so before we took off on our trip, we took Frances into the garden. The laburnum tree had, according to Lew, gone mad.

"I try and chop it down, but it keeps coming back, bigger than ever!"

"It's like Jack and the beanstalk!" said Mum with great pride. The tall spindly tree had reached my bedroom window, its branches hooped and curved under the weight of thousands of tiny yellow teardrop-shaped flowers, like endless canopies of dappled sunlight.

"Right, then, are we going to be off or not?" Lew was impatient to go.

We finally set off just after ten. The traffic was blissfully light, and, within half an hour, we were over the Dartford Bridge that spanned the ever-widening Thames as it was pushed nearer to the sea. We left Dartford and its grisly industrial estate, complete with cement plant and mundane housing covered in gray soot and grime, and headed south. We piggybacked part of our journey along a relatively new and efficient highway destined for the seaports of Dover and Folkestone, glimpsing some of England's most beautiful countryside. Unlike my home county of Essex, which is essentially flat, the county of Kent, as far as I could see, was endowed with more than its fair share of verdant green hills and downs, valleys and winding rivers, orchards, castles, and stately homes. Kent is called the Garden of England, and for good reason. It grows all manner of fruits and vegetables, even grapes for wine-making by optimistic viticulturists. Hops for beer are also grown in the county, and we saw many of the large hop kilns that once dried the crop. Nowadays machines have replaced the sun in this process and the oast houses are no longer used, but these odd, slightly conical-shaped brick and iron buildings remain in place, their unique outlines an integral part of the Kentish landscape.

We were all surprised how quickly we got to Canterbury. We were within earshot of the cathedral bells in just under an hour. Although parking was expensive and complicated to find, we managed to snare a space within walking distance of all the sights, just inside the ancient city precincts. Canterbury was a walled town and, despite the best efforts of the Luftwaffe, the cathedral was mostly undamaged during World War Two, and much of the town's medieval ambiance had remained intact.

Set within its own grounds, Canterbury Cathedral is an ornate, gray-stoned edifice surrounded by patches of green lawn and clumps of trees. Of course, this cathedral is most famous for the archbishop who was murdered near its altar. Although Henry the Eighth dismantled the shrine around the place of martyrdom, the spot where Thomas à Becket was slain is still marked. Or so we were told. On the big, black, studded doors, a little typed notice informed us the cathedral was closed for some event of a religious nature.

"Bloody unlucky, that is! I mean, it's not as if it's Sunday, is it? Coming all this way!"

Lew sounded more than a bit miffed, convinced religious events should only happen on the day of rest. But the weather was pleasant, if a little cold, so we decided to walk around the cathedral's precincts. The soaring towers, ornate windows, and perching gargoyles were still worth seeing. I could easily imagine how, upon its completion seven hundred years ago, this building would have had a profound impact on the pilgrims of the day. Especially since practically all the buildings in the immediate vicinity were squat and lowly dwellings of thatch and clay and cow dung. How imposing, yet how incongruous this towering edifice must have appeared, with its walls of windows and sweeping stonework: the physical manifestation of God's glory, or man's folly.

Hard by the cathedral was the King's School, founded by Henry the Eighth. This is a public school, what Americans would call a private school or a bastion of privilege. Alumni include Kit Marlowe, Hugh Walpole, and a writer I admire, Somerset Maugham. Even though he hated his time at King's, Maugham left money to the school and some rather bizarre bookends, for buried within the walls of the library are his endowed ashes.

"I wouldn't mind whetting my whistle. And your mother, you know what she's like."

Lew pointed to Jessie, as if I had forgotten who she was or was not quite attuned to her unspoken desire for a libation of an alcoholic nature. Fortunately there were many pubs nearby so we entered one at random and whet a number of whistles. In England, as a rule of thumb, the bigger the church, the more pubs, or inns, are clustered around. This came about from the days of pilgrimage, when people showed up in droves looking for room and board. Apparently, they still did. After we left the pub, we found any number of restaurants in less than a minute, including a huge selection of ethnic eateries.

"How about a kebab, moussaka, something Greek?" I said, somewhat teasingly.

"I wouldn't mind trying that." My mum surprised us all. Lew started laughing.

"I'm not eating that foreign muck." He shook his head at our blatant stupidity.

"Come on, Dad, you like Indian food, can't get more foreign than that now, can you?"

Ghrrr.

That was his only reply. Ghrrr. A guttural mutter laced with impatience and dashed with a splash of venom. Lew often used "ghrrr" when words failed him. Lew fell back on "ghrrr" a lot. Sometimes this throaty grunt was rounded off with a smile and an affectionate "go on, get out of it, you little bugger," or it would end in a stone-gray stare, or a look that said, "you'll bleeding well drop me right in with your mother, you will," but this did not happen very often. I decided to let him off the hook. Indian food. I had teased him about it, but to him, it was not foreign—it was the food of his youth.

The early nineteen thirties were the twilight years of the British Raj, and Lew knew about it first hand. I was fascinated by it all. As Somerset Maugham was downing Singapore Slings in Raffles Hotel and writing about bored and frustrated planters and their jaded wives in one corner of the empire, Lew was sweating in another, earning the King's shilling. He had married Jessie in the early thirties, but could not find any steady or reliable employment. With the Great Depression, which affected Europe even more than the States, employment grew even scarcer. The future looked grim for a working class lad. So Lew joined the army and was shipped out to British India. Ironically, almost five decades later, I faced a similar dilemma. I was not making it in Britain, but I did not join up. I packed up and left for America.

Lew was always reticent about his army experience, no matter how hard I pushed. His recollections were always tantalizingly sketchy. He was a gunner in the Royal Artillery. In those days the guns were still pulled by teams of horses, so Lew learned to ride. He often told me stories of his horses and one in particular, called Judy.

Lew wrote to Jessie about Judy and his fondness for her, but for some unknown reason he forgot to mention that Judy was a horse. Understandably, this incensed my mum, for the last thing Jessie wanted to hear were stories about how Lew bathed Judy, rubbed her down and, dare I say, rode her. This led to many letters of mortified explanation and, as there were no phones or airmail service for enlisted men, this misunderstanding took months to unravel.

I tried to eke more stories out of Lew. The earthquake in Qatar. The monsoon. The riots. The *shite* hawks, the aptly named kites that circle the skies looking for carrion. What was it like? Being in India? Boring, he said. Most of the time it was boring. Life, everyday life, filled the gaps in his stories, but, occasionally, he would drop tantalizing snippets of information such as, I read Milton in India. I got malaria. No explanations, just statements of fact. No amount of prodding could elicit more information. Most frustrating. And then, inexplicably, a day later, six months later, he would pick up the thread he had so easily dropped and begin once again to knot together the little snags in his ancient memory.

~

Canterbury was a settlement, of sorts, long before the Romans came. Yet, despite the ancient cobble, the lopsided medieval streets, and the odd clump of Roman mosaic, the town is not above pulling a fast one. Namely, we noticed more mock Tudor buildings than real ones, built at the turn of the twentieth century and festooned in an array of fake timbers and mottled plaster. So upon finding the Elizabethan Tea Rooms, Frances wasn't as excited she might have been. Located on the high road, covered in a forest of blackened timber, this seemed like another turn-of-the-century knock off. But on closer inspection, the Tudor rose moldings and fat, scantily clad cherubs set in stone seemed suspiciously like the real thing. The building even bowed slightly in the middle. And inside, the oak paneling and pebble-thick glass windows spoke to the building's ancient provenance. As it turned out, this wonderful pile started life as a private house in which Queen Elizabeth the First actually stayed, dithering over whether or not to wed a foreign dignitary, wondering, I'm sure, whether or not she would have to rename the American colony of Virginia. Today, this old house was a tearoom serving light lunches, various savory things on toast, as well as steamed puddings, bread pudding, jam rolls, all served with moats of custard. And teacakes, flattened buns with currants, toasted then slathered with butter. And, of course, pots and pots of tea.

When we arrived back in Dagenham, the first thing Lew did was put the kettle on, my parents proclaiming they were gasping.

"Have a kip," said Lew. "Forty winks, go on, do you good."

"Are you going to nap?" I asked Lew.

"Naaaw, we'll be alright, we don't need to nap, me and your mother, we'll be alright."

An hour later I woke up, padded downstairs, and found my parents passed out in front of a muted television. A large organ-like gas fire was blasting heat into the small room. I almost passed out myself. This front room was our family's lounge and dining room in which guests, usually relatives, were greeted and Christmas dinners eaten. Naturally, this room displayed Mum's treasured possessions, including colored glass animals in a glass-cased zoo, and a plastic gondola, from Venice, of course. Above this sat a bright crimson and gold-painted sherry decanter with two matching glasses. Two chromed statues that looked like Rolls Royce hood ornaments stood on the sideboard. On the mantelpiece were two blue enameled vases and a pair of empty liqueur bottles shaped like African princesses with pointy bosoms. Mum liked to have things in pairs so everything "matched up," except when it came to wallpaper, where nothing matched anything. One wall had a trellis motif with tulips incongruously growing up it. Another wall featured pots of red geraniums and a third had red and white stripes. A window took up most of the fourth wall, an oak table stood in front of it. The most eye-catching feature, apart from the chandelier, was the carpet that covered most of the floor, fire-engine red with the pinkest roses the size of beach balls. And yet, for all its gaudy flash and mismatched colors, the decor countered the dreariness of the street outside perfectly. It was my parents' Aladdin's cave. I had just never realized it before. The chandelier shimmered slightly, its crystal nipple glinted and winked at my sleeping parents. Not wanting to tempt fate, I left the door ajar and tiptoed out.

~

"So, where we going today then?" Lew feigned interest.

"Chislehurst. It's not too far." Frances was very excited about this particular trip.

"Never been there before. What's in Chislehurst?"

What indeed! I would never had gone there. But Frances had discovered, in an obscure book, a six thousand year old mystery nestled in a nondescript suburb of London on the south side of the Thames. The caves of Merlin.

"They are very old caverns. Ancient," said Frances, sensing a general lack of enthusiasm.

"Never heard of it." Mum was a typical North-of-the-River Londoner, any suburb south of the Thames was alien to her, almost foreign. I felt much the same way.

The approach to the Chislehurst Chalk Caves was unprepossessing. There was a convenient car park, a garish sign, a ticket booth, even a little cafeteria selling tea, coffee, calcified cakes, and sugar-coated donuts hard and cold. And yet, miles and miles of ancient caves were within, dug out or formed thousands of years ago. Frances told us the caves contained an ancient Celtic shrine, the very stuff of legend. She could not wait to go inside. We bought tickets and, with Frances in the lead, edged our way forward.

The opening caves were large and became somewhat smaller, but never small enough to have to stoop. I was beginning to catch a little of bit of Frances' excitement, and I was not alone. Much to my surprise, and much to their credit, my parents decided to come in with us. Resisting help, they stepped into the outer cave, where the only light came from the lamp held by our guide, and that was not much. Bravely, Lew and Jessie walked a few yards and stopped.

Ghrrr.

The unevenness of the pathway, the rocky gullies, and the jutting rocks that occasionally burst through the uneven surface of the cave floor unnerved them. I carefully retread my way back to where they stood clutching each other in stoic terror.

"No good, son. If I take a tumble, I won't get up again. Nor your mother."

We helped them from the chilly interior back onto the level gravel path. Kindly, their admission money was refunded, and I escorted them to the cafeteria.

Issued with portable lamps, we followed our guide into this labyrinth of chalk caves. Even I was beginning to think this could be fun. We were the only visitors in the party, and that added to the spookiness and excitement of the occasion. Some people, explained our guide, believed the Chislehurst Caves were haunted, and the voices of children had been heard laughing and crying. Others swore they had seen a hunchbacked old crone. Roman soldiers had been sighted, and a lady in a long blue gown had been seen floating from the center of a haunted pool. In some respects, the ordinariness of the vicinity beyond the caves enhanced the mysteries we could imagine within.

After a few minutes, we arrived at the Celtic Shrine, believed to be thousands of years old. Its high altar, once used for human sacrifices, was flanked on either side by chapels or crypts. Yet, despite the caves' bloody, pagan past, they still managed to possess the grandeur and stillness of their above-ground Christian counterparts. The guide flashed his light around the crusty, dry walls, then collected our lamps.

"Now stay here. I'm going around the corner." Our guide left us in the dark, in more ways than one.

"Okay—"

We waited. The total darkness stretched and teased out the seconds the guide, and the light, was away. The dark was velvet thick and seemed as impenetrable as a stone wall. We could not see our hands. Half a minute seemed liked two, which seemed like an eternity. It was eerie, almost frightening, to be enveloped in such blackness and silence. Quite suddenly we heard a loud banging sound that echoed and resonated for perhaps half a minute, an indescribable noise bounced around the walls until the dark slowly swallowed it up. Then the guide shuffled back towards us and handed back our lamps with a grin.

"What do you think?" he asked excitedly. We were speechless.

His sudden reappearance was almost as startling as his banging on the tin can. We moved on, past the haunted pool and a small antechamber.

"Jimi Hendrix. He was here. Singer. If you can call him that. And…" He then spoke, slowly, dramatically, "Doctor Who!"

"Really," I said.

"Oh, yes!" He smiled smugly. "The Doctor Who people were always filming down here."

Our guide obviously felt more comfortable with an alien space traveler than a big-haired rock star. We were not much interested in either. Frances was more interested in a big-haired magician.

"And Merlin? What about Merlin?" she asked, hopefully.

"Well, you know, these tunnels, they go deep, for miles they do. People have been lost, you know, and some of the caves have been boarded up," he said, avoiding the question.

"Yes? And Merlin?"

"As for Merlin, well, that was a long time ago."

He instructed us to move on, and, dodging our questions about Merlin, he led us back out.

"See any ghosts?" Lew was laughing at us. He pointed to the tea lady. "We've been talking to missus woman here—"

"Worked here for over thirty years. And she's never been inside them caves. Not once!" My mum was impressed by the tea lady's lack of curiosity.

~

From Chislehurst, we traveled in a southeasterly direction towards the village of Downe. We stopped by the village green, then headed for the pub across from the church. Time for lunch. We had a round of drinks while we waited for our food. After insisting he was not hungry, Lew ordered a steak and kidney pie. Mum chose a salad and was brought a few limp pieces of lettuce, quartered greenish tomatoes, and a few chunks of cucumber, accompanied by a jar of salad cream, ersatz Mayo. I had shepherd's pie—ground beef and mashed potato, grilled until the potato topping is crispy and brown. Frances had a ploughman's lunch, a plate with French-type bread, soft and soggy, a big wedge of cheddar cheese, and a few sprigs of salad.

"Another schooner of sherry, Mum?"

"She doesn't want anymore. Are you mad?" Lew seemed angry.

"Oh, you! You shut up, you!" Gathering her breath, Mum reared up, then leaned across the table, emitting a loud rumble of discontent. "He's always trying to spoil my fun, he is—"

Ghrrr.

After lunch we drove just beyond the village, turned a bend in the road, and suddenly Down House was upon us. I almost missed the entrance. Although the house was very close to the road, a high box hedge blocked it almost completely from view.

Off the beaten tourist track, Down House was a very large Victorian abode with tall windows and a whitewashed stucco exterior. Not a grand house in the English manor house tradition, and not a very attractive one, but then we were not visiting the house so much as paying tribute to the man who lived here most of his life.

"What is this place again?" asked Mum.

"The home of Charles Darwin. Frances just read a book about him. Wanted to see his house."

"Darwin. The evolution waller, wasn't he?" said Lew.

Charles Darwin, Charles Darwin—I could almost hear the Rolodex in Mum's memory flapping around, but not stopping. She smiled and shrugged and turned her attention to the huge wall of boxwood that separated the small driveway from the road beyond.

"Look at that, almost as big as the house. Look at that, Lew!"

We were shown inside by the curator, a pleasant, studious-looking young woman, with an open round face and prematurely graying hair. She was unaccustomed to visitors, but even so, she made us feel most welcome. A work in progress, Down House and its gardens were being meticulously restored. Apart from the museum-like quality of the conservatory, the rest of the house and grounds seemed remarkable for their genuine intimacy and refreshing lack of show. Each room appeared to have been left much as it had been in Darwin's lifetime. As we were the only visitors that day, we had the house very much to ourselves.

"Very few people come by."

Even though the curator smiled sadly, I could detect a touch of relief in her voice. Unlike most historic houses in Britain, Down House was apparently unknown to the general touring public. Lew looked around approvingly, as if he knew the house and the previous owner. I was pleased that he appeared to be enjoying himself.

"You're not from 'round here, are you?" Mum had been troubled by the curator's accent.

"I'm from the States, but I live here now, in this house."

"Ooowhaa!" My mum rendered this sound whenever an expression of surprise, fear, or disbelief was called for. "And you've come all this way, to live 'ere? Well, I never!" Mum feigned surprise. "Goes to show…"

"Well, yes—"

"And my son, my son, that's him! He lives over there now." Mum pointed with her finger in a disdainful arc. "In America, he does."

"It's different in England. Takes some getting used to, but I like it here."

"See that, she likes it here." Mum shot me a glance. "Rather be here than in America, she would."

"Mum—"

"And she's American!" Mum turned to the curator, her unwilling foil, and smiled her most winning smile. "Bet-you-don't-know-where-I-come-from!" With every word, Mum's Cockney accent thickened. It is a mistake to believe that only young people are indulged. My mum had been indulged, deferred to, and emotionally cosseted for as long as I could remember. She had a sunny disposition that was easy to warm to, if things were going her way.

"I come from nowhere near here. You'll never guess where—"
She made it sound as if her journey from the rust-flattened industrial landscape that marred the banks of the Thames across to the

bucolic hills and dales of Kent had been a journey of epic proportions. For her, perhaps it was.

"I'm from London, I am. Lon-don." Mum enunciated the two syllables very carefully.

"I can tell." The curator smiled and proceeded to show us around the house exhibits and the restored rooms on the ground floor. We walked over to a glass case and saw some pinned butterflies.

"How ghastly!" I muttered.

"Oh, come on, didn't you catch butterflies as a kid and pin them down?" asked Frances.

"I did not do that. Anyway, there are no butterflies in Dagenham. Well, none that I saw."

Apart from the butterfly pin-ups, we looked at a few family portraits on the walls, some sea urchins and large seashells in a case, a few fossils, and not much else. The curator repeated that the place was being renovated. Most of the upstairs rooms were closed for this very reason, not that this stopped us from poking around. Nothing much appeared to have been done yet.

In the conservatory, back on the ground floor, was a large dining table featuring a display of pictures culled from a TV series of Darwin's voyage on the Beagle. I dutifully looked at the display of stills of various actors hanging from ropes, digging up things, collecting samples.

"Darwin's sand walk? Is it still there?" Frances had done her homework. This was the famous thinking path Darwin trod down for years, counting his turns around the path with pebbles. Every day, he would walk in quiet solitude, or with visiting scientists, perhaps to think through the theories that would change the world's view of creation for all time. Or was it simply to escape his bustling, hectic Victorian household, filled with relatives, visitors, and children of all ages, for a few precious minutes of contemplation and exercise? We could not wait to find out and to follow in his footsteps.

"It's through there, at the back of the garden." The curator ushered us gently onto the patio, then left us to fend for ourselves. My parents sat down and enjoyed the sunshine and the view of the

garden, while Frances and I tramped past flower beds brimming
with all manner of foliage and fauna. The garden was neither wonderfully chaotic like a cottage garden, nor formal or austere. Definitely a place where the young Darwin children could have once run
around, playing ball, croquet, or cricket. The garden also served as
Darwin's alfresco laboratory, filled with a variety of plant life and
exotic flower specimens, grasses, even a wormery.

We found the sand walk at the very end of the garden. The path
had been soaked and muddied by rain and seemed to be covered
in mulch, not a bit of sand in sight. We followed the path as it
meandered onto a neighbor's land, then through a densely wooded
copse. In just a few minutes we had walked in the footsteps of great-
ness, and I spent most of the time pirouetting and leaping across
cow pats and ankle-deep mud pools in order to keep my pristine
cross-country trainers in shape for hardwood floors and carpets
and other such rugged indoor terrain. The path was a lot shorter
than we had imagined, and Frances left a little disappointed. As we
headed back to the house, we passed a rectangle of jumbled plants
that resembled cornstalks and yellowing dry grass. My parents were
still basking in the sunshine.

Like a salamander carefully eyeing his surroundings, Lew suddenly sprang into action. He jumped up and started stirring Mum,
who snuffled and snorted awake.

"Where to now then?" she asked.

"How about a nice cup of tea?" I asked.

"And some cake!" added Frances.

"Tea? A bit of cake? What a bloody good idea. Come on, Jessie.
We're in luck!"

In our walk around Darwin's thinking path, good thoughts had
not eluded us entirely.

CHAPTER 3

From Chartwell to Aldeburgh

VERY CLEVERLY, Frances had put Chartwell on her list of places to see. This was Winston Churchill's home, and, as I was an admirer of the old curmudgeon, she knew I would be happy to go along with her planned excursion. Again, we headed across the Thames to the green hills of Kent. As with Down House and Canterbury, it took less than an hour to get there from Dagenham.

Quite unlike Darwin's abode, Chartwell is always besieged with coachloads of tourists, even during the week, even during the cold months of spring. But I really did want to see the place so, reluctantly, we joined the touring hordes, but only for a moment.

We soon discovered that, because of the number of visitors, only timed tours of the house were being given. Not much time for musing, reflection, or much of anything else. And the hour-and-a-half wait to get inside was not appealing to any of us. We decided to forego the congested and expensive house tour and headed instead for the grounds of the estate. And I am glad we did. Just wandering around, I got a real sense of the place and the man who helped shape it. Churchill spent a lot of time in his garden, and it was not hard to see why: the views across the Vale of Kent were both stunning and commanding. From Chartwell's high vantage point, we could see a patchwork quilt of meadows and farmland stitched together by ancient hedgerows that stretched for miles and miles. I was glad to be out of doors.

"You go ahead. We'll wait in the car. Take your time."

"What do you mean, wait in the car? Oh, come on, Dad, at least you can have a look around the gardens, see the black swans and everything. You and Mum, you love gardens. Come on. This is the great man's place!"

Ghrrr.

We moved Lew and Jessie across ankle-breaking boulders of gravel and onto paths stoned with smaller, more manageable pebbles, obviously ground down by decades of tourists. We descended a couple of steps onto a much safer flagstone path. Frances and I pointed out views and scenery to them, obligatory murmurs of delight followed, and they soon began to take an interest. Lew pointed out specific flowers to my mum. She, of course, corrected him and made him look at plants that were her favorites. With Mum's arm hooked in Lew's and his stick setting the pace, they soldiered on along the path. Reluctantly, gradually, they were starting to enjoy themselves.

"Alright now, we're going to have a sit down over there." Lew thrashed the air with his cane. "You and Frances, you go off. You can find us over there when you're done looking."

"Don't you want to see the—"

"We've seen enough! And if we want to see more, we'll see it from over there." He was insistent. "It's lovely out here. We're stuck indoors all day—nice change, this is."

The day had indeed turned lovely. Like a weather vane in a hurricane, the micro-climate had changed and changed again. A sudden downpour had evaporated and bright stamens of warm, gold sunshine had burst through the slate-colored sky. Even so, we could never be sure, so coats were worn or carried, just in case. Leaving my folks to meander at their own pace, we visited the gardens, lakes and ponds, the outdoor rooms Sir Winston had created. Not many people were in the gardens, and that was fine by us.

We found the famous seat where the old man had fed his fish. The black swans still swam dutifully in the lake. Roses were lined up for inspection, and brick walls sprouted around the estate like weeds! Some were used as embankments and some as windscreens. Some had been given to Churchill by his children. We even found brick walls Churchill had laid himself. I wondered why he had built them; what was he keeping out, what was he keeping in?

Deep in the garden, we found Sir Winston's art studio. Venturing inside, we found a compact room, rather like a small cottage without a bedroom level, with paintings lining the walls. Despite the obvious contrivance of a cigar left in an ashtray and a paint-stained smock across a chair, there was one very authentic touch beside the easel: stacks and stacks of Havana cigar boxes filled with tubes of paint. Churchill's paintings were bold, brash, energetic, exuberant South of France landscapes. To me, they all seemed to be tantalizing self-portraits, yet only partly revealing. More time was needed, but others wanted to gape, and we had to push off.

We caught up with Jessie and Lew, patiently sitting on a bench near the car park. We drove to nearby Westerham, a large village with pubs and antique shops brimming with Chartwell visitors. Despite the bustle and crowds, we found seats in a wood-paneled village pub filled with hunting and riding bric-a-brac and prints. We settled in for a steak and kidney pie lunch. Frances had a shandy, a pleasant mixture of pale ale and lemonade, Lew had his Guinness, Mum her requisite schooner of sherry, and I had a cider locally brewed from Kentish apples, strong with a clear golden color and filled with flavor.

"Well, what do you think, Dad? Great place, Chartwell, don't you think?"

"Nice to see where he lived." Lew seemed pensive for a moment.

"Not that far from Dagenham, really," I said.

"No, I suppose not, if I'd known—" Lew shrugged.

"Got to have a car though," said Mum. "We never had one, did we?"

"What you talking about? You never wanted a motor. I said about getting a motor, you weren't interested." Lew was trying to be patient, but inadvertently rolled his eyes.

"Who said that? I never said that!" Mum's eyes blazed. "You never wanted a motor. I wanted one, but you, you—"

Lew's face tightened into a ghastly stare, his pointed finger jabbed the angry air between them both, but he said nothing.

Ghrrr.

The food arrived before the bitterness could foment, and bubbles of pub chatter warmed up the frosty silences. Lunch proceeded without further incident. Even so, Frances and I thought it might be nice to have a little time alone.

"Good idea! You go off and enjoy yourselves!" Lew said, with gruff enthusiasm.

~

After breakfast the following morning and just before we hit the road, I called some pals in London, including one of my oldest friends, just to touch base. For years, Isabel had rejected boots and suits and remained wonderfully glamorous in paisley tops and big looping earrings and jeans tight enough to wilt a rock star's wiggle.

When I first met Isabel, I was looking for someone to illustrate an album cover. A mutual friend told me she was very talented, talked a lot, and I would like her. About an hour later Isabel came bounding into my friend's office, talking a mile a minute. Swathed in a tight denim jacket with jangly silvery bits, she looked madly arty. I remember thinking, if she illustrates as well as she looks, we're in business. She did. And we were. The album project was heartbreakingly killed, but our friendship was forged of stronger stuff. Mind you, her very up-market voice had at first been a bit intimidating for an East End kid like me. But she quickly overrode my prejudices with her down-to-earth manner. And here we were, years later, picking up where we left off, words and laughter spinning out of control, spanning time and distance in a matter of minutes.

I told Isabel that Frances and I were heading to the fenlands and an overnight stay in Aldeburgh. I pronounced it as it is written, All-der-burg. Gales and gales of mirth ensued. She could barely speak for guffawing.

"Oh, Denis, you've been away *su-ch* a long time! It's not All-der-berg, it's All-braah!"

More laughter, interspersed with wishes for us both to have a lovely, lovely time. She talked happily, words accelerated past one another and sped beyond my unaccustomed, untuned ears. The faster she spoke, the less I understood. Not that I let on, of course.

So, by about ten, we headed out on a clear road for "All-braah" by way of Woodbridge. Frances had booked ahead for lunch at a fancy restaurant just outside the town, in an ancient Elizabethan manor house. It was all going to be quite grand. Seckford Hall dates from the time of Henry the Eighth, and his daughter Elizabeth held court there on more than one occasion after she became queen.

We entered through a heavy oak door studded with iron bits that would have looked better in a torture chamber. Inside, the flagstones were smooth and shiny with age, and various antiques and museum-quality chairs, not suitable for sitting, were carefully arranged. Even the assembled suit of armor didn't seem out of place. To one side of the castle-like reception area was a delightful bar that looked like a snug country pub. The floors were covered in red carpet, the walls beautifully oak-paneled, with mullion windows overlooking the gardens and framed by gorgeous amounts of wisteria. We approached the restaurant and another cozy sitting area in front of another roaring fire. We were greeted affably by the restaurant manager, who indicated we could wait in the sitting area and peruse the menu.

"Why?" I asked, genuinely curious.

He smiled. "We have to prepare your table, sir."

"Not ready? Oh. Well. Really? But we did make a reservation."

"It is Mr. Lipman?" His eyebrows rose in anticipation. "We do indeed have your reservation. Always good idea." He nodded sagely. As if by magic, he produced two menus the size of large game boards. We ordered our lunch. Many minutes later, we were told our table was now prepared. Another waiter guided us into the restaurant, a large, airy garden room with about thirty tables. Except for one table, the place was completely empty. The lone table was occupied by an old fellow with a large bulbous nose the color of port and a slightly younger woman in cardigan and pearls. They were seated by the window. Even though every table was set exactly the same way, for some unknown reason, our table was by the door.

"I'm glad we made a reservation," I said.

The waiter smiled enigmatically, oblivious to irony.

"Where is everyone?" Frances seemed as bewildered as I was.

"A little slow today, modom. One never knows—"

It was a little slow, especially the service. We waited obediently at our table, wondering why we had been asked to order in advance.

"It's probably a delaying technique to sell you more drinks." I was not impressed.

"Go with the flow," said Frances. "When in Rome—"

I was getting riled up. Angry. Frances told me to relax and stop acting like a twit in a snit. Another ten minutes went by, and then our first courses showed up. A plop of cold rice stuck with parsley and unripe slices of tomato for me, lukewarm, orange-colored soup for Frances.

Just as we started to eat, the tweedy gentleman with the ruby red nose began farting. Perhaps in a filled restaurant, his outbursts would have melded with the ambient noise, but in this deserted room his wind-breakers resonated, almost echoed, loud and clear. Each time he let rip, we thought a chair was being scudded on a floor. We looked over, but apart from the rising and lowering of his posterior, we saw nothing moving. The flatulent diner's partner chose to ignore his outbursts, or perhaps she was simply deaf or inured to them, but not, it seemed, to our reaction. Looks of withering disdain greeted our peels of laughter.

Seckford Hall itself was much better than the food, except for the coffee and cookies we had in the lounge. Perhaps we should have remained in the bar for a pub lunch, but then we would have missed the fireworks. Missed the laughter. After lunch, we strolled the grounds for a few minutes. The magnificent mansion was made of brick about half the size of conventional brick, dark and rust colored, slightly curved with age and covered with ivy. The thick, bottle-green glass windows were leaded in the traditional cross-hatched style. On one side of the roof were wonderfully elaborate chimneys twisting and twirling upwards like ornamented puff pastry. On over thirty acres of gardens, we saw ducks on a pond, a willow tree, and rose beds galore. Unfortunately the weather was turning rather brisk, so we decided to press on towards our final destination. I had been practicing saying "All-braah" since leaving Dagenham, and it seemed to be working.

Aldeburgh was built on an apron of land just above sea level, with the obligatory promenade and the high street running parallel to the beach. On either side of the town, we could see the skinny coastline, rugged and unspoiled. In the distance, a Martello tower, built for the feared invasion of Napoleon, could be reached by a path that snaked along the seashore.

The coastal town was the home of Benjamin Britten, one of England's greatest composers, who drew inspiration from the surrounding land and seascape. I could see why. The entire locale was remarkably dramatic. The skies were huge and wide and the iron-gray sea dominated and sharply defined the horizon. The flatness of the land made the sea appear bigger, scarier than it would be along a more sheltered part of the coastline. The sea was inescapable, whipping up waves that crashed across the beach, raking and sucking fist-sized pebbles into smooth submission. It was easy to understand how Britten could conjure up its malevolence and potent force in his music, for he had grown up listening to its relentless song.

I quite enjoyed Aldeburgh, even though it was not the kind of place I would have chosen for a traditional beach vacation. The North Sea looked as if it never got warm, the wind blew virtually all the time, and the pebble beach was definitely not made for bare feet. Not surprisingly, this was a favorite seaside resort for the austere and health-conscious Victorians, desirous of maintaining their decorum and lily-white complexions. Holidaymakers came to this stretch of shore to feel the effects of the bracing air and take long, invigorating walks. No sun, fun, or sand castles for them.

In times past, the lack of cliffs and huge rocky outcrops brought the sea threateningly close to the land. In fact, parts of the coastline were swallowed up by the waves entirely.

Sinking into and walking through the pebbles that filled the beach, we could see the outlines of deserted cottages. Farther along were seaweed-covered concrete blocks imbedded with rusty yet working winches attached to drums of inch-thick cable used to haul in fishing boats laden with their catch. Hard by these boats were small, sturdy huts built of wood, old ships' beams, planking, and corrugated iron. Fishermen sold their briny wares right off their boats. I noticed various flat fish, including sole and skate, as well as ugly monkfish and halibut, open-mouthed and angry looking. The fish was not the cheapest, but you could not buy it any fresher.

If you could not cook it yourself, the fish and chips shop at the end of the high street was the perfect alternative. This is where Britten took visiting friends. No sit down service here. Strictly take out, with fish wrapped in paper. When the fish was fresh in, there was always a line outside. We saw diners sitting on seawalls and nearby jetties, happily munching on cod and chips with their fingers. It's a classic way to eat this most English of dishes, and one day I may yet eat my fish that way, but not yet. I prefer using cutlery. My wife marvels that I am the only man she knows who eats pizza with a knife and fork. She also marvels that I have survived so long in a world of finger food and paper napkins.

For a bit of a splurge, Frances had reserved a room at the Wentworth, one of the grand dames of Victorian seaside hotels. Nothing much seemed to have changed in over a hundred years. The hotel was set in the comfy aspic of a bygone era, a little worn and musty with age but still quite charming. E.M Forster, Somerset Maugham, or Benjamin Britten would have felt quite at home when they stayed there. The vestibule and lounge area was enclosed within what appeared to be a conservatory offering comfortable views of the ocean. We had requested a room with a seaview, and we got one, with a high ceiling and tall windows. Pastel-colored furniture complemented the faded ivory wallpaper featuring jolly yokels in pastoral scenes. I looked out and saw the reflected sun glinting like bits of silver paper on the water.

As recommended, we had made a reservation for dinner. I was feeling lazy and enjoying the fusty ambiance and atmosphere of the Wentworth, so we thought it might be rather fun to eat there. But first, we decided to stroll around the town and take advantage of the unexpected warmth of late afternoon. When we returned, I hooked back the thick velvet and brocade curtains at the windows. I wanted to see the morning sun rise across the ocean. Frances thought I was mad, but she indulged me. We leisurely changed for dinner, then stopped at the bar for a drink.

The ruddy-faced man who had unloaded our bags was now busily laying tables for dinner. A few moments later, the same fellow had changed into a gray tuxedo to become our dining room host. He escorted us into a long, narrow, terraced room with huge windows overlooking the sea.

"Any recommendations for dinner?"

"The codling, sir, with new potatoes." He moved on ahead and busied himself flicking imaginary specks from a table.

"What's codling?" Frances whispered.

"I don't know, baby cod?"

"Anything else?" asked Frances, not wanting to cause offense.

"Whatever you wish, Madame. Follow me, please—"

He beckoned us to sit down. On the table was an ornate place card holder bearing our room number. Very organized. Then the waiter bowed and disappeared. And there we were, sitting right by the door. Again! We were far from any window, far from any view of the sea or the reflection of a waning sun upon it. And we were also far away from the main dining room, which was almost empty.

A smiling waitress appeared. Before she could reel off the night's specials, if any, I jumped in.

"I wonder…sorry, but would it be possible to move a little closer to the windows?"

"But this is your table—it was assigned to you when you booked the room, sir, you see." She paused. "Shall I take your order now, sir, or would you prefer to see the wine list?"

I took the wine list. I ordered a bottle of red. All I could see was red. The waitress smiled and left. We looked around. I hoped it would not be a replay of lunch.

With a white tea towel draped over his forearm, our ruddy-faced maitre d' now played sommelier. He dribbled wine into my glass to taste.

"Oh, just pour away," I said impatiently.

The wine was poured. We were still the only people in that section of the dining room.

"Excuse me, do you think we could move to a window seat?" Frances asked.

"But this is your table, Madame."

"I know it's our table, but we're the only ones here, so can we please move?"

Smiling and retreating, he uttered vague assurances, then disappeared into the kitchen area. A moment later our waitress reappeared.

"If you would follow me, sir."

We picked up our half-filled wine glasses and were led to a small table with a lovely view of the water, right by the window. We had made it in time and would catch the last glowing embers of sun as we set to our first course.

"Would this suit, sir?

It would. Despite the fact that we were just about the only diners, the food was surprisingly good. As we signed the check, the waitress informed us, slowly and carefully, no doubt thinking we were either eccentric or slow-witted American tourists, that our lovely window table would be our table for breakfast. We had been reassigned. She smiled and departed. We could not have been more pleased.

After taking our time over coffee and mints, we went for a walk, then slowly climbed the stairs back to our room. The bed had been turned down, and the thick curtains I had opened earlier had been pulled shut. This was probably the most easterly part of England, and I imagined sunrise here could be among the grandest. I wanted to see it, so I reopened the curtains.

"Do you have to do that?" Frances asked wearily.

I smiled knowingly as I fumbled with cloth and hooks and gold-braided cord.

"Darling! We're facing east so we can see a day break on the water, remember? Just imagine it, with this huge sky." I enthused dramatically. "Can you just imagine it?"

"Twit."

"I want to get up early, go for a walk on the beach, and catch the sun. Don't worry, darling. Fear not, you will be undisturbed!" I was trying to be amusing.

"Just don't forget to close the curtains, and lock the door behind you."

"Fear not, my darling, you won't be disturbed!"

～

"Aaaaaaaaaaaaaaaaaah—"

A battery of searchlights had been aimed straight into our room. I groaned and furrowed my eyelids into impenetrable slits. I waited for ack-ack guns to fire. So much for slender rays of amber sunlight dappling across my sleeping face. After the dazzle of sunlight had penetrated my brain, I was shot through with panic. Oh, Christ, I thought, it had to be past noon. Bugger. We'd slept through breakfast! Worse, we would be late for the family get-together my parents planned for us, and they would be worried.

"Maybe we can still get some coffee—"

"Oh, my God—"

"Maybe a croissant or something?" I sounded very apologetic. Very whiny. I was halfway dressed and heading for the door.

"Stop!"

"I'll see what I can rustle up—" I babbled on.

"It's four o'clock in the morning!" Frances shouted.

"What?"

"Four o'clock. It's four o'clock in the morning!"

Frances repeated the ungodly hour a couple of times, in case I wasn't getting it. I stopped dead in my tracks. I grabbed the watch from the side table. I blinked, stared in disbelief.

"Four o'clock?"

My watch came into focus. Frances was right. It was four in the morning, and the sun was ablaze. Momentarily confused, then I remembered we had traveled to the far eastern end of England, where the day's dawning was obviously not a slow, meandering affair.

"Now you know why the curtains are so thick!" Frances is very logical even half asleep.

"Ah, yes, yes, that makes sense," I said, rather lamely.

As we were up, we decided to go for a walk on the beach. Half an hour later we walked back through the deserted hotel. We muttered again about the ungodliness of the hour, the strangeness of the weather, then went back to sleep—thank goodness for thick blackout curtains!

~

A few hours later we went downstairs for our traditional English breakfast. We dutifully followed our hostess to our newly assigned table by the window. We sat down and were immediately caught by the glare of the blinding morning sun. Like religious converts in a painting by Rubens, we squinted, we shaded our eyes, we turned aside, but to no avail.

Although a few tables were occupied by hearty breakfasters, many others were empty. As discreetly as we could, we moved to another, not quite so close to the window but still with a view, grateful to be out of the sun's glare. A moment later our waitress from the night before appeared. Her face dropped when she saw us, the bright smile nose-dived into a distressing quiver.

"But this isn't your table; your table is that one, number five. We've moved you. Don't you remember? Your new table is by the window, there. It's what you wanted—"

"Yes, I know, I know, sorry, sorry, but it's too bright. The sun." I indicated foolishly. "It's quite blinding."

"But we changed your table especially."

"Yes, I know, but—"

"But this is not your table!"

"There are lots of empty tables, what's the problem?" Frances asked with a smile.

"It's not the point, is it, madam?" The prim accent slipped into a slight Suffolk drawl as she went on, "And we 'ad to change everything, special like. Oi'll see what can be done." With a slight sniff she turned and fled. I scowled away the moments until the waitress returned. A bit of a smile hung from the side of her mouth like a worm in a bird's beak.

"That'll be alroight, surr, you can stay where you are fer now." She bit her lip and looked at us with earnest resolve. "You won't be changing back tonight…will you?"

"Don't worry. We'll be checking out after breakfast," I said.

Her face brightened. "Oh, well, that's alright then, isn't it? Two for breakfast?"

"Yes. I'll start with the kippers!"

"Roight away then, sir."

"Kippers?" Frances stared at me.

"Herring. Smoked locally, apparently. With lots of vinegar, pepper, and hot buttered toast! Can't wait!"

"Weirdo."

Apart from the locally smoked kippers, which I ate alone, we both ordered the full English breakfast. Only tourists can eat breakfasts in England and live to tell the tale. Not for the faint of heart, but even so, our morning feast was a splendid thing, with fried bacon, fried black pudding, fried pork sausages, fried eggs, fried mushrooms, fried kidneys, and that cornerstone of English cuisine, fried bread, not forgetting baked beans rimmed with congealing bacon fat! The only healthy thing on my plate was a limp piece of parsley draped across the fried tomato.

After we finished eating, we strolled up and down "the front," stared out at the sea, then came across the tiny Tudor Moot Hall, which was closed. From the outside, it looked like a half-timbered doll's house. Rather uncharitably, I thought it might make a nice beach hut. We stared at this postage stamp-sized bit of history for a brief moment before turning back to the hotel. We took one last look at the sea and packed up the car.

On the way back to Dagenham, we decided to stop by Dedham, a village on the banks on the River Stour that inspired the landscape painter, John Constable, over two centuries ago. A truly beautiful place, its wide, winding streets opened onto a village square of sorts. Quite suddenly the memory of a museum landscape became fresh and vivid and inviting, and we were walking into canvases with the paint still wet.

Although most of the houses were built in Elizabethan times, many were refaced with Georgian, neo-classical fronts in the eighteenth century, rather like dowdy kitchen cabinet doors are refaced in the States. It worked. The high street offered us a picture of uncluttered elegance, surrounded by a soft blue sky that framed it all quite perfectly. We strolled aimlessly and window-shopped. It was Sunday and, apart from the pubs, the town was shut. Even so, we managed to peer into a number of antique shops, greengrocers, and cottage homes, all beautifully preserved and happily lived in.

"I love your rosemary. Delicious!" I called out as charmingly as I could.

We were passing a small cottage with an abundance of this wonderful herb spilling over the garden wall. Frances hurried along, pretended to ignore me as I tried to curry favor.

The home owner looked up quite suddenly and smiled. I smiled back.

"Have some, have some," my new friend insisted, as if reading my mind. "It grows like a weed here! Take as much as you want!"

I thanked her profusely and made off with a swatch of the spiky yet tender green leaves. The aroma of lemony pine and mint clung pleasantly to my hand long after I had stuffed the rosemary into my pocket. I was determined to keep this culinary treasure for our next lamb dinner. A few minutes later we reached the river bank. We saw a few toddlers splashing about at the water's edge and prostrate day-trippers with trousers rolled up over chalk stick legs. Oblivious to all and sundry stood chocolate-colored cows, slowly chewing on the warm air. A few stood away from the herd, in the middle of the river, up to their udders in the cool water, blissfully unaware of the visitors watching them, or the constant roar of nearby highway traffic that cut like a scythe through two hundred years of tranquility.

CHAPTER 4

To Barking and back

WE ARRIVED BACK later than expected. My parents had arranged a little party for some of my aunts and uncles to meet my bride and toast the happy couple. The door opened almost as I knocked. I think Lew had been waiting in the passageway for our return. He pulled himself up, chest out, and stood before us like the sergeant major he had been.

"What time do you call this, then?" Lew was all dressed up in his fancy lemon-checked waistcoat, shirt, and tie. His hair, still nut brown, was brilliantined. Years back, my mother and I had laughed that Lew parted his hair like our dog Rex, straight down the middle.

We shrugged and said hurried hellos as we clambered in. Lew sounded scolding, but he was smiling. "Come in, the both of you, we're all waiting. No excuses."

A small collection of relatives was gathered in the tiny front room. My brother Tony, his wife Tricia, three of my mum's sisters, and my cousin Pam had arrived much earlier. Dad's brother George, his wife Doris, and their son, my cousin Paul, had shown up just before we had. At such family gatherings, beer and sherry would be served while food was prepared. Cheese and pickle sandwiches, ham and mustard sandwiches, watercress sandwiches, sausage rolls, sliced pork pie with a boiled egg in the center, anchovy sandwiches, and gherkins with little onions on sticks was the usual bill of fare. After this, Mum would serve tiny chocolate-iced cakes, mince pies, a cream sponge cake, or a currant cake and a jam roll. Everything was store bought, but my mum was complimented nonetheless. Lots and lots of tea would also be poured. Once tea was served, out would come the gin, my mum's cherry brandy, or both.

Like all such occasions, this one started off a little stiff. The two sides of my family never mixed well, partly because they never really saw much of one another except at funerals, or at weddings. Regardless, it was nice to see this gaggle of relatives gathered up to meet Frances. Not wanting to put her on the spot, everyone feigned interest in foreign holidays in the sun. New grandchildren. Even each other.

"Oh, so you're Lew's brother. George, is it? Yes… Well, we must have met sometime or other," said Aunt Flo, one of my mother's sisters.

"Oh, I'm sure of it," said Uncle George, Lew's younger brother. He said nothing more.

"Enjoying your trip? Jessie told me you've been gallivanting around." George's wife, Aunt Doris, made the effort. We filled in the details.

"Got the weather for it. Lucky. It's been bad, over here. The weather." Aunt Flo enunciated her words. She laughed nervously. Uncle George nodded sagely but said nothing.

"Never know what it's going to do. Ay? Ay, Jessie? You never know, do you?" said Aunt Vi.

"I wake up cold, I do, I know that. Cold of a morning, I am."

Mum shook her head, and Aunt Vi gave her a sly look. "Long as I've got a drop of drink, I don't care. Keeps me warm. I haven't got a big man like you, Jessie, to keep me warm. Bet he keeps you warm, ay, Jessie, ay, ay?" Vi verbally nudged Mum, who bristled.

"Listen to this one! Listen to this! Bloody hell next!" said Tony, pretending to be shocked.

"Doesn't keep me warm. No meat on his bones." Mum seemed put out.

"Well, Jessie dear, if you don't want him—" said Vi, airily.

Vi was one of my favorite aunts. She was my mum's younger sister but looked on first glance to be older. She had silvery gold hair spun as thin as cotton candy and set on a vivid pink skull. She had a wizened chin, rounded at the end like a small doughnut. And when she smiled, her jaws caved in thanks to ill-fitting dentures. But her eyes twinkled with the mischief of a sixteen year old. Vi quickly changed the subject back to things meteorological.

"I bet the weather's all lovely where you are, Denis, ay? Ay? In America, isn't it, Denis? Like in the pictures, innit? Hollywood. Lovely. Love it over there, don't you, Denis?"

I had never lived in Hollywood, or in California for that matter, but when Vi thought of America, she thought of sunshine and glamour and excitement. I suppose anywhere in America was a kind of Hollywood back-lot, if you had not been there. I changed tack.

"So, how's John?" I inquired about her son, an older cousin.

"Given up the tally work. Hacking a cab now, he is. The things he gets up to—"

"Shame he couldn't make it here. I wanted to see him—meet Frances."

I could trace my intellectual exodus from Dagenham back to cousin John. When I was about ten, John gave me a box of magic tricks. From that I developed a passion for conjuring. I joined a young magicians' club in London. I met funny and fascinating and sometimes eccentric people. I made interesting friends, not just my own age. I even rubbed shoulders with a few celebrities. Cousin John's box of tricks helped me reach beyond my years, beyond the limitations Dagenham imposed upon me.

"He wasn't invited, was he?" Aunt Vi announced. I was confused. She continued, "He would have liked to have seen you again. But there it is—"

"Dad said John couldn't make it. Or he couldn't get hold of him. I don't remember."

"Didn't want to, more like. I'm sure he never invited him."

"Dad?"

A shadow crossed Lew's face. He said nothing. He tried to slope out, back to the kitchen.

"I'll get the sandwiches," he muttered, eyes to the ground.

"Dad! What happened? I did tell you. I wanted to see him again."

"Well, I didn't! I saw John a couple of years ago. Had a fight. That was it."

Lew was angry. He had been caught in a lie. He moved out into the kitchen. I sighed. Lew had a tendency to lie, if only to curry favor with the person he was with at the time. He should have been a politician except that, to his credit, he was a bad liar. He always had been. When I was a boy, he gave me a beautiful wooden sword, flat with beveled edges and curved at the end like a scimitar. I was going through my Sinbad the Sailor phase, so it was the perfect gift. It had to be painted, but other than that it was perfect. I was thrilled. "Who made it?" I asked. He said he had. And I knew it was not true. He was no woodworker. His work shed in the back garden was littered with badly constructed, unfinished, wobbly objects. He was as clueless in his work shed as Mum was in the kitchen. "Did it on the lathe at work."

"Great job, Dad. Really good!" I often wondered if he knew I could chew on a paddy-whack of lies as well as he could.

~

"What's all that about a fight? What fight?" I was clueless. Aunt Vi shook her head.

"Your dad was telling John to behave himself. Treating him like a child, he was. Patronizing. Your father, well, you know what he can be like. And John was drunk as a lord. Almost came to blows. Things were said. Bad it was. Your father walked away from him, hasn't spoken to him from that day on."

I shot a quick glance at Frances, smiled reassuringly, but she did not appear all that reassured.

"Well I'm sure things will blow over. In time, you know. Give it a bit of time."

"What time you wanna give it, Denis? This wasn't a couple of years back. The fight your father's talking about happened almost twenty years ago!"

I looked at Frances. She looked relieved.

"Got a memory, your dad. For a lot of the bad—for all the good it does." Vi sighed.

I poured her a large glass of wine. My family drank hard spirits, usually gin, so when anyone drank wine it was in a sherry or a liqueur glass. I had bought a few wine glasses on a previous trip, and I handed her one of those. Vi's eyes widened like gob stoppers.

"That's not a glass—it's a goldfish bowl!"

"Too much?" I asked.

"Don't worry, Denis, I'll manage. And I'll tell John you said hello. Funny old bugger, your dad is, isn't he?"

"Yes, he's a funny old bugger alright."

"Cup of tea, Mum?" Pam moved her mother's walking cane as it slipped from her side.

"Oh, don't fuss, Pam!" Aunt Flo sounded a bit dismissive, almost cold.

"I was just asking, no need to go on, Mum!" Part foil, part dutiful daughter, Pam was always close to being taken advantage of, but she took her mother's curtness with grudging acceptance. Pam was genuinely fond of all her aged relatives. For some odd reason she found their extreme and sometimes erratic behavior entertaining. Pam was unmarried and in middle years though still very attractive, with long blonde hair and smiling eyes. She seemed happy to play nurse-companion to her mother, happy to escape from her father.

"So, how's Tom, Aunt Flo?" I asked. Tom was Flo's husband. Apparently old age was not having a mellowing effect upon his nature.

"Nasty. Cantankerous. Well… You know, hasn't really changed, actually—" Pam leaned across and spoke even more softly than normal. "I think he's getting worse. If that's possible."

Then she laughed and playfully tapped Flo's knee. "Horrible little man, isn't he, Mum?"

"Glad we left him at home," Flo said.

"Always good for a laugh! Ha, ha! Uncle Tom!" Tony's voice bubbled with salacious laughter of half-remembered naughtiness. "What a character! I should say so! Funny little sod."

"Well, then—" I said. "Another drink?"

"You making more tea or what?" said Mum.

"Tea! Who wants?" barked Lew, clambering to his feet, looking from one to another. Suddenly everyone was muttering about having a nice cup of tea.

More tea was served, more sandwiches, and then more drinks. Frances showed pictures from our wedding, and pleasantries were dutifully clucked. As the snaps were passed around, I tried to catch up with my family as best I could. Drinks flowed along with conversation until suddenly someone checked a watch, mentioned the last train, and that was that. It was time to go. With some effort everyone tottered to their feet. They had been sitting down for the best part of five hours, not moving except to go to the lavatory.

Everyone swayed and steadied themselves as if disembarking from a ship. Lew started to faffle around for coats and canes, and soon everyone was on their way. Hands were pumped, hugs were exchanged, smiles were flashed, faces kissed. The front door was opened, and the smell of talcum powder, sherry, and perfume mingled with the cool night air. Cars were started. Lifts to Becontree Station were arranged for some to catch the last train back to town. We waited in the doorway and waved. Final bursts of chatter and laughter, and then they were gone.

"Alright, come on in, you two, or you'll catch your deaths." Lew shepherded us back inside. The farewell moment tucked safely away, I smiled. I was flattered so many had turned out to meet Frances, and it had all gone surprisingly well.

～

On our last day, we went to nearby Barking. Although enveloped by the Dagenham housing sprawl, Barking retained a lot of its original mundane and charmless appearance and was, to me, quite interchangeable with a dozen or so county towns that cling to London's burgeoning perimeter.

Needless to say, I hated Barking as much as Dagenham. Hundreds of years ago it was probably different, only because nothing was there except flat farmland slanting towards the Thames, working sail barges on the river and, in the far distance, the green-smudged hills of Kent. Today, the busy town of Barking hankered neither to the past nor the future. The Barking Creek was now a concrete sludge-way. The fishing fleets were long gone, and so was the farmland. We did see the remains of Barking Abbey, originally looted and destroyed by Henry the Eighth in a fervor of Protestant greed. This tiny ruin, with its tiny tower and itty-bitty crenulations, contained a small chapel that, two centuries earlier, became a famous local landmark when Captain Cook was married there before embarking on the Endeavor for one of his many voyages of discovery. That was the high point of the Barking visit, but there were lesser sights to see, and Frances was game to see them.

I played reluctant tour guide. There's the cop shop where I once waited for my mum when I got lost in the local street market. And there's Poole's, the butcher's. Brian Poole? Twist and Shout? The Tremeloes? No? Oh. There's the municipal indoor pool. There's Pesci's fish and chip shop. That's where the local Odeon Cinema was. And see that? It was a football stadium for Barking United. Looks like a shopping mall now. Oh, well. And here's the Spotted Dog, where Lew told us to go for lunch. And look, there's Dick, right on time.

My old friend from music days was meeting us for lunch. Years before, we had written songs together. He was also a good-looking lead singer who could actually sing. Yet, despite some early success, Dick had remained in Dagenham, not two blocks from where my parents lived. Since my last visit, his hair had turned unnaturally blond, and he now sported mutton-chop sideburns that matched neither his hair nor current fashion.

"What's with the sideburns?" I felt compelled to ask. "Is this for a fifties revival?"

"If only it was, Den. I'm fronting a glam band. You know, all that glitter shit from the seventies. I'm only doing it for the dosh. It's either that or it's a job on the light railway."

"So, how's it working out for you?" asked Frances, trying to keep a straight face.

"Well, actually, Fran, oh, oh, Frances, sorry, sorry. Well, what can I say?" He leaned forward and continued in a matter-of-fact tone of voice, "It's demeaning. Really quite revolting. And fucking vile. Did I say it was demeaning?"

Frances and I lost it, and Dick started laughing so hard, he put his hand to his mouth as if something was about to fall out. Then, nearing hysteria, he recounted his painful show-biz experiences with the enthusiasm of a self-flagellating penitent.

"You should see me in the Lurex trousers, the glitter! I look such a wally! But they lap it up, Den. They really do! And I hate it. I have to get pissed out me brains just to get up on stage!"

After he calmed down, Dick drank some of his beer, then sighed heavily. His smile shrank to an angry pout. He fisted his hands and went on to berate the state of pop music and moan about how hard it was to get gigs. Waiting for the phone to ring was the hardest, he said. Contacts, Den, you've got to have contacts. Ironically, he had written songs for a movie that failed in Britain, but had been a huge hit in the States. Instead of following up on his American success, he chose to hunker down in Dagenham. To wait for the phone to ring. For his luck to change. Never knowing, his luck had already changed, a long way from home, a long time ago.

The food in the pub was not very good. I had a pie with gristle bits and gravy. Frances had soggy fish and chips. Since the advent of mad cow, Dick had sworn off meat. Have the fish, I said. Polluted. Okay, I suggested poultry. He refused, hands waving frantically, a look of fear in his eyes. No, no, no, he said, smirking at my innocence and gullibility. The government is poisoning the chickens, Den. Apparently the government was behind everything. And what we didn't know about, they were covering up. Needless to say, Dick ended up chasing lettuce leaves around his plate, massing them into a little grassy knoll of his own making. Not a good lunch, and not much of a reunion.

～

"You went to the wrong one! It wasn't the Spotted Dog. I told you. It was the Barking Dog. The Barking Dog. That was where I told you to go!" Dad shot Frances a look, mustering an ally. "He never listens."

"There are two dog pubs, across from each other?" asked Frances.

"Well, the town is called Barking, innit," Lew said, with a slight smile.

"It was alright, Dad. It was alright. Wasn't too bad."

"Have a lovely lunch, they do. At the Barking Dog. Oh, well, never mind, eh! We'll have a nice tea here."

But first, Frances insisted on exploring the immediate vicinity. A quick walk before dinner. It was where I grew up, she said. She was curious. I was not. But then, maybe I was. A little.

The landscape in Dagenham had no contours, except for the occasional tarmac hillock to accommodate London Transport on its bold thrust eastwards. Yet, even with its flatness, Dagenham didn't have a big sky like Aldeburgh. It narrowed at the edges of one's horizon, cowering in one corner and skulking in the other. And so it was with Castle Green, the vast playing fields located a few blocks from my old home. Frances and I went for a walk there, following the path I took years ago with Rex, our family dog. We headed diagonally across an empty expanse, past a muddy soccer field and the sagging narrowness of an unkempt cricket pitch. Past the brick sports building that was always locked and always reeked of pee because the local soccer players could never get to the inside toilet. Past the wooden notice board with pasted-over information of long-gone events. Nothing new to announce. Nothing I did not know about.

Castle Green had always been completely devoid of trees. Rex could never wait to scamper across it. And who could have blamed him.

"Rex! Over here, boy!" I used to call out. Part Chow, part Husky, Rex would circle back toward me, panting loudly, his mouth open in what looked like a permanent smile, his curly fan tail swishing wildly. He was a handsome dog, broad-chested, strong, and fearless. He also sported what appeared to be an Elizabethan ruff made of fur that ringed his ginger-colored teddy bear face. He would sidle up close, I would slip on his leash, and we would leave Castle Green, cross over Ripple Road, and head towards the Ship and Shovel. This pub was positioned where the marsh ended and the boundary of the Dagenham estate began. My parents, Rex, and I would often walk over in the evening. Kids were not allowed in public houses in those days, so I was condemned to stand in the doorway with a bag of crisps, a glass of sticky lemonade, and Rex for company. No one thought twice about leaving young children outside pubs. That was the way it was. So there I stayed for an hour or two, staring silently at other kids in a similar predicament. Occasionally, out of sheer boredom, Rex and I would venture onto the marsh. It was night-time, but if we stayed to the tufted high ground it was quite safe. Except once.

Thinking it was a patch of emerald grass, Rex jumped into a deep, wide bog. He sank for a moment, then thrust his head through the bright green slime. He trod marsh water for a panic-stricken moment before swimming through the reeds onto a mud slick. I slid down and hauled him back to the path. And there we sat, out of breath and much relieved. Rex stank of marsh and gasoline but he was wagging his tail and, after he had shaken himself, I soon smelled as badly as he did. I looked up and heard the squalling of river birds, misplaced seagulls streaked with brown sludge, poster birds for animal rescue groups. Fly away! Escape! Get preened! They never did.

On the near horizon, old cargo boats slipped silently and slowly down river. I watched them until their languid shadow-black profiles had drifted beyond the massive Ford car plant, its furnace glowing in the night sky like a manmade daybreak. In those days, the furnace worked day and night and was only turned off during the break in summer, aptly called the "Ford Shutdown." This marked the annual holiday for virtually every Ford worker. Two weeks away from it all.

I had just spent a week back in it all. And now it was coming to an end.

"Want a drink? They may even let you inside this time." Frances smiled. I smiled back. We looked across the road toward the Ship and Shovel. The flatness of the skyline, once shaped by the occasional steamer, was now buckled into permanence by houses and flats that stretched down to the water's edge. The new housing estate was called Thames View. More cars. More shops. More people. More of everything. But less of what I remembered. We did not go into the pub. Instead, we turned back; it was almost time for dinner.

~

"Right on it? You going to put it right on it?"

My mother was mortified. I had produced the rosemary I had charmed from the lady gardener in Dedham the day before.

"Yes, Mum, the rosemary will impart a lovely flavor to the meat. Delicious. You'll like it."

"Ghrrr. That's French. That's what that is. French!" Lew said it as if it were a slur. And he was looking at me as if I were an aesthete nancy boy bent on perfuming lamb! Hell, next!

"Dad, you can't write off a whole country."

"I've been to France. Twice." A dark scowl swept across his face. Lew did not need to remind me what "twice" meant: Dunkirk, then Normandy. I tried to lighten his mood.

"Didn't you go to Paris with Mum once?"

"Oh, yes, that time. Oh, yes—" He recalled the visit with happy rancor. "We were walking and we were that knackered, we couldn't walk anymore. So we sat down on these two seats near this cafe. And this little bleeder came running over to us. Jabbering on in French, he was. Then, he starts in English. Broken, mind you. You know what? He wanted to charge us just for sitting there! Lovely place though, Paris. Never went there during the war. Never got close enough. Too many Germans that time. Right, I'll get dinner."

Moments later Lew was hurrying in with plates of English lamb, Yorkshire pud, roast spuds. Mum had served Brussels sprouts with every evening meal that week, so we were relieved to see a different vegetable.

"Ah! Marrow fat peas, marvelous!" I beamed with childlike enthusiasm.

"Marrow fat peas?" Frances stared at the small mound of bright, marsh-like greenness piled up on one side of her plate. When my parents left the room to get more plates and condiments, Frances whispered, pointing to the peas, "They smell. The peas smell like—"

"Urine? That's why you need the mint sauce. Covers it up, mostly," I said, smiling casually.

Frances tasted one of the starch-engorged peas, then immediately scooped the remaining ones onto my plate when my parents were not looking. Coward.

The following morning Lew gave us packages of tea to take home, and Mum gave us two jars of her blackcurrant jam. The currant came from a bush at the bottom of the garden. Every two years its canes would bulge with tiny balls of fruit like giant globs of black caviar. Like all of Mum's culinary adventures, her jams were hit and miss. Sometimes the preserves would set perfectly, an explosion of bright flavor that burst in the mouth, combining tartness and succulence with the wonderful aromas of tangy chocolate, oranges, and a kind of woodiness. In off years, Mum's jam was syrupy and runny, but if it could not be spread on buttered bread, it could at least be poured on ice cream. No one complained.

Along with the jam, Lew gave me a stack of cassette tapes featuring my favorite radio show, *The Archers*, a daily soap opera produced by the BBC for over fifty years. *The Archers* was set in the village of Ambridge and revealed the everyday life of country folk, farmers, landowners, laborers, vicars, poachers. Ah, the pastoral life! The English countryside! Admittedly, I did not have much experience of it. But it was real enough. It was there. I had made the odd day trip. And I wondered what it might be like to stay longer. Now there was a thought.

As we left, Jessie and Lew stood at the door and waved and waved as they always did. I could see them in the rear view mirror. They did not move. I turned the corner at the end of the street. Again, I was pulling away from my home, from them.

A Tudor Cottage in East Anglia

CHAPTER 5

From Dagenham to Rattlesden

WE ARRIVED in the drab outer suburbs of London at a time when only the most foolhardy of sparrows felt compelled to sing. We were shuffled down endless black, corrugated rubber mats. We had hand luggage, piles of diapers, a six-month old baby, no stroller, a very large and very heavy bottle of Jack Daniels for Lew, an orange liqueur for my mum, lots of photographs, and a large, frozen prime rib roast packed within our clothing. Frances and the baby were more than a tad cranky. I limped along beside them, bags crushing my shoulders, prematurely curving my spine, bashing against my legs with every other step. Against my wife's saner judgment, I had insisted on carrying everything. This was my sodding country, I had dragged my family here, and I should bloody well be punished for it. We finally reached Immigration.

"Is your trip business or pleasure, sir?"

"Neither. I'm visiting my parents."

"Shall we consider that pleasure then, shall we, sir?"

"Pleasure? They should have another category, don't you think?" I aimed what I thought was a witty aside at Frances, who tried to smile but yawned instead. She had heard all this before.

"Where are we staying, sir?" said the official, obviously not one to banter.

"What?"

"Why do you need to know that?" Frances moved to the counter.

"I was talking to sir, madam."

One does not call a Barnard Woman a madam. They are not to be trifled with, even by a bureaucrat of the same sex.

"Why do you need to know where we're staying?" Frances was now dog to the bureaucrat's bone. I admit I, too, was impatient and also a little angry, but my anger was tinged by my working class fear of officialdom in all its wondrous forms. I was cowering, my wife was blossoming.

"What if we were touring? Going around the country?" she asked. "Other democracies don't ask you were you are staying."

Good point, I thought. Good point.

"We may have to contact you in case of an emergency."

"Look," I said. I was timid. "We're visiting two ancient people. It's no good calling them in an emergency. In fact, if there's going to be an emergency, it'll be because of them. D'you see?" I smiled wanly and waited for a reaction. None came.

"Where are you staying? Sir?" The woman stared at me. I panicked.

"I don't know, we are staying at the 'Bird's Nest' or something like that. We're meeting someone there, by the Vicarage Wall, or somewhere. And we're going to be late. Late! Late!" Now I was sounding as batty as the White Rabbit.

"Just write in that you're staying at Buckingham Palace," Frances said, not too helpfully.

"Not a very good start to your holiday, madam, lying to Immigration."

How very true! I scrawled my parents' address, where no one would be, certainly not us. Certainly not Jessie and Lew.

"Have a pleasant holiday, sir." Venom dripped triumphantly from thin lips stretched into a smile of sorts. Frances was still mad as hell and had made no attempt to kowtow. Good for her. But I had humbled myself before this bastion of official idiocy and couldn't look my wife in the face for quite a few minutes.

～

Driving on the left side of the road was not all that difficult, as I am left-handed, "cack-handed" as Lew would say. My parents lived in the extreme East of London, so, to me, driving through London seemed a logical choice. Frances suggested we take the Orbital, which is not a dental exam but is, in fact, the highway "orbiting" the city. Naturally, I ignored her suggestion. This was my country. My city. I knew best.

When we hit Central London, the back-up was appalling. I started to wish I had taken the Orbital, although I would never have admitted it. I was, after all, an Essex boy, born and bred on the edge of the edge of the city. I knew my way around London, or thought I did. Of course, when I lived in town, I had been a pedestrian, a user of public transport, an occasional taker of taxis. But now I was in the driver's seat. And I was clueless. I did not know where I was going, so I did what comes naturally to any savvy pedestrian: I followed the buses.

With joy and relief I found a 38 bus heading vaguely in the right direction. This was my favorite bus. I knew the route it followed—I had hopped on and off that bus for years. At last I knew where I was going. Then the bus entered a bus-only lane. A new innovation. But I was not fazed or panicked. I recognized Park Lane with its aging hotels on the left and Hyde Park on the right. I swerved around Hyde Park Corner and passed various landmarks in quick succession, Buckingham Palace, Trafalgar Square, St. Martins in the Fields, until we found ourselves on the Strand. Happily, I connected with a number 22 bus, another route I knew well, heading east. I became cocky and overtook it.

I saw the dome of St. Paul's, which meant we were entering the City of London, the original square mile that now contains London's financial center, its oldest buildings, and the fewest residents, except during business hours when the population swells from a few thousand to over a million people. Beyond the City with its own jurisdiction, its extra-tall policemen, and its own way of doing things, was the East End and, eventually, my old home.

We sped past St. Paul's Cathedral, then Mansion House, home of the Lord Mayor of London. I pressed on until we arrived finally at Aldgate East Station. I now decided to follow the District Line of the London Underground, eastbound to Dagenham. For a while, my unique navigational system seemed to be working. Whitechapel, Bethnal Green, Mile End: the road traffic appeared to be following the below-ground rail system. I sped on with renewed confidence. The next stop on the District Line was Bromley-by-Bow. But my next train stop turned out to be Stratford East. My above-ground bearings had come adrift from the underground map.

Stratford East is in no way connected to Shakespeare's neck of the woods, but as far as I was concerned it might just as well have been. I was now following the Central Line, heading northeast and away from our destination. A few minutes later I pulled over. We were in a rancid-smelling, litter-strewn street in a part of London called Seven Kings, aptly named in my case, for I was now royally off course and hopelessly lost. I asked the first person I found for directions to Dagenham.

"You're a long way from 'ome, aren't you, mate!" He was a grizzled, slightly stooped old duffer, but cheerful. He seemed to take some small measure of delight in my obvious discomfort. "Can't direct you to Dagenham, would Ilford do you alright?"

"Thank you. Yes!"

As he was already stooped, my helpful navigator simply swung himself parallel to the driver's window and started jabbing the air with his pathfinder's hand.

"Now, you go up there, right, left, right. Got that? Right! When you get up there, you'll come to this thing we call a 'roundabout.' Got that, yeah?"

He talked slowly. He talked loudly. We realized he thought we were foreign. He thought I was an American! He said again, but slower, "a 'ran-da-bhat.'" Bloody nerve.

"Anyway, you'll come to this 'ran-da-bhat' and—"

He never explained what a 'ran-da-bhat' was exactly. Instead, he started making large circular movements with his oddly bent hand and arm. If I had been American by birth and not by choice, I might have imagined he was describing a carousel with gaudily painted wooden horses placed on the highway to amuse passing commuters, rather than a traffic circle. I stared at him. He smiled, nodding, looking like the amiable idiot he thought I was.

"Yes, yes, I know what it is. I've been 'ere before." I thickened up my Cockney accent.

"Sorry, mate, I thought you was a Yank. Anyway, don't go right a-rhaand it. Turn off before you do, and that'll get you on the Ilford Road. Can't miss it."

I thanked him, and we were on our way. I knew Ilford. Not the most direct route, but after the jetlagged, mishmash of a journey we had just taken we were finally headed home. Home! Oh, God!

~

"Where is she? Where is she!" Lew was gruff and proud-sounding.

Aaah.

"Let me look at her! Come on, you, out the way." Mum pushed Lew aside and put her hands out to touch the baby.

Aaah.

"Oh, bless her! Lovely, lovely she is!" Mum chirped gaily.

Lew was momentarily speechless, but he was smiling.

"The wanderer returns! The prodigal is back!" I assumed a dramatic pose, trying to attract attention, but old eyes were on the new.

"There she is, there she is. 'Allo, Katie. 'Allo, Katie. Oooh-oooh! Oooh-oooh!" Frances and I received congratulatory hugs and handshakes, but my parents were still looking at Kate.

"Welcome home, son."

"Well, Dad, what d'you think?"

"She's marvelous, she is. Marvelous."

Lew seemed lost in thought for a moment. Then it passed, and he got straight to business.

"Bet you want a nice cup of tea!"

"Put the kettle on." Mum waved at Lew, who was looking again at Kate.

"Yes. Yes, don't worry your arse." Lew huffed and shuffled lower for a better look.

"He's funny, isn't he? Isn't he funny? He's a funny old stick, isn't he!" Mum was smiling and pointing out Lew to Kate. She talked about him as if he wasn't there. Lew didn't mind a bit.

"Oh, Dad, remember, Frances doesn't take milk," I called out as he took off for the kitchen.

"I remember, I remember, no milk." Pointedly, for my mum's benefit. "Hear that? No milk! No milk! Gawd save us!" Lew chuckled as he returned with a tea tray.

"Right then, so, Mum, Dad? You both packed and ready?"

"Are we packed? Packed!" Lew laughed, a hackle, hackle, hackle, kind of laugh. "We've been packed for a week!"

I stared at them both, excited as kids on their first day of camp. If renting a cottage and hosting my parents for a week had raised any doubts in my mind, they did not loom up then.

We consulted a local map to find the best way to get to our country cottage. Frances suggested we take the highway. I was skeptical. Lew smiled his slightly patronizing smile and slowly shook his head, but Frances was insistent.

"Now steady the buffs, steady the buffs." Lew spoke forcefully and with quiet authority. "No need to get all worked up. We're going the direct way there!"

Frances did not know what to say. She was outnumbered by Lewis and Clark and decided to go with the flow. Lew was, after all, the man on the ground, so she deferred to his judgment and navigating skills. She should have stuck to her guns, for although Lew had worked at Ford's for decades, he had never owned a car and knew very little about driving. Certainly he knew nothing of traffic patterns. Or highways. Or byways, for that matter. If I had asked him to look for a spur in the road, he would have looked for something small, shiny, and pronged.

The only time I recall Lew driving was when he rented a car one year, on our annual holiday. I was about seven years old. We were staying on the Isle of Wight, in the far South of England. Lew had trouble changing gears, because he always attempted to perform this feat without the aid of the clutch. Consequently we found ourselves lurching in a cartoon-like manner from one cliff view to another.

"Oh, bugger it!" Lew slapped the steering wheel and pulled over. Realizing he had gone the wrong way, he decided to turn the car around on a headland curve. This maneuver required backing up on a sharp incline. Regrettably, Lew couldn't seem to get the car out of reverse. The car backed up on a crumbling curb, then over the tufted grass at the roadside. The car jolted back over rocky gravel, ever closer to the cliff's almost vertical incline. Despite the erratic lurching, we were now, surprisingly, pointed in the right direction. Lew slammed on the brakes, the car juddered and then stopped. He peered though the front window and could see a small bit of road beyond the grassy tufts. He smiled. "Alright now," said Lew, as he revved the car's engine.

Mum and I looked out the back seat window, and all we could see was sky.

"I wanna get out. I wanna get out!" Jessie sounded firm, her voice an octave higher than usual.

Lew was angry at Jessie's lack of faith in his driving abilities. For my part, I was a little surprised by my mother's lack of maternal concern.

"I wanna get out!" Jessie yelled.

Lew started yelling back, trying to convince no one in particular that all would be well. I looked out the back again and stared down. And down. All I could see was greenish, frothy water. And large rocks that looked as small as pebbles. What had been scenic had now turned horrific.

"LEMME OUT! LEMME OUT!" Mum had become hysterical.

"Don't panic yourself, woman. I know what I'm doing!"

Young as I was, I was beginning to have my doubts. I had never seen my mother so scared. Her face was as white as the eternal Cliffs of Dover. Then Lew stalled the car. Without a backward glance at me, Jessie fumbled with the door and clambered to safety, leaving me behind. Her instincts for self-preservation were truly memorable. I remained frozen in my seat. What to do? Lew started the car again.

"Good luck, Dad!" I jumped out and ran towards Mum. Again, I heard the sound of metal being torn and shredded as Lew changed gear. I had not closed the back door properly, so it swung open and flapped, useless as a broken wing, as the car lurched forward, back over the gravel, the grass, back over the curb, and onto the road again.

"Don't know what you were all so bloody worried about! I knew what I was doing!"

Tactfully, or prudently, we remained silent. Lew grumbled and mumbled as he stared into the windscreen, not daring to look at us. We continued grinding our way upward. Walking would have been faster. Steep hill, he muttered, steep hill. Then he looked down and released the hand brake, which seemed to help our ascent considerably.

Ghrrr.

From that day on, he never drove a car again. But standing in the little passageway of my old home, thirty odd years later, Lew had inexplicably affected the expertise of a seasoned racer. Stirling Moss! One last time, Frances tried to make the case for the highway. Not the most direct route, she conceded, but definitely the fastest. Again, Lew looked at her kindly. With apparent reluctance, he shook his head and emitted a wheezy chuckle punctuated by bronchial commas.

Hackle, hackle, hackle.

The very idea of going out of one's way, even slightly, to get to somewhere faster was an alien concept to Lew. As it was to me. To her credit, Frances did not gloat, at least not openly, at our navigational error. We drove and drove. We did not seem to be getting anywhere. We just seemed to be driving from one "ran-da-bhat" to another, some as close to each other as Olympic rings. In one stretch, I counted six roundabouts within a mile. Some had gardens in the middle. Very nice. Others were covered over with grass and some were just painted circles in the road. One was little more than a foot in diameter, I have no idea why they bothered with that one.

Deeper and deeper we plunged into the Essex countryside. Motoring down country lanes, we swerved and veered past giant hedgerows and saw nothing except twisted bracken and hedge leaves. Villages appeared as signposts to the left or right of the curving, apparently endless road that twirled and opened up before us.

Beyond the impersonal sameness of Sudbury, we lost our way. Lew had been studying the map in silence, and what knowledge he may have gained from its study, he kept to himself.

"Okay, everyone, we're looking for Great Waldingfield," I finally said.

"Great Waldingfield, you say? Not Little Waldingfield?" Lew spoke with apparent sagacity.

"No," I said with equal conviction. "Why?"

"Doesn't matter, doesn't matter." A moment later Lew casually mentioned that we had passed Great Waldingfield about ten minutes earlier.

"Bugger."

"So, Little Waldingfield, would that be any good to you?"

"Well, it might be. Why?"

"Well, we just went past that one a few minutes ago."

"Why didn't you tell me?"

"Because you didn't want to know about it!"

I shot a glance at Frances for support. Failure.

"We're right up a gum tree now, aren't we, son." It was no question. Lew was stating a fact in his normal pessimistic way.

"Thanks, Dad. Thanks! Great! If I remember rightly, you're supposed to be navigating!"

"How you doing back there?" asked Frances, turning around, trying to lighten the mood.

"Don't you worry about us, gel, you just carry on," said Lew.

My parents were jammed up against the doors, dwarfed by what was probably the largest child's car seat ever built, a cross between a giant throne and a commode. They could barely move, scared of disturbing the little princess who was sleeping, blissfully unaware of anything untoward.

"I need to go," said Mum ominously.

"She needs to go," Lew repeated, pointing and nodding his head as if to underline the veracity of her statement. The map fell off his knees. He tried to catch it, but the map fluttered down to the floor like a giant moth.

"Oh, bugger!"

"Don't worry, Dad, leave it where it is. We've gotten this far without it," I said with some degree of resignation. I looked out at fields of yellow stuff. Occasionally I glimpsed the odd bus shelter, a rusty gate, but no signs of life. Certainly no signs of relief for Mum.

"Lavenham! Look! A sign for Lavenham! Found it. There it is. Almost there now. Hold on a bit longer, Mum." I stared at the roadside. "Now we're looking for a turn off to Cockfield. That's it! Look! That's it! This will lead us straight to Rattlesden."

Lew was jubilant and cried "Hooray." The sign even cheered me up a bit. Rattlesden could not be far now. Like so many of the rural roads we'd passed, this one was neither straight nor fast. But things were changing, the hedgerows getting a bit smaller. Mum's need to "go" had momentarily, thankfully, passed. She looked around, quite unimpressed with the scenery.

"Couldn't live in the country, meself. Too quiet. I like a bit of life, meself."

We shot around a bend and turned past a gas station. No neon oasis here, just a small lean-to with one pump, a quaint relic from another age, when motor cars, in England at least, were the playthings of the rich and titled. I could imagine the likes of Lord Peter Whimsey or Mister Toad roaring up to it, all grins, goggles, and gauntlets. But the day we showed up it was closed. It was the weekend, after all, and this was England. Then we saw a sign. Rattlesden. Finally. And just as well.

"It's a long way away, isn't it? Don't think I can hold it much longer!"

"I'm busting, meself. Cor strewf!" Lew joined in with some urgency.

A local saw us. No, no, I don't need petrol. I'm looking for The Bird's Nest. I couldn't believe I was actually asking someone for a bird's nest. I was almost embarrassed, but it didn't strike the villager as strange in the least. A flicker of recognition flashed across his face and he started giving directions. We were very close. He, too, spoke slowly. He, too, thought I was an American. Strange. Or maybe he just associated helplessness with being a tourist. But my helplessness had more to do with being in the countryside than anything else. Growing up, no one I knew gravitated towards hamlets and green hills and dales. To us, this was all an alien landscape. To my mother, it still was.

"Is it much farther, son?" asked Lew, leaning forward, his face creased in stoic panic.

We drove on about a hundred yards or so, and then the road forked. The left side of the fork sloped away into a small gravel track, on which the Bird's Nest nestled. Our rental was one of three Tudor-frame cottages built during the reign of Elizabeth the First. This tiny piece of history sat on the edge of the gravel as if in repose, shrunken a little with great age yet still inviting and cozy. The thatched roof lay across it all like an immaculately shaped hay rig. Tiny red bricks like so many red plums formed the chimney. Although the beams were hard and solid black oak, here and there they curved and buckled ever so slightly, giving the cottage a more rounded, softer, friendlier feel. Red roses were growing around the leaded framed windows. Reluctantly, I cracked a smile. Frances could not wait to get inside. I had to admit, if this was it, we would have a wonderful week.

CHAPTER 6

From the Bird's Nest to Stowmarket

"YOU MADE IT THEN. I was beginning to wonder what happened to you all."

Dave, the keyholder, ambled over to us. I apologized for our late arrival.

"You didn't take the motorway? Should have taken the motorway, you would have been here in an hour. Hour and a quarter at the outside."

I apologized again. Frances smiled, said nothing. Our journey had taken almost three hours.

"No problem. I've been doing some odd jobs around the village. I was checking back every now and then. No harm done."

I had gotten out of the car as soon as I could to readjust my spine and reacquaint myself with the rest of my anatomy. Frances had taken Kate out of the car and was heading for the cottage. Lew was stretching his legs and pulling his arms back like a semi-trussed chicken.

"Forgotten all about you, have they? Come on, darling." Dave opened the car door for my mum and gently pried her out. He smiled and she cooed appreciatively.

"Better not forget about me!" She smiled at Dave. He helped her into the cottage.

"Now, you set yourself down here, my love, and we'll get you a nice cup of tea."

As Dave went off to make some tea, Mum immediately began to sing his praises.

"Lovely! Lovely chap, isn't he? Lovely."

"Yes, Mum, yes—"

I smiled and rolled my eyes at Lew, but if Mum was happy, he was happy, and Mum was ecstatically so. She loved it when anyone other than Lew made an outrageous fuss of her. We lay Kate down at her feet, and she smiled and stared at the baby.

The front parlor, what Frances would call the living room, was even smaller than the one at my parents' house. Everything about it was minute, but in perfect proportion to the house, except for the support beams that crisscrossed the low ceiling. Jutting out at various points around the room, these large lumps of oak were like molded barricades.

"Oooooooow!" The sound I made was followed by a curse.

The beams were five hundred years old and did not give. I kept forgetting they were there, although I received several painful reminders. I was reduced to hunching over and lurching around like a latter-day Quasimodo minus the bells. This worked well, until I felt the need to straighten up. Then I would promptly forget the ceiling's irregular topography and crack my head again. I was too stupid to be a Pavlovian dog, but at least I had ibuprofen.

To the left of the front door were stairs so steep they looked like steps in one of those Gothic castle towers in which half-mad relatives are sensibly walled up. They shot upwards into the roof of the cottage. Under the eaves were two small bedrooms. The one for Frances and me, although snug and sloping, was quite lovely. The adjoining one, Kate's room, was so teeny tiny it could best be described as a glorified dresser drawer. But as Kate was less than two feet tall and did not walk or even crawl, this room was also well proportioned. Except for the door, which had been hung for a gnome.

"Dad, you should come up here," I shouted down. Lew took one look at the steep stairs and decided against rappelling towards our airy nest.

Beyond the living room with its unlit inglenook fireplace was a small but charming dining room. To the left was a bedroom for my folks, with two narrow twin beds. We found a modernized kitchen and a bright breakfast area, as well as a small conservatory with a bathroom and a self-contained, all-in-one shower unit. From the breakfast area, a door led out onto a narrow garden, fat with grass and flowers and hedges that framed the church on the hill in the near distance quite perfectly. I would have to explore. But first things first. Tea.

Dave poured. Delicious. In addition to tea, he had thoughtfully stocked the kitchen with bread, milk, butter, eggs, and bacon. Dave was a jovial countryman with a wind-burnt face and quite knowledgeable about the outside world, aware enough not to get involved with it unless he really had to. He did odd jobs around the village, a general handyman who tended gardens, made deliveries, and occasionally worked at the local pub. He had grown up in the neighborhood, a Suffolk man born and bred.

"So what brought you here then, to Rattlesden?"

A good question. This was deepest Suffolk, not the Cotswolds or the more obvious tourist destinations of rural England. We explained that we were somewhat limited because we wanted a bedroom on the ground floor so that Jessie and Lew would have a break from twisting and difficult stairs. That being said, we did not feel the cottage fell short of expectations. We had done our homework. And, although Rattlesden was off the tourist trail, Frances had already identified several sights, including some of the most beautiful villages in England.

"And it's not that far from where my parents live," I concluded.

"Even closer if you take the highway!" Dave smiled his winning smile, then turned to Lew and my mum. "D'you miss him then?" He grinned, knowing what the answer would be, and nodded in concert with their grumbles and mumbles of resignation and slight resentment.

"Well, you've got him now, haven't you?" Dave, who obviously had a knack with old people, went on, "And look at the beautiful baby he's brought over for you."

"Of course she is. Beautiful. Beautiful, she is—bless her!" Mum smiled and waved at Kate, who obligingly waggled her limbs at her doting nanny.

"Looks like you, Mum." Kiss up from the gallery.

"Blonde, she is, like me."

Kate was as bald as a fuzzy peach. Undaunted, Mum went on.

"I was always blonde, meself. And she's got my eyes, she has. Two lovely blue eyes." She started singing. "Two lovely blue eyes, two lovely blue eyes," then la-la-lahed the rest of it. She looked up at Dave and smiled. "Do you have any children?"

"Just the one," said Dave.

"Is that all? Just the one?" Mum was a little surprised, a little disappointed. "I had two meself. Would've been more, you know, with him, but I put me foot down—"

"Not now, Jessie." Lew was firm. He looked at me, his glance heavenward.

Mum eyed Dave. "So, you've just got the one then, have you? Having any more?"

"My wife has M.S., so we better not have any more children." He was matter-of-fact.

"Why not?" said Mum, unaware of the acronym for the dread disease.

"Because she's sick, Mum. She's sick!"

"Oh. Oh, well, then. Well, if she is—she is!"

Silence.

"You finish your tea before it gets cold," said Lew, pointing to her cup.

"Don't you tell me what to finish. I'll finish you! Always bossing me around, he is. Well, he tries to anyway. But I don't let him!" She laughed nervously. Lew rolled his eyes and his throat rumbled and emitted that well-worn sound, devoid of words.

Ghrrr.

"Can we get something to eat in the pub?" I asked, eager to change the conversation.

Dave downed his tea and stood up. "Got that covered. Thought you might be late, so I had a word with the landlord. I'll go over now, see if it's ready."

And then he was gone. I finished my tea. We did a bit more unpacking. Now I felt I could relax, but not quite. Mum looked flustered, a little panicked.

"Where's Dave?"

"Jessie!" Lew sounded impatient now.

"What's a matter with you then? I'm just asking."

"Hello, hello, settling in alright, are we?" Dave had returned. He told us our late lunch was all set, and went on to describe the impromptu feast. "Smoked salmon, fresh baked bread, salad. Be alright, will it? Be ready for you in about ten minutes." As Dave was leaving he turned, as though remembering something. "Take a paper, don't you? Of course, you do. They don't have newspapers here. You have to order them. I take the *Sun* and the *Mail*. I'll bring them over when I've finished. Save you a couple of bob on petrol."

Lew did not normally read the *Mail* but he did not mind. Any newspaper that carried a racing page would do just fine. Both my parents loved the gee-gees, the horses. Gambling was their one shared passion, one of the few times they ever talked to each other, as words did not normally feature too loudly in their vocabulary. A forceful kind of sign language filled the vast stretches of silence that landscaped their lives. They pointed and stared and eye-rolled and grunted and snarled and huffily ignored one another. Then, sometimes, inexplicably, they would hold each other's hands for the longest time, without ever saying a word.

I broke out the colossal bottle of Jack Black I'd brought over for Lew, the Cointreau for Mum. Dave told us that if there were any problems, not to hesitate and call. If he wasn't there, I was to leave word for him at the village shop or at the pub. I poured him a large shot of Jack, which he downed with a toast to our stay. Dave then smiled all around and was gone, along with my mum's memory of his visit. Spilt milk. I poured Mum another drink. Lew quietly issued a cautionary request for me to take it easy. Mum noticed, and a shadow of anger eclipsed her sunny personality.

"Don't listen to him. This is my medicine, this is. And look at him looking. Look at that face! Just look at it! I have to live with that."

Mum pointed to Lew then tittered nervously. He said nothing. He sat in gnarled resignation, his skinny jaws and chin clamped shut in a vice-like grip. Wanting to speak, but scared of what he might say.

"Come on, everyone, I'm starving. I could eat a horse!"

Time for our smoked salmon and salad. We were lucky to get it. This, after all, was Sunday afternoon. All the pubs and most restaurants had spent their all earlier in the day, preparing the ubiquitous Sunday lunch of a roast meat served lukewarm and revived with brown, immovable gravy, leather-like roast potatoes, a Yorkshire pudding that stretched when torn, and a sopping wet assortment of formerly fresh garden vegetables. But when it is done right, nothing can beat a rib of beef, pink-to-rare on the inside, crusty on the outside, with a freshly made Yorkshire pud, crispy vegetables as well as meltingly roasted potatoes and parsnips. This feast is a thing sublime, with the looks, aromas, and flavors of Thanksgiving and Christmas all rolled into one.

Until recently, pubs could only open on Sunday from noon until two thirty in the afternoon. Then they would, by law, have to close until seven in the evening. Pub licensing laws were instituted during the First World War because the ruling class feared that if the loutish working class were allowed to drink all day, they would somehow subvert the war effort. Quite possibly, the English Sunday lunch evolved around these inane laws. Mum would pop the roast in the oven at noon. She would put her feet up, and Dad would take off for the pub. At two, Dad would return and start hacking away at the joint, and slices of beast, overcooked vegetables, and a fat-soaked pudding would be consumed. Afterwards, the kids would play, Mum would do the washing up, and Dad would nap until the pubs re-opened at seven.

Not that this scenario ever played out in our house. Mum's job on Sunday was to supervise and harangue Lew as he cooked. Her only other job was to mix and bake the Yorkshire pudding. She was not always a bad cook, but she was always a surprising one. Sometimes her puddings would rise like golden mountain peaks; other times they would lie there, in a pool of meat fat, looking and tasting like a rubber bath mat. There was no way of knowing in advance. Although inured to Mum's culinary failures, we were buoyed up by her erratic successes.

After our late lunch, while many of my countrymen were sleeping off a boozy meal, Frances, Kate, and I slept off our jet lag in our delightful little cottage. We woke about seven thirty, starving. Where to go? Dave came to our rescue again by suggesting an Indian restaurant in nearby Stowmarket. He was just passing by on his way to the pub, which had now reopened to serve the regulars, but not hungry tourists.

"Dad, would you put you teeth back in?" Using the skills of a master magician, he had managed to palm both racks of teeth out of his head without anyone noticing. "Please. You'll scare the baby."

"Do I have to? They make my gums sore; they don't fit right," Lew whined with conviction.

That was true. The bottom rack wobbled, and the top rack was worn down into an acute triangle, creating an irregular gap on one side of his mouth.

"Then why didn't you get a new pair?"

"I'll be dead before I get the benefit of a new pair, so what's the point?" Every year for the past ten, Lew had come up with the same mournful end-of-the-road lament.

"Yes, Dad, but what if you're not dead anytime soon?" I asked, as I had been asking for years. "What if you don't peg out?"

He looked sullen. I tried to jolly him along.

"Ah, come on, Dad, you'll need them for your curry. For those big prawns you like."

Ghrrr.

A moment later his teeth reappeared, once more filling out his face. He grimaced and growled, and I smiled my thanks.

Stowmarket was only fifteen minutes away and quite easy to get to. By eight thirty we were perusing the vast and varied menu of the Taj Mahal Restaurant. Kate was fast asleep in her stroller. Indian music, akin to the sound of a cat being gently throttled, played in the background. Red velvet flock paper with shiny gold bits adorned the walls. Sparkly beaded curtains covered doorways. A picture of the Taj Mahal was framed and lit in a plastic wooden box with plastic foliage sprouting beneath it, all pleasantly fake except for the aromas that came from the kitchen. These were pungent, exotic, delightful, authentic. Lew peered intently at the menu. I'm not sure why, because he always had the same dish, but he studied the menu nonetheless. Mum looked a trifle lost, but she smiled at me.

"What are you having, son?"

"Don't know yet, Mum, but I don't think I'll have a curry."

"But this is a curry house. Gotta have curry in a curry house." Mum was emphatic.

I said I might have the tandoori chicken instead. She wanted to know what that was. I explained it was chicken marinated overnight in yogurt, lemon, and various spices, then thrust into a specially constructed oven for a few minutes. I enthused and said it was delicious. Mum appeared distrustful and reiterated her previous observation.

"But this is a curry house." She implored me to see sense and order a curry.

"Let him have what he wants, if that's what he wants. He's big enough and ugly enough to decide for himself. I know what I want. King Prawn Madras! And your mother will have the lamb madras."

"No, I won't!" said Jessie.

"What do you want then, woman? A row of houses and a battleship?"

"I dunno yet. What you having then, son?"

"Like I said, Mum, I'm having the tandoori chicken."

"What's that, then—?"

Ghrrr.

Thankfully, distraction came when the kitchen door opened. A chef popped out to use the pay phone, located close to the bar. When mum spotted him, she became quite animated.

"Ooowah! Lew! Lew! Look, look!" Mum was beside herself. Throwing all political correctness to the wind, she blurted, very loudly. "Look! A white man!" Frances and I hurriedly turned away. If we could have hidden behind the hedgerow of flock wallpaper, we would have.

"A white man? A white man!" Lew growled, but his interest was aroused. "Where?"

"There! Over there!" Mum was pointing eagerly.

"Mum. Mum!" I whispered loudly.

The entire restaurant was now listening while Lew, careful not to twist his neck, resettled his entire body to point himself in the direction of the chef making a call. Like aging children, my parents were the center of each other's universe. Right or wrong, they shared no sense of restraint. They spoke their minds and spoke them loudly, and not just because they were going deaf. They just did not possess any awareness of anyone else being around them. Ever. Lew turned his glance from the chef and emitted his chuckling, condescending growl.

Hackle. Hackle. Hackle.

"That's not a white man, Jessie." He took a deep breath and bellowed, "That's a wog!"

Oh, Dad—

The entire restaurant laughed good-naturedly at the remark, and at my acute discomfort. They knew. Perhaps they had parents just like mine. I tried to curb his enthusiasm and loud lack of tact.

Moments later, a waiter in a tuxedo showed up, and Lew starting talking at him in a smattering of half-remembered barrack-room Hindustani. The waiter's face cracked, eyes widening with mock surprise. He smiled a mouthful of gold, waggled his head, and took the dinner order from Lew. It was all very *pukkah*. Phrases of an exotic language filled the air. The waiter muttered replies. Maybe he understood Lew, maybe not. The scene had played out before. I was suddenly ten years old again, in Veraswami's in the West End of London. This restaurant was one of the first and probably the most famous Indian restaurant in London. And really quite swanky. My dad was holding forth, and I was happily riding a chair shaped like an elephant, ogling sticky-looking, vividly-colored desserts on a stainless steel Ferris wheel.

"You don't want any of that muck!" Lew had said, but I did. But I also knew my parents. They were not rich, and this dinner was a big treat for the family. Incomprehensible lingo had filled the air amid smiles and patronizing bows. The waiter in his silken tunic and embroidered slippers had shrugged his shoulders, as if to say, "Well, I tried," then he smiled at Lew and withdrew with his lavish, syrupy concoctions. "He knows what I was saying, son. He knows."

The language Lew spoke to our waiter in the Stowmarket restaurant was just as I remembered it from thirty years before. And Lew looked more than pleased with himself. We ordered dinner. We ate. I left a large tip even though Lew insisted on paying for the meal.

Later that night, safely back at the cottage, I had a glass of Jack Daniels with Lew. I had lots of ice with my drink, Lew sipped his neat. The ladies had long gone to bed. We didn't speak. But I was happy because the trip was going well. And Lew was happy because I was home.

CHAPTER 7

To Lavenham and
Saffron Walden

THE FOLLOWING MORNING the iron gray clouds had clanked away and the sky was clear. The weather was a little brisk, but ideal for touring. I woke early, and popped out for a quick walk. From what I could see, Rattlesden was a real English village. No cream teas to be had. No sightseeing coach stops. No trinket shops or farm houses selling beeswax candles, pillows of potpourri, or homemade jam gussied up for the tourists. Not even a stately home to visit. Rattlesden was a small, working community with a church, two pubs, and an ugly, oblong community shop. There was a village school, a number of old cottages, a derelict brick barn, and a few farm buildings. The entire place oozed with honest toil and animal smells.

When I returned, I heard the crisp rattle of cups. Lew was up and about. He was making tea. I smelled toast.

"Is that all you're having? You should eat breakfast. Fruit. Bran. Drink milk."

My healthful tips were lost in a barrage of questions and comments. Fancy a nice cup of tea then, son? How's the baby? Sleep alright, did you? Your mother was out like a light. Slept well, I did. Unusual that. And Frances, is Frances alright?

I smiled and nodded. Lew continued arranging cups as I walked out into the garden. The grass underfoot was lush and thick and emerald green. I looked across the way to a small, steepled church built on a gentle incline in the near distance. At the edge of the garden, the grass had grown tall and flaxen and red, and a wild array of flowers and plants was growing within its tufts. A washing line ran parallel with the narrow path down the garden's center. Tucked in the corner, a small garden shed and some patio furniture had been dappled with morning dew. It was all so blissfully quiet.

I went back inside and found everyone scurrying around. Frances had brought over ground coffee and, using spurts of boiling water, was patiently filtering it. As much as I loved my tea, since meeting Frances, morning coffee had become a happy and invigorating ritual, not to be missed, not even in the land where tea is always on the brew.

"All ready then, are we?" I looked at Lew. "Where's Mum?"

He grunted and jerked his head.

"I left your mother on the toilet."

"Okay. Fair enough."

Then Mum appeared in the kitchen, cooing "Oooh-oooh!" to all and sundry. She wore a bright green suit and knitted white hat atop silvered ringlets. She was all set for a day out.

"Alright, Mum? Ready to go?"

"I'm ready. I've done me business. Where we going then?"

"We're going to see some old buildings. Maybe a church. Cottages. And I don't know what else!" Lew was enjoying himself, jokingly disparaging. He thought we were wasting our time. He could not understand why we were not at a beach somewhere, and I was inclined to agree with him.

"It's your holiday, son, you do whatever you want to do." Mum was equally benign. Then, suddenly, a moment of panic. She shot a look towards Lew. "How you going to put my bet on then?"

Lew picked up the paper and betting slips and waved them so she could see. Mum looked relieved. Putting on her bet was much more important than visiting villages brimming with charm and beauty.

So we went to Lavenham in pursuit of history and a betting shop. When we arrived we found a well-preserved town with streets of half-timbered houses dating from the early part of the sixteenth century. Frances loved it from the moment she saw it. No beach in sight but, I had to admit, good views from any direction. We parked along the high street, then gently made our way around to the market square. Interestingly, not all of Lavenham's Tudor half-frame buildings were starkly colored in black and white. We discovered a cream-and-apricot colored guild hall, musty ochre-colored houses, and bay-windowed shops awash in muted Suffolk pink. All were dramatically framed by black oak timbers interspersed with high-gabled windows, sloped and gracefully curved with age.

My parents trotted along at their own pace, arm in arm. I looked back at them from time to time and, every time I did, Lew waved me on with his walking stick.

"We're alright, son. You go on, you enjoy yourself. And find us a tea place!" he commanded cheerfully.

Firmly dismissed, we ventured forth, our baby in the stroller, in search of a suitable hostelry. As we walked on, we marveled that these beautiful structures were not museum pieces but were still worked in, lived in. We walked past the Swan Hotel, which was the original Wool Hall, a hive of commerce, the seat of wealth and power in medieval Lavenham. Looking up, we saw ornate and colorful woodcarvings etched in the black oak gables and corner joists. The hotel was built over an archway, underneath which was a cobblestone courtyard festooned with geraniums, but it all looked a little too stuffy and fancy for our mid-morning nibble. So we toddled on a bit farther and then we found our tearoom. This was a classic Olde Worlde, hickledy-pickledy kind of place. Just what you would expect to find in a village that was thriving when Shakespeare was still an undiscovered playwright.

Across from the teashop was a private house gloriously over-run by a dazzling array of purple and white wisteria. On closer inspection, I saw that ancient branches of the tree had sprung from the pavement to enclose the lower part of the house in its gnarly grasp. But from just a short distance away, the effect was magical—the house appeared to float on a huge bed of fluffy petals. The perfect backdrop for our "elevenses," the mid-morning break when tea or coffee is slurped down with cakey things and hot buttered toast.

"A cup of cawfee will do us."

Lew was warning us in advance. Mum confirmed his story, insisting that she didn't want to "overdo it," but she did not sound terribly convincing.

Frances parked the stroller, then we slowly edged my parents over to a table. We ordered coffee and toast and Dundee cake, a rich fruit concoction strewn with slivered almonds. As the name implies, this sweet cake originated in Scotland and, with luck, is impregnated with that golden highland beverage. Frances ordered tea and scones, which arrived with strawberry jam and a pot of thick, bright yellow, velvety clotted cream.

"No, no, darling, you don't put butter on 'em!" Lew snickered, but in good humor.

"What do you mean? How're you supposed to eat them?"

I cut a scone in two for her, applied a layer of jam to one half and topped it off with a dollop of clotted cream.

"There you go! No butter!" I said. "Bon appetit!"

We all watched with approving smiles as Frances started to eat her perfectly layered scone.

"Oh, it's so good—taste?" She did not have to ask twice.

"Have you put my bet on yet?"

For certain things, Mum's memory remained quite sharp, especially when it came to having a flutter. When the gee-gees did not run, usually in the depths of winter, my folks bet on the dogs. They loved to gamble on just about anything. Even bingo! On most Saturday nights, they went off to a converted movie house to play for cash prizes. They never spent very much, and now and again they actually won. But their first love was always horse racing. On "the flat" or over "the sticks," both my parents loved to bet on the horses. I grew up in a household where shouts of "Gee up! Gee up, get on up there!" were heard virtually every day. Lester Piggott, Scobie Breasley, Willie Schumacher, Yves Saint Martin, I knew the names of all the top jockeys. And I knew enough to know that if Piggott had his horse in front at Tattenham Corner, even by a nose, he would win the Derby. Always. But it isn't called horse racing for nothing, and sometimes my parents lost. "What a bah lamb! He let me down, the bah lamb let me down!" As a child, I could never understand why my mum waved her fists at the horses and called them sheep. Years later I discovered that "bah lamb" was Mum's creative way of calling a losing horse a bastard.

~

"Right you are!" Lew swung round to me and began to clamber out of his seat. "I better find a betting shop, or there'll be hell to pay."

He slurped down his coffee and, before I knew it, was making for the door. I went after him.

I caught up with Lew as he stepped into the street. Forcefully, I told him to go back in and finish his cake and coffee and relax. I would place their bets. Finish, as he would say. He smiled his thanks. The betting shop, or turf accountant as it was euphemistically called, was close by. I placed their bets, and when I returned everyone was ready to leave.

Fortified by our mid-morning feast, I felt we'd be able to tackle a fairly steep hill at one end of the village, just beyond the teashop, to visit the imposing Norman church of St. Peter and St. Paul.

"We going up there? Aaaw mah Gawd, you'll put us in a early grave, you will," Lew rattled on. "And I've seen more churches than you've had hot dinners."

"Then one more won't make much difference, will it?" I said, trying to sound reasonable.

Ghrrr.

The church was a gem. Built in the perpendicular style of the medieval period, its construction was paid for by wealthy wool merchants, a pious way for them to give back to the community, show off, and curry favor with the almighty all at once. The imposing stone and timber roofed church was richly decorated and beautifully illuminated with stained glass, story-book windows, and beautifully carved wooden pews in which the rich prayed and gave thanks.

"Bleeding cold in there. See the vicar?" Lew pointed to the robed figure by the wishbone shaped doorway. "He was smiling at me, he was."

"He probably likes old buggers like you, thinks you might put a couple of bob in his box."

"Naaaw, he was looking at me as if to say, 'You might as well stay here, mate, you ain't got much longer.' Sizing me up for *my* box he was, not for his collection box!"

Hackle. Hackle. Hackle.

The smiling, white-collared vicar watched us as we proceeded at a leisurely pace down the hill. Frances was anxious to explore more of this unspoiled and picturesque town. But my folks had other ideas.

"I'm thirsty. Are you thirsty, Jessie? Yes, I thought so! Denny! Denny!" Lew cupped his hand and waggled it back and forth in front of his mouth.

"Fancy a drink then, Dad?" I took the hint.

"Thought you'd never ask!" Lew grinned at me like Mister Punch. We proceeded to find a pub. It was lunch time and Frances and I were hungry anyway. And I had to admit, the thought of a libation was tempting. We were, after all, on holiday. We found an old, timbered pub, neither crowded nor smoke-filled. We sat in the saloon bar, the more salubrious side of the hostelry, and looked up at the blackboard menu. I got a round of drinks, Guinness for Lew, a large schooner glass of sherry for Mum, a lager for Frances, and a big glass of ice cold cider for me. I always drank cider in England. Unlike American cider, it's fizzy like beer but with a clean woodsy flavor of autumn and baked apple. I found most commercial cider in pubs really rather good and not too alcoholic, unlike homemade apple cider, which is called scrumpy.

Someone offered me this brew once in a country pub near Stratford-upon-Avon. I remembered, all too well, the pub guv'nor's sweaty purple-red face, bulbous nose, and sly grin as he poured the cloudy yellow liquid from a white enameled jug into a pint mug. I also recalled the scrumpy's strength and unpleasant after-effects, and how it was made. Windfall apples studded with maggots and mush are pressed and left in a vat for months. I was told that, for additional flavor and fortification, barrels of scrumpy are left uncapped, in the hope that a rat or mouse might inadvertently fall in and drown. If a passing rodent proved elusive, the brew was seasoned with a lump of uncooked meat, preferably pork. I have not drunk scrumpy since then.

"What do you want, Mum? How about a steak and kidney pie? Is it freshly made?" I smiled at the barmaid.

"It's all homemade here, the pies that is," she said without looking up, polite but uninterested.

"Just get for yourself and Frances, and leave us out of it." Lew sipped his beer with earnest concentration. Mum reached for her sherry.

"Don't you want a bite of lunch? Mum? A bit of salad?"

Lew swiveled towards me, a skinny bag of nails about to burst.

"Look, we don't eat lunch. We don't need lunch. We don't want lunch. Finish!"

I ordered another round of drinks, and food for myself and Frances. Mum caught my arm.

"What you having then?" Mum asked. She decided to eat something after all, explaining that she did not want to be left out. Not surprisingly Lew also decided not to be a gastronomic gooseberry and ordered himself a steak and kidney pudding.

While my folks finished their drinks, I nipped around the corner, got the car, and drove back to the pub. Everyone was waiting outside, replete and smiling. We arrived back in Rattlesden mid-afternoon, time enough for a nap. Frances took Kate upstairs.

"We don't nap." Lew molded himself to the armchair. "We'll watch the racing on the telly."

About an hour later, I crept out of the charming upstairs bedroom, swung around a ceiling beam, and climbed backwards, sailor fashion, down the steep stairs to the front door. My parents were sprawled out in the tiny living room, Mum prostate across the sofa and Lew pinioned to the armchair, in the shape of a hook. Their eyes were shut, their mouths were open, and for a moment I thought they were both dead. Oh, bugger! Fortunately, I started hearing rustles of rasping breath. With some relief, I quietly closed the door and went out for another walk around the village.

The air seemed a little damp, but I was grateful it was not raining. Patches of green velvet moss crisscrossed the sidewalks and walls of the red brick buildings I passed. A black-and-white cat ambled across my path and went down a deserted alley. I walked towards the pub on the main village roadway. The only traffic was a few parked cars. No wonder the small filling station was still closed. I was beginning to think the garage was just an outdoor museum. Its oval petrol pumps were reminiscent of my childhood toy set.

"Settling in alright?"

It was Dave. He was fixing a window frame in a nearby cottage. I smiled and waved. Apart from the cat, he was the only living creature I saw on my walk, and that was perfectly fine with me. The village lay inside a soft-sided gully, too narrow to call a valley, more like a wide dip in the land. On one side of this gully was the community store, where I bought some tiny, waxy new potatoes, leafy greens, and Cadbury Flakes for Frances. From this store, I could also have ordered a newspaper, mailed a letter, bought stamps, fruit, batteries, cakes, and, if I'd lingered long enough, I'm sure I could have picked up some local gossip. The shopkeeper seemed eager to chat—he knew I was renting the cottage—but I was more inclined to explore a bit farther than on my previous walk.

Across the dip, on the other side of the community shop, I climbed up to the church, a modestly imposing structure made of limestone. This was the same church we could see from the back garden of our cottage. I walked inside. The musty fragrance of the flowers that decorated the pews from the previous Sunday's service still permeated the air. The church was deserted, but I sensed the presence of people, a small congregation. The pews smelled of fresh wax. The candlesticks smelled of metal polish. Everywhere were plaques in memory of various villagers long gone. Tucked away in a small enclave, I found a brass eagle with an inscription beneath it. This plaque had been placed there by the village, in memory of the American airmen stationed nearby who were killed in combat during the Second World War. The eagle gleamed a little in the scant deflected light. The plaque had been recently polished.

I ambled back to our little nest. I found Lew recalled to life and in the kitchen, making tea.

"Well done, Dad. Did you have good nap?" I couldn't help but ask.

"Naaaw, I didn't sleep, just closed me eyes for a bit, that's all."

He faffled around and then poured tea. Mum was still asleep. Frances was putting a small load of clothes in the tiny washing machine.

"There's no dryer! I looked everywhere." Frances was bewildered. She had never seen a washing machine without a dryer.

I looked into the garden and saw the clothes line. It was not there as a decoration. We started hunting for clothes pegs.

⁓

About nine the next morning Dave showed up with newspapers. We were finishing breakfast and getting ready for a new expedition. Mum was waggling fingers and blowing raspberries at Kate.

"So where they taking you today then, darling?" Dave asked.

"Oooh, I dunno, I just go along with whatever they're doing," said Mum, happily incurious. She turned to the racing page and gave it her undivided attention.

"We're going to Saffron Walden, then we'll backtrack from there," I said.

Kate spluttered and cried a little until we adjusted her bottle.

"Well, at least now I can say I heard the baby cry." Mum peered over her newspaper, "You and Frances going to have another one?"

"No, that's it for us, Mum." I sighed through my smile.

Suddenly Mum looked up and pointed at Dave. "That's you, innit? Dave!"

"Certainly is, darling."

"Have you got any children?" Mum smiled innocently.

"Just the one," Dave said, standing up.

"Just one? Why's that, then?"

"Mum!"

"I'm just asking! I'm only asking!" Jessie sounded defensive and a little shocked by my reaction. Lew muttered off into the kitchen. Patiently, and without missing a beat, Dave retold the story, again without remorse or self-pity. I saw him to the door and smiled apologetically. He nodded, smiled with great understanding, and said he would see us later. Dave was a good sport.

"Lovely man, isn't he? People like that can't do enough for you, can they? Can't do enough for you. So nice to have a conversation with someone nice, one of your own kind, isn't it?"

A moment later, in the kitchen, Lew grasped my wrist tightly.

"I'm sorry, son, but there's nothing you can do. I tell her something, then two minutes later she's forgotten what you've told her. So I tell her again, then a bit later she asks me what I said, and I tell her again. Then a bit later she starts asking me what we were talking about. Sometimes I can barely remember meself. So I just give up and turn on the telly. It's all I can do."

Even though Lew did try to elicit more sympathy than was perhaps warranted, her condition was especially hard on him. For a long time, Lew had simply thought she was becoming more forgetful. This was not like a cold or lumbago; memory loss was not something she could take to the local doctor. And of course, my family avoided the doctor and the National Health Service as much as possible. So Mum never went. And her illness became akin to a personality quirk, something to be lived with, occasionally suffered, occasionally considered, best forgotten. In our family, things unremembered were best forgotten.

~

The sun was shining. The weather was warm. And there was virtually no traffic on our way to Saffron Walden. The interesting section of the town, the medieval part, was compact and quite easy to tour on foot. Mum smiled her smile of happy disinterest, Lew wore his grim grin-and-bear it expression, but they tottered around with us uncomplaining.

Beautiful carvings adorned the outside of many buildings. Some were covered in gilt, some set in plaster. These were signs of wealth. Like Lavenham, Saffron Walden was a prosperous town in the Middle Ages, its wealth and name derived from the saffron industry that grew up around the area's crocus fields. A burning amber gold was extracted from crocus stems and turned into a liquid dye that adorned and enhanced the clothes of the rich and powerful, not only in England but all over Europe. But, of course, the idea of using this precious resource as a subtle flavor enhancement did not gain much ground. It would take the advent of holiday travel to Spain before people like me and mine would discover the culinary pleasures of paella and chips and the difference a pinch of exotic saffron could make.

"A maze? What you want to see a maze for? You saw one of those at Hampton Court," Lew said, somewhat impatiently.

"Dad, we want to see the maze here. It's very ancient."

"And totally different," Frances added.

Frances had read about this particular maze in another obscure book about Merlin. We were both, at the time, reading books about Stonehenge, the Druids, and the Arthurian Legend. This maze was another possible link to a time of romance and ancient myth. Unlike oral histories that seeped down to us from those far-off days, the maze at Saffron Walden was written in earth, a real find. Imbedded. It could have been set in stone. Even I wanted to see it.

"What if you get lost?" asked Lew darkly. "You got lost in Hampton, you did. The little man in the middle had to guide you out." Lew smiled, then turned to Frances. "What a carry on that was!"

We continued to walk through winding streets, past a perpendicular-style church and an eleventh century Norman castle keep hedged by a set of ruins from a more recent era. Beyond that was the very large village green, and across the green was the ancient turf maze Frances and I wanted to see.

"We're not walking across that, son. Bugger that for a game of soldiers," Lew protested.

For once, I was inclined to agree with him. The village green was more like a common, a large oblong of "common" land with green and brown bits, hemmed on all sides by houses, usually flat, bordered by trees and quite unkempt. The common in Saffron Walden stretched on and on. Even without the stroller, traversing this large clump of untamed nature would take at least thirty minutes. For my poor parents, it would be a death march.

"Alright, don't worry. I'll get the car 'round."

"Thank Gawd for that!" Lew looked as if he'd just recovered a winning betting slip thrown out by mistake.

Mum suddenly wanted to know where we were going. She sounded concerned, almost fearful. Lew told her again, and she seemed satisfied. We parked across the street from the maze.

"Do you want to come and have a look? Mum? Dad?" I asked with feigned eagerness.

"No, no, you and Frances, you go on, leave the baby here. We'll look after her, and you can see your maze. Go on, you go have a good time."

Hackle. Hackle. Hackle.

We got out of the car and walked across to the ancient site. We found turf squares, cut in a circular pattern. An enigmatic structure, possibly of Druid origin, the maze was literally thousands of years old. And yet it was totally uninspiring. It reminded me of a hundred gnome-sized cricket pitches swirling around a tiny field. Beyond that whimsical leap of imagination, we could evoke nothing to sustain our curiosity. Was it a druid temple site? Was it used to count out soldiers during a muster? Was it an ancient meeting place? Why was it called a maze? Did we care? We tried our best to appear interested, especially for the beady-eyed bugger gazing at us from the car. I just sensed Lew watching us as we walked around, looking at the ground, apparently looking intently at nothing. And I was right. I looked up and there he was, laughing. I could imagine Lew's commentary. "Look, look at them walking around in circles, staring at the ground. The things they do, I ask you!"

Hackle. Hackle. Hackle.

Mercifully, it started to rain and we were able to hurry back to the car. Kate was holding an ancient hand in each of hers. Quite the diplomat. And my parents were singing to her, "Beautiful Katie, oh beautiful Katie, you're the only little girl that we adore—" My folks hummed most of the tune, and Kate enjoyed it. Then we all applauded, and she enjoyed that, too.

"So, how did you both get on?" asked Lew.

"Fascinating. Really interesting. No one knows why it was created!" Or why anyone would want to see it, I could almost hear Lew thinking his reply, seeing through my veneer of enthusiasm.

"Just so long as you saw what you wanted to see, my son," Lew spoke very slowly, patronizing as ever. "As long as you are satisfied—"

"Alright, alright. Let's look around. Then we'll get lunch, maybe go back to Lavenham."

"Oh, no! I told you before, son. We don't eat lunch!"

"But we do!" I snapped back.

Ghrrr.

～

"Dad, Dad, what are you doing?"

He was peeling those lovely, tiny new potatoes I had bought from the community shop.

"What's it look like I'm doing? I'm peeling 'taters. Why did you get them so bloody small?"

"You don't peel those potatoes, Dad! You leave the skins on. Taste better."

Hackle. Hackle. Hackle.

"You hear that, Jessie? Our currant bun doesn't want me peeling the taters!"

Mum looked at us and blinked, fascinated by another one of our strange little ways. She tut-tutted gently. Frances was intrigued by "currant bun," Cockney rhyming slang.

"You know, currant bun—son." I shrugged it off. "He gets into it sometimes."

Lew was smiling to himself, gently shaking his head at my daft, incomprehensible ideas about cooking. He went on peeling the potatoes. That evening, those spuds were going to accompany the huge slab of beef we had brought over with us.

"Bought some fillet of steak the other week, a pound-a pound it cost me—never had it so cheap! Giving it away, they were!" Lew huffed.

"Good for you, Dad!" I said.

"Mind you, they say if I get mad cow, I could go barmy in twenty years." He stopped peeling for a moment. "I'll tell you, son, if I'm still here in twenty years, I *will* be mad."

"Well, you know all about mad cows, Dad. You've had to deal with Mum and her sisters for over fifty years!"

Hackle. Hackle. Hackle. Whaaaagh!

His laughter overwhelmed him, and he became wheezy and breathless. He nodded. His face, the color of a plum, creased into a grin, but he could say nothing. Which was just as well as Mum was hovering nearby.

"What's he laughing about, then? Let us in on it, I like a good laugh, I do."

"How are your sisters, Mum?"

"Alright, I suppose. I only ever see them once in a blue moon."

Not the closest of families, but when my mother and her sisters got together it was as if the years had never parted them. Dowsed in cheap perfume and talcum powder, hemmed in by corsets, covered by glittery decorations and bits of rabbit fur, these aging girls were ready for anything and always fun to be around. I could just sit and watch my aunts flattering each other, laughing at one another, and finally teaming up to have some sport with their customary prey— the men they had married. My father and my uncles were the objects of my aunts' outrageous scorn, emasculated spear carriers or, in their case, drink carriers, in a kind of Chekovian drama rewritten by Chaplin. These hapless husbands responded with much eye rolling and exclamations of, "Gawd help us!" and "What can you do?" and, finally, "What chance have I got with them?" They hated these women, but they loved them too, and in their humiliation was born a sense of pride, even a sense of wonder. What bloody chance did they have? None.

"What you talking about then?" Again Mum quizzed Lew with some degree of hostility.

"Nothing, nothing, I'm not talking about you."

Lew recoiled from her withering looks and threatening gargle. He looked at me. His eyes betrayed the unspoken words. What bloody chance have I got? None.

CHAPTER 8

To Long Melford, Woolpit, and Cambridge

THE FOLLOWING MORNING, I was holding up the shower head for Frances while she tried to bathe. The plumbing fixture had collapsed on her like a demented metallic dragon spewing dangerously hot water. So I found myself holding the shower head in the fashion of Lady Liberty, while Frances hurried to escape. We then summoned Dave, who appeared with a bag of tools within half an hour.

"Hallo, darling, how are you this morning?"

"All the best for seeing you! I mean, I ask you, look what I have to put up with!" Mum was delighted to see Dave once more. She waved her paw at her somber-faced husband as if to ward off an evil spirit. "Look at that face. Look at that face! I have to live with that." She tut-tutted, then cocked her head towards Dave, smiling broadly. "Just as well I've got a sunny personality."

"I could tell that, just by looking at you." Dave had most certainly been working on the art of flattering old people. Jessie gave him the perfect opportunity to hone his skills.

While Dave fixed the shower, Mum continued to extol his many virtues. And so did I, and with good reason. But I could tell Lew was getting a bit sick of it, feeling a little jealous of the attention Dave was getting. Jessie knew it, of course.

The weather was overcast and moist. Hanging soggy clothes on the line did not seem an option. Dave volunteered to take our laundry and run it through his dryer at home, then wished us a pleasant day and took off.

"You okay about staying here, Mum?" Lew had told me they wanted to take it easy today. I could not blame them. The leaden sky looked like a giant gray paper bag filled with water and about to burst.

"I'll go along with whatever you want. It's your holiday."

"She wants to stay here." Lew was emphatic, which meant *he* wanted to stay put but would never admit it. He slowly sprang to his feet, weaving slightly like an old jack-in-the-box, then hauled Mum out of her armchair. Once on her feet, Mum tottered over to Frances, who was holding the baby. Small, doughy fingers were gently waggled by old veined ones.

"There she is, bless her. Yooo-hooo! Oooh-oooh!" Mum grinned at Kate, then looked up as if she had just remembered something. "Has the baby been christened yet?"

"We're not—" Frances stopped, shook her head. "She's not going to be christened."

"Why not? Denis was christened." Mum seemed perplexed.

"Mu–m." I said, hanging on the word, "I told you, Frances is Jewish, and—"

"Jewish? Is she Jewish?" She sounded more than a little surprised.

"Yes, Mum," I said, wearily.

"On both sides?"

"Yes, Mum."

"But you were christened. At Saint Albans!"

"Well, Kate won't be. So drop it!" Lew was firm.

"I'm only asking—" Then she reached through the fog of her memory. "I'm a Christian, I am! And Denis, you were as well!"

"You're absolutely right, Mum. When I was thirteen," I smiled at Frances, "I wanted to be a missionary, an evangelist. I wanted to be Billy Graham. I tried to convert my friends and my favorite teachers at school."

"Poor them," said Frances.

Poor them! How I prayed for them all. I prayed for Jessie and Lew. For Tony and Rex. And once, apart from praying to Jesus to forgive my many sins, which I did on a regular basis, once, just once, I had a Denis-of-Lourdes moment. I prayed for a cure. I prayed harder than hard for Jesus to heal my athlete's foot. When I woke up the following morning, my foot was still inflamed and my toes still horribly cracked. And there had endeth my religious phase. I gave up Sunday school and reverted to being a young teen filled with sinful thoughts and not much else.

"Right! Better be on our way!" I said. As we pulled out of the gravelly path to the village high road, my parents were framed in the rose-covered doorway, waving good-bye.

Under a threatening sky, we arrived in Long Melford about forty minutes later and started to walk. Both sides of the village high street were festooned with antique shops. Frances and I are avid browsers, occasional collectors, and Kate was small enough for us not to worry about the unwritten "you break it, you've bought it" law of shopkeepers worldwide.

The first place we discovered, on the edge of the village, was a delightful teashop with an adjoining bric-a-brac shop. We gazed and grazed. Next door was a potter's studio, complete with a genial potter. After buying a couple of blue and white wall vases, we began our walk through the village. Long Melford was deadly serious about antiques. There must have been over thirty shops selling the stuff. We found emporiums jammed with dressers, spindly side tables, ornate corner pieces, china cabinets, and bureaus representing hundreds of years of genteel wear and very little tear. Many of these overly cramped salons were part-commercial enterprise and part-museum. We entered several establishments and invariably found a couple of antique dealers whispering to each other, utterly uninterested in us. They somehow knew we were not serious buyers, just mere collectors of well-worn trinkets.

As we left one shop, the large gray inflated bag in the sky above suddenly burst.

"Oh, come on! It's only a village street. Melford Hall is just off the village green. How far can it be? And Beatrix Potter awaits!" I spoke with forced jocularity.

We were heading for a residence in the grand style in which Beatrix Potter, famous for writing about rabbits and other farmyard creatures with a penchant for human clothing, spent many a summer.

We marched on. It continued to rain. We continued to walk. Then a cold wind picked up, hard and blustery, that turned the rain into ice-like pellets that splattered our faces and dampened our spirits. Flopsy, Mopsy, and Cottontail suddenly seemed a long, long way away. Our footsteps dragged heavily, and still no village green appeared. We stood under an awning. We checked our map. Long Melford was apparently well named, with the longest village high street in England, about three miles long. A fair walk on a good day, utterly miserable on any other. Typical, I thought. Now we're wet through, cold, and miserable, and we'll probably get sick. Bloody place. Bloody damp. I seethed. I ranted. Frances tried to make me see reason, but I closed my eyes to it.

My black cloud was returning. Annoyingly logical, Frances suggested we turn back and pick up the car. I fumed and complained but complied. As wet and uncomfortable as I was, Frances also insisted I cheer up. If I did not, the weather would only get worse. So she said. But then, Frances did have an uncanny knack about things meteorological. I faked a smile that stuck to my face as tenaciously as the freezing rain. I felt wretched. As we walked back to the car, the rain slowed to a drizzle. By the time we had driven the length of this stretched-out village and reached our destination, the rain had stopped and the merest hint of low-wattage sunlight appeared. Frances smiled with hidden knowledge.

Melford Hall was a three-storied, rectangular mansion. We entered a forest of varnished wood cleaved to walls, with a wide staircase that could easily accommodate a Broadway chorus line. As we crossed the foyer, a museum flunky jumped into our path.

"Sir, sir, excuse me, sir, no prams. Not upstairs, sir. You can borrow this for the baby."

He waved "this" in front of us, a giant sling in which to cradle infants instead of broken arms. Naturally, I balked and grumbled, but the sling device actually proved to be quite a boon. Much better than lugging strollers up endless wooden steps.

With Kate securely slung, the stroller stowed, we ascended the wooden hill. On the way up, we passed several suits of armor and a row of uninspiring portraits. Huge, black-and-red urns of Chinese origin were dotted around the place. I looked up at the wooded scrollwork that adorned the ceiling. I also noticed one or two oriental screens, along with prints and pictures of eastern origin. I was beginning to detect a theme.

We walked down a long corridor and approached two bedrooms overlooking an ornate garden. They were the only upstairs rooms open to the public, at least that day. Although cordoned off with red ropes, we could see a period four-poster bed in the larger room, replete with white draperies that hung in furls like sails on a dainty galleon, a night stand, a cabinet, other bits of expensive antique furniture. The room, like the house itself, appeared drained of color. We dutifully peered inside, but found nothing to stir our imaginations. Then, next door, in the smaller room, we saw something that did evoke our fanciful imaginings, in spite of the weather. On the walls were framed watercolors and sketches of scenes from Miss Potter's stories. And there, on an overly stuffed chair, was an overly stuffed child's rabbit. Was this young Beatrix' stuffed animal? Was this the model for one of her creations? Was this indeed Peter Rabbit? Was this, in fact, the very bedroom Beatrix Potter slept in when she spent her summers here? We turned to an attendant perched on a chair, on our side of the red ropes.

Frances asked her, "Can you tell me something about this room?"

"It's a bedroom."

The bed was a dead giveaway. Frances quizzed the attendant a little further.

"Do you know who the person was, who slept here?"

"I dunno." The furrows on the attendant's brow twisted and deepened, as if pausing for thought. "That was before my time."

"Oh. Do you know anything about Beatrix Potter. You know, Peter Rabbit!" I insisted, trying to jog a memory. Frances was trying not to giggle.

"Oh, the children's stories. Oh, yes. Yes. Yes." A glimmer of recognition wafted across her face. Again she smiled. "No. Never read them meself."

And then the dam burst and Frances started laughing, quite loudly. And it was funny. With merriment in our eyes, we swapped the sling for our stroller and were on our way again.

∼

The following afternoon, through a break in the clouds, the sun playfully pointed a finger of light in our direction. We left Kate in the front room with Jessie and Lew and took off to forage for fish and chips. Dave had told us that the nearest fish shop was in Wool-pit, a nearby village only slightly bigger than Rattlesden.

When I was a young boy, every fish bar in and around London seemed to be run by Italians. Times change. Today, many fried fish shops are run by immigrants from the Pacific Rim. And who knows? A tempura-like fish batter might not be so bad. The shop was doing a brisk trade, so we ordered. In broken English, the young, diminu-tive couple said they would fry the fish there and then, and it would be ready in a few minutes. Perfect. With a little time on hand, we decided to amble about the village.

We discovered that Woolpit derived its odd name from "a pit to trap wolves" and had nothing to do with sheep being clipped or dipped. The old English name for Woolpit was Wlfpeta, which sounded like a medieval animal rights association but, in fact, harked back to the time of the Vikings. Regardless, the village was not without charm.

We walked into St. Mary's churchyard down a cobbled path edged with moss. Adjoining the church we passed through a large medieval porch built in the fourteenth century. The carved porch-way was made entirely of wood but its rippled and splintered skin was as hard as stone. The church proved even older, constructed two centuries before in the Norman style with a high church steeple that dominated the immediate landscape. Inside, the church seemed somehow smaller, more intimate. Peering up and through the dark musty light, just below the mighty beamed roof, we saw carved wooden angels, jesters, eagles, and dragons trapped haphazardly in a wooden web of timeless silence broken only by our intrusion.

Across the village green we passed municipal buildings made of red brick. Woolpit was once famous for making bricks, both red and white. The white brick was exported the world over, and some say the White House in Washington, D.C., was originally made of Woolpit brick. We ducked down a side street and, although we didn't find any red or, come to that, white houses, we did see several ancient cottages awash in Suffolk pink framed by blackened Tudor beams. We noticed one of the end units was for sale. It was going for the price of three lavish cruises. Fortunately, our hunger overrode our impulse to buy anything more than skate and cod. We picked up our freshly cooked dinner and drove home.

Lew was distraught. When we came into the cottage, he was hovering over Kate, crouched low, his elbows stuck out like trussed chicken wings, as if to help keep his balance. When he saw us, he turned towards me.

"There he is, there he is!" Mum waved from her seat, happy to see us.

"I'm so glad you're back, son." His worn face was a mixture of distress and relief. "I couldn't pick her up. I just couldn't."

I told him everything was fine. And it was. Kate was on her mat and crying, but when Frances scooped her up, the tears started to evaporate.

"Thank Gawd for that!" said Lew, almost breathless. He went on, as if he had to explain himself, "See, if I'm down, I need both me 'ands to get meself up again, let alone picking 'er up. Can't manage it anymore. Sorry, son." He tried to demonstrate what he could no longer do.

"It's alright, mate, no harm done. Really. Sit yourself down; you look knackered."

~

All children think their parents are old, but mine always were, exceptionally so. Obviously, they weren't born old, but they were old when I was born. By the time I became conscious of age and generational differences, they were already in their fifties.

Because of my parents' age, I missed several generations of popular culture: Elvis, Marilyn Monroe, Ban the Bomb, Beatniks. My parents missed them, too. My points of reference were Fred Astaire, the Gershwins, Bette Davis, Charlie Chaplin, Bob Hope, Bing Crosby. Not a problem unless I ran into a parent of one of my school friends or a friend would meet my parents. That was always a shock for everyone. When my parents dressed up to go out for the evening, they always looked like Nick and Nora or any movie couple from the thirties. Mum wore lots of rabbit fur and hats with feathers and smelled of talc, and Lew always wore double-breasted suits with baggy trousers. He was always clean shaved, always had a short back and sides hair cut brilliantined like Ramon Navarro—whoever he was.

Now, seeing my parents with Kate, they were looking frail beyond their years, looking into an uncertain future, as though life had suddenly raced ahead of them, leaving them both behind, somewhat baffled by it all.

I helped Lew over to his chair. He looked physically exhausted, reigned in by the frailties of old age. Only his gray eyes appeared less than accepting of his condition. They still seemed shot through with the strength and anger of a younger man. I gave him a small glass of Jack and smiled. Lew nodded his thanks and quietly sipped his drink, happy to be sitting down. Frances and I exchanged glances, mindful not to put that kind of responsibility on him again.

"Panic over! Panic over," said Mum. "Don't I get a little something?"

"What would you like, Mum?"

On the kitchen table we carefully unwrapped our fish and chips from the swaddling-like paper sheets, ominously rendered transparent by oil. The fries were as soggy as wet noodles. The fish was awash in cooking grease, and the batter looked soft, limp, and thick. I peeled back this yellowish shroud in search of fish. Instead of plump, white, flavorful cod, I found a thin layer of mysterious gray stuff, attached to a lump of black skin that resembled wet tarmac. I dressed the fish again in its oily jacket and touched it no more. Frances and I played with our soggy chips, ate bread and salad. Mum announced, with some ardor, that this was the finest fish she had ever tasted. She was either being unbelievably contrary, or old age had robbed her of her last remaining taste buds. I wasn't sure.

Lew rolled his eyes but said nothing. Kate drank formula, and we happily drank more Jack Daniels.

~

The bustling county town of Cambridge was ringed with car parks that became progressively more expensive the closer we got to the city center. With eighty year olds and a baby, parking closer was infinitely better, and we figured the parking fee was the price of admission to such an historic town.

Cambridge itself was rather small, so getting around proved quite painless despite the lack of motorized transport. The university, like the delta of a limestone river, sprawled through the entire city. Down alleys, streets, passageways, across bridges, beyond greens, university property ranged from colleges anchored to chapels, to bikes chained to fences. And because of its age, the architecture encompassed everything from the Tudor to the flashy and futuristic metal-and-mirror style. But despite those differences, the college area had an overall religious feel. New or old, the buildings seem to emanate a sense of worship, dedicated, I assumed, to the Gods of Learning. Lucky are those who worshipped there.

The streets surrounding the colleges gave way to warren-like passageways filled with cobblestone, bottle glass, and wrought iron work. We spotted the occasional gas lamp and flower baskets that dripped with pansies and geraniums. Dark and mysterious, the pedestrian byways of Cambridge were inviting, but where did they lead? These were the same streets and turnings that Isaac Newton, Lord Byron, and Charles Darwin ambled down.

We walked towards the river Cam and crossed a small, hump-backed bridge. Beneath it were several young men in straw boaters with neckties swung around their waists to hold up their white flannel trousers. These would-be tour guides, local students, playfully accosted us as we passed by, extolling the virtues of viewing the River Cam from the inside of a punt. Unlike a gondola, a punt is completely flat-bottomed from stem to stern. It resembles a miniature barge that is devoid of ornamentation and comfort, save for a few ratty pillows. From the riverbank, we watched one glide past. It all looked effortless, which in my experience is the first indication that it is anything but. I watched the next punt with great care. The boatman dipped a long pole into the water until it connected with the river's muddy, shallow bottom. Then the agile punter would push off, extricating the pole from the mud, pulling it upwards before the boat moved away, leaving the punter stranded midstream clutching his pole. Regardless, clutching and jerking poles around, especially in public, was not my cup of tea. Much better to watch. And so we did, from a hotel conveniently located just over the hump-backed bridge.

The hotel had a lovely terrace and verandah, and from there we happily slurped tea and gazed upon the tranquil river traffic and the ancient spires of Cambridge. A little later, we ambled back over the Cam and made our slow progress across a large lawn, towards those hallowed halls of academe. The first college we came to was closed because students were sitting for an exam. Such nerve. We decided to walk on to Saint John's College. Lew was preparing for the march with all the resolve and determination of Scott returning from the South Pole.

"It's just here, Dad. We're right here. It's not that far."

"It's not that, it's just your mother hasn't been yet. I hope there's one inside."

Lew's concern with finding bathroom facilities and suitable places in which to drink tea, or Guinness, tended to occupy most of his time away from home.

"Alright. Let's go inside and have a butcher's. You alright, girl?" asked Lew.

Mum shrugged, then smiled. Frances looked at me quizzically. More Cockney rhyming slang. "Butcher's" was an abbreviation for "butcher's hook," which meant, "look." As I finished explaining, we arrived at the college. The entrance to Saint John's opened onto a beautifully lawned quadrangle, beyond which was a kind of miniature Bridge of Sighs that spanned the river, a knockoff of the Venetian original. For some reason, tourists were not allowed over this covered walkway, but we saw it well enough.

"That's the rose of Henry the Eighth, that is."

Lew was looking at a wall and there, indeed, was a Tudor rose carved in wood. Unlike our cottage in Rattlesden, built of Tudor oak and wattle, the college was mostly built of red brick, perhaps from Woolpit. We walked towards the college chapel, built in 1511 by Henry's grandmother, Lady Margaret Beaufort, and still famous for its choir and recordings of seasonal music. But on the day we were visiting, apart from the sound of small muted echoes caused by tourists like us, the chapel was bare and silent. Sunlight barely trickled through the vaulted stained glass, causing dust particles to dance attendance. It was very dark inside, the heavy, dark wood looking like a giant, ornately carved jewelry box with tiny wooden compartments.

Outside in the sunshine, Lew sat down on a seat in one of the courtyards separating the college buildings and looked around. As he gazed into the distance, Frances snapped his picture, immovable and seemingly at peace. I watched him for a moment, wondered what he was thinking. For hundreds of years young men had been gaining a higher education just a few yards from where he sat. Lew left school at fourteen to make a living, but I don't think he looked around him and saw a missed opportunity for himself. It was a world in which he felt he could never belong, the world of Milton, Tennyson, Hawking, a world beyond his horizons, his class. But not beyond the ambitions of his family.

"Your granddaughter may study here one day, Dad."

Lew's face crinkled into the semblance of a smile. He nodded. I prepared myself for a bitter comment, a wistful phrase tinged with regret.

"I'm knackered. I'm truly knackered," he growled as he got to his feet. "There's a pub up the road. We'll go for that, me and your mother. Come on!"

"Sure you don't want any lunch, Dad?" I walked along with him, inwardly smiling.

"I've told you before! We don't have lunch! Now you listen, you and Frances and the baby, you go off, have a look around, have your lunch. Take all the time you need. We'll see you back here in an hour." Lew hooked his arm out for Jessie to take. "Come on, girl!"

I did not argue. We had our marching orders, and we took off. We had one hour.

After perusing a teddy bear shop that interested me more than my daughter or wife, we headed off in search of smoke-free dining. A few minutes later, we were sipping wine in a surprisingly airy cellar restaurant. The food was very good, the service fast, and we managed to get back to the pub forty minutes later. The other colleges, along with the village of Granchester and "the backs" down by the river, would have to wait for another time.

My parents were looking for us out the window. Once she spotted us, Mum started waving frantically, beet-root faced and smoochy-mouthed. Although we could not hear it, we could tell she was making "oooh-oooh" noises for Kate's benefit. She then fell against the pub window in a merry daze. The palms of her hands turned white as she smacked and shuddered the window. Luckily, she was unhurt and did not sail through the plate glass, but she did leave palm prints. Behind her, I could see Lew rolling his eyes and rocking a cupped hand back and forth in front of his mouth, to indicate the amount of beverage Mum had consumed. When we got inside the pub, I noticed his sudsy Guinness glasses evenly matched her empty schooners of sherry.

"Have a drink with me, son." Mum waved her handbag at Lew.

"You've had enough," Lew said in a low grumble.

"I've had enough of you, that's what I've had!"

Lew reluctantly sidled up to the bar for another round. About an hour later we got back to the car. On the way back to our cottage, Mum passed out and slept as soundly as Kate did.

$\sim$

Our last night in Rattlesden was spent in our "local," the Brewers Arms. We ate in its home-style restaurant, drank, talked, and listened to a pianist pounding out old favorites on the upright piano. A bit later some traveling musicians and Morris Men showed up and started a sing-song and dance. Mum joined in. Her evening was complete when Dave eventually showed up. We bought him a drink and toasted our stay in the village. Then we said our goodnights.

Arm in arm, Lew and Jessie, Frances and I, made our way back to the cottage with Kate's stroller before us, tacking like a sailboat many sheets to the wind. That night, I cannot recall hitting my head on any beams.

The following morning we settled up with Dave for the odd phone calls we had made. He wouldn't take any tip; he would not even take money for the newspapers or the life-saving laundry service he had so thoughtfully provided. We said good-bye. Dave gave Mum a big hug. Moments later, the car was crunching gravel on the old path beside our tiny cottage. Then we were on the slightly sticky smoothness of tarmac. Our village was gone. With our remaining few days, we intended to stay with friends in London. But at that moment, with the highway looming ahead of us, our holiday seemed to be over.

CHAPTER 9

London

"Now, what if Katie slept hayer and you and Frances slept over thayer."

Isabel pointed aloft, and bangles rattled gracefully down her elegant, suntanned arm. Frances and I looked where she was pointing. It was a light-filled platform above the landing. A large bed filled most of the space, giving the impression the room was entirely upholstered. To enter this bedded nest required climbing a tiny, wrought-iron, spiral staircase—the kind found in backstage Hollywood musicals from the nineteen thirties. It looked charming, perfect for two young love birds. But the thought of climbing down those twirling steps in the middle of the night to change, feed, or comfort our newborn filled us with dread.

"Isabel, it's fabulous. It's so—dramatic! Got anywhere else?"

Undaunted, Isabel trooped us into another room, much less romantic but far more practical.

"There's a bed!" Isabel pointed, then mused aloud, "But what about Katie? Don't have a crib. What to do? Ideas? Thoughts? I know!"

Isabel whipped out a big leather suitcase from a closet and, like a magician performing a trick, flung it open and started producing sarongs, silk scarves, and the odd boa or two. The case was finally empty and surprisingly large.

"Big enough? Thought so. I'll get some blankets. Sheets. Kate can sleep in this—brilliant!"

Well, it was. With sheets and blankets suitably folded and tucked in, the high-sided suitcase was soon transformed into a bassinette. All very theatrical. Shades of Ernest Worthing being left in a handbag. Kate did not seem to mind one bit.

Located near Kensington Park Road, Isabel and Colin's Georgian row house was reminiscent of a slightly squashed mansion.

The house was very narrow, with high ceilings and lots of floors, rooms with balconies, and narrow stairs sharply zigzagging from the top to the bottom. Isabel was a painter, and her flair for decor and color was evident in every room and alcove and landing. Despite its bold and florid elegance, the house looked perfectly lived in, as if a horde of children with a finely tuned sense of style had gently blown through the place the weekend before. After bathing, we settled in, had a relaxing dinner, and talked until very late. We caught up on past times, and then the conversation got around to our week in the country.

"I don't believe it!" Isabel exclaimed. Her words careened out even faster than normal. "You see, I was there, too! Visiting my father. Lives three miles from Rattlesden!"

"Woolpit?" I asked.

"Woolpit! Oh, no! Such a coincidence. If we'd only known! How maddening. When I was a student I worked in the chemist's shop in Woolpit, handing out pills with dodgy prescriptions. Had lots and lots of old age pensioners queuing up when I was on duty, I can tell you. Quite irresponsible, of course. Jolly funny though. Can't believe we were so close. How absolutely brilliant of you to find Rattlesden!"

I couldn't argue with that.

The following morning after breakfast in the basement kitchen, Frances and I drifted into the tiny walled garden, lush with lilacs and budding roses, and sat around the bistro table to soak up a bit of morning sun. Colin bade us farewell, he was off to do financial things in the city. See you later? Yes? Good. We drank more coffee. Isabel was already in her attic studio working away. We found her there, sizing up a subject, drinking black coffee. She held her brushes like darts while talking to us non-stop. Then, suddenly, she would strike, filling a section of her canvas with paint, her brushes hurled with the expertise of a circus knife thrower.

"So what are you planning today? I've got to work. Can't stop. We'll do stuff later? Yes?"

"No problem. We're seeing an old friend for lunch, from my music days. Then we'll potter around town. Back mid-afternoon?"

"Brilliant!"

~

We decided to walk across to Covent Garden. It would take some time, at least an hour, but the sun was shining, and we could go through some lovely parks. With Kate in her stroller, we walked up Kensington Park Road, then into the broad expanse of Hyde Park.

We headed down towards the rust-colored Palace of Saint James' and along Pall Mall toward Trafalgar Square. We strolled through flocks of pigeons and hordes of tourists, passed a sparkling new addition to the National Gallery and the creamy, cleaned Nelson's Column. We looked up and saw Saint Martins in the Fields, still veiled in centuries of black dirt like a spinster aunt at a funeral. From there we headed down the Strand.

Finally we reached Covent Garden, immortalized by George Bernard Shaw and his flower girl, Eliza Doolittle. The grand piazza built of glass and iron was still in place, but the old flower market had long since moved to a more mundane and functional abode just south of the river, at Nine Elms. A few years after the original market moved out, the area was turned into an upscale shopping mall with the obligatory boutiques, knickknack shops, market stalls, pubs, and wine bars. But it all seemed to work. Over a pint or a glass of wine, visitors enjoyed street performers, from magicians to string quartets, even opera singers. Very touristy, but the area was also thronged with locals. And there, quite near the grand piazza, we were meeting Sally for some traditional English fare.

"Ah jus' noo ya loved bein' pregnant, did ya not love it, lass?" Despite years in central London, my friend's Scottish accent had remained as thick and pleasingly impenetrable as porridge.

"No. Not really." Frances smiled, but Sally had her mind made up.

"Aaah, but I know different. Deep down. I can sense things, that I can."

Sally had always been certain of herself. Confident. Years back, she had worked for one of my song publishers. She had been extremely efficient, protective, forthright, and tempestuous. People had been scared of her. Friend or foe, she never really looked at people, she scowled at them. Sally had thick, wavy blonde hair and bright blue, startled eyes that still made her look a bit scary. There was a wildness about her, something of the gypsy. Sally looked at Kate with a benign smile. No scowls, that was a good sign.

"Aaah, she's a beautiful wee lassie. I'm getting a good sense of her."

"That's good." I said.

"Well, I would, wouldn't I? Get a sense of her. Remember, I'm a witch. You do remember that, don't you, Denis?"

"Oh. Yes. I do indeed. Shall we order?" I wanted to avoid the occult, magic, and mystic beliefs, but Frances appeared interested.

"Aahm the seventh daughter of a seventh daughter!" Sally went on.

"You believe in all that?" Frances asked, fascinated, never one to leave well alone.

"I don't believe it, Frances. I am it."

Since I had last seen Sally, the sharp, angular figure had softened with age, but she remained sure of herself and her place in the world of mortal men.

"The lamb and apricot pie sounds good, don't you think?" I tried to refocus, move the conversation back to the more mundane, less supernatural. Frances ordered a chicken and mushroom pie. Sally had a cock-a-leekie pie without the cock. Like my friend in Dagenham, she, too, had become very wary of all kinds of dead flesh. I ordered more wine.

"If you like, I'll give Katie a blessing. You wouldn't mind if I did that, would you?"

We saw nothing wrong with a pagan blessing for our child. Mind you, I was a little fearful of Sally's zeal. Then again, I did not want to incur her wrath, so I said nothing and let her get on with it. She muttered a few words then looked at me, beaming happily.

"All done. Let's eat!" she said, eyes agleam with true belief.

Amen did not sound appropriate, so I said, "Cheers." We then tucked into our designer puddings and pies. Two bottles of plonk and eighty English pounds later, we were walking back through the market to where Sally lived, in nearby Long Acre. She was a little unsteady on her pins, the effects of lumbago, she told us, a cold climate, indifferent health care, and possibly the wine, not that she complained about that. We said our good-byes, and Sally promised to keep an astral eye on Kate.

Sally's building was a new apartment complex at the top end of Covent Garden. At one time, the area had been a bit shabby and run-down. Not anymore. As we looked around the teeming streets and alleyways, I could tell the renovation had recaptured the vibrancy, the color, and the commotion of the old market, minus the flowers and vegetables. The one thing missing was the silence, the quiet emptiness of the old market in the afternoon. From about three o'clock onwards, "The Garden" became a harbor of solitude in the heart of London, shuttered and empty. Smeared and trodden remnants of flowers and leafy greens clinging to the cobbles were the only indications of the thunderous commercial whirlwind that had swept through the place just a few hours before.

But the old Covent Garden was not just about flowers and vegetables. It was also home to one of the biggest printing and publishing companies in the country, the Odhams Press. This enterprise occupied a huge chunk of land, a colossal, red brick building filled with yellowy, dirt-shut windows. When the Odhams Press closed, so did a number of the cottage industries it had spawned. One business that had suffered but survived was a small bookbinder and machine rule shop in nearby Nottingham Court.

"What's a machine rule shop?" asked Frances.

"It's where we're going," I said cryptically. We walked over to the courtyard and stood where the old shop had once housed the strangest printing press I had ever seen.

Built in the Victorian era, of boxwood and metal, this particular machine ruler was a loom-like contraption that looked like the inside of a giant piano. A huge leather belt connected all the wheels and levers, making a thuck-thuck sound as it turned and drove the beast into life. Large, blank ledger sheets were hand-fed beneath its strung interior. Pins of red ink would descend, inscribing lines on the paper, which then were collated, folded, and bound into marble-edged daybooks, receipt books, or large hard-backed, leather-covered ledgers.

"Must have been fascinating to watch, the printing. The whole process."

"It was, it was..." I smiled. "And I saw it operating loads of times."

As a teenager, I worked in a private studio in nearby Soho that sold equipment to professional magicians. I would often be sent to the machine rulers' in Nottingham Court to get paper cut or to pick up privately bound books on conjuring. I was always greeted by the cheerful owner, Derek, his effervescent mum, and the dour-faced George, their sole employee. And they always made me a nice hot cup of tea. Mrs. B. made wonderful tea, which we drank huddled around the small gas fire. We nattered away, but the subject always turned to the weather.

We all agreed it was bitter, bitter cold, but what could we do? Mrs. B. never took off her overcoat, Derek and George always wore sweaters. Even in summer the building was freezing. But it had its advantages, they told me, especially when they had the elephants in. Elephants? I was baffled. They went on to describe the pong, and how much worse it would have been if the building were anything other than freezing. Oooh, yes, yes! What a smell! Oooh, the smell! Mrs. B. and her son sounded uncannily alike. Elephants? They noticed the quizzical look on my face and laughed. Old George explained. Down the stairs, along the court, were stables where they kept elephants whenever they performed *Aida* at the Royal Opera House.

And now, walking along Nottingham Court with my family, I remembered the custard-colored gas lamps that had shimmered across the shiny wet cobblestones. The damp, swirling fog. It was another time. Even the pedestrian balustrades set into the pavement were vestiges of a bygone age. These were upturned barrels of cannons that last saw action during the Napoleonic wars, their deadly roars now spiked by concrete. Thirty years on, pink and green signs hummed across the courtyard like neon graffiti. A glass-framed bridge spanned the court's narrowness. I sniffed the air—it reeked of the new and the brash. Thick, teal glass walls. Fiercely scrubbed brickwork. Brush-chromed doors barely contained the money-making buzz within. Media companies. Ad agencies. All that glittered. The stillness that once cloaked Covent Garden in the late afternoon was gone. So too were the bookbinders, the rule makers, the craftsmen. And the elephants.

~

The following day was our last in England. Isabel took us for a stroll around her neighborhood. We walked up Church Street to a large indoor antique market. Our pace slowed perfectly. There's something about looking at antiques that forces relaxation. We browsed and talked about nothing in particular. Sometimes just being with friends, reaffirming steadfast relationships, can be enough. We bought a wonderful sauce boat made around the beginning of the nineteenth century. Isabel bought Kate a silver spoon crafted, very appropriately, during the reign of America's last sovereign.

Frances enjoyed this part of London, filled as it was, not with the obligatory monuments and postcard views of the capital, but with the people who lived there. We strolled through streets lined with creamy-colored terraced homes and pillared entrances, window boxes crammed with flowers, and tubs of lush green plants by doorways. Mary Poppins could have dropped in and felt right at home and, as we were pushing a baby stroller around these leafy streets, so did we.

~

We left Isabel and Colin's bright and early the following morning. Our cab sped through West London, veering past the odd bend in the River Thames as it snaked its way towards narrower, more tranquil banks. We made it to Heathrow with enough time to visit the various duty free shops.

I called my folks just before we took off. We happily recalled Rattlesden. Then Lew put Mum on the phone.

"Good to get back home. Missed me old bed. I can't sleep when I'm away from it."

"You did alright, Mum. You settled in nicely. Slept like an angel. Can't fool me."

"Always good to see you, son," she said.

There was a slight scuffle on the end of the line.

"Get off out of it, you!" Mum was scolding Lew, who was muttering and growling away in the background. Clonk. Clonk. Clonk. The phone had been dropped.

"Now look what you made me do!" It was Lew, blaming Jessie for his fumble.

Silence followed. A few more banging sounds as the phone, I felt sure, was being hauled up from the floor by its long extension cord. The phone finally clattered onto the telephone table, landing like a big plastic red snapper. I heard the sound of rasping breath.

"Everything alright?" I asked.

"Did you get your tea? Didn't forget it, did you?" It was Lew again, gulping air between every other word he spoke. I assured him we had bought enough tea to fill a small scale clipper, as well as chutneys, some fruit sauces, and Frances' favorite, crumbly Cadbury Flakes.

"Did you like the cottage, Dad?"

"If we can see you and Frances and the baby, you can put us in a tent in Barking Park." He avoided the question, but I smiled at the sentiment.

"Great! Well, then, we'll do it again next year. Frances wants to go somewhere different."

"If we're still here."

"What d'you mean, if you're still here? Where the hell do you think you're going, then?"

"Someplace warmer!"

Hackle. Hackle. Hackle.

I assured him Old Nick would wait, and suggested he should stick around for a bit longer.

"Miss you, son."

I jumped on that one, closing the floodgate before it opened completely. I told Lew to get a pair of shoes that were not made of molded plastic. I also told him, as sternly as I could, to buy a set of teeth that would not rattle around his mouth like castanets. He could not see me smiling.

Ghrrr!

It was just the reaction I was looking for. Always good to leave home on a positive note.

Hard by the Master's House

CHAPTER 10

In Windsor to Winchester

We arrived at the usual ungodly hour. Cleverly, we had decided not to journey for hours in search of a welcome pillow and a reviving nap. Instead, we picked up our rental car and drove to Windsor, a few miles from the airport. Blissfully, we traveled in the opposite direction of rush hour traffic and arrived at Queen Elizabeth's second home within half an hour.

We located our hotel, a large, Victorian abode in a nondescript street in the suburban part of the town. The front door was open and, as we walked in, warm air mingled with the smell of air freshener trying in vain to hide the odor of staleness and age. It was dark inside. We looked around. A glorified bed and breakfast without chintz or charm. Plastic flowers rattled in a vase on the hall table. Stiff, yellowing doilies were draped across gravy-brown furnishings.

We were shown through the hallway by a vaguely disinterested little man with a cardigan over rounded shoulders and brown tartan carpet slippers. He looked like a disheveled mouse. He complained about the unseasonably hot weather, then shuffled around the back of a tall desk.

Upstairs, The Mouse showed us a room with a four-poster bed. It was really quite nice. Not that we could have it, the current occupant had not moved out as scheduled, but our host thought we might like to see it all the same.

"Ascot week," he said, knowingly.

"Ascot week?" asked Frances. "Oh, you mean, like in *My Fair Lady*, when everyone wears those big hats?"

"Yes, well, the ladies do dress up a bit. For the occasion, as it were... The Queen has several horses running," the Mouse went on, warming to his subject. "And the Queen Mum, of course. Likes her racing, she does. Windsor fills up. Can't get a room for love or money."

He showed us an unbearably stuffy, high-ceilinged room. Ours.

"You could open the windows, but it's going to be quite noisy, I'm afraid." The Mouse then reminded us, with another knowing look, that it was Ascot Week. I guess he thought we were lucky to get a room at all.

I remembered Royal Ascot, not from the Hollywood movie but from watching the real thing on TV, with my parents. The Queen, along with her mother and other horsy royals, would watch from the glass-enclosed Royal Box. This regal podium was adjacent to the Royal Enclosure, where the privileged few paraded their finery. Ascot kept the toffs within thrilling proximity to the reigning monarch. Like the Queen, they drank champagne and nibbled on cucumber sandwiches. As in the movie, the women wore outrageous gowns and fancy hats, the battier the better. The men wore morning suits and gray top hats, a bit like the Monopoly man. These affluent race goers milled around the Enclosure, looking at the horses with pretended interest and at each other with pretended indifference. The bookies and hard core punters were not allowed in this rarefied section and had to make do with the public bleachers where, ironically, the view of the racing was a lot better.

I smiled as I thought of my parents watching it all on TV, hopefully backing the winners.

Just as The Mouse was about to scurry out the door, he stopped and turned.

"Oh, yes, I meant to tell you. I have to give you a key later. A chap who works here was using the room. Popped off with the key. I'm sure he'll turn up with it."

"What if he comes back while we're napping?" Frances was more alert now, a tad alarmed.

"He won't disturb you. He's Turkish, you see." As if that explained everything. "I'll put a note on the door, saying the room is occupied and to come down to the lobby and give me the key." The Mouse tried to sound encouraging as he backed away down the stairs.

As soon as the door closed, Frances suggested we barricade ourselves in. I looked around. The furniture was big, cumbersome, and quite immovable.

"Look, don't worry," I said, trying to reassure her. "The Mouse is pinning a note on the door, so the Turkish Delight will take the key to reception. We'll pick it up later."

"Can he read English?"

"If he couldn't read, why would The Mouse write him a note?" Brilliant logic, I thought. Reluctantly, Frances agreed.

I suggested we try and nap before Kate woke up. My smile oozed confidence and Frances gave up, perhaps reassured by my complete lack of concern. We kicked off our shoes and fell onto the bed. Sun streamed in. Fortunately, the curtains were thick and heavy and obliterated most of the glare. Not the traffic noise, however. Too tired to care, I closed my eyes and went to sleep.

~

"Hello, what is it? Yes? What is it? Excuse me!" Frances was calling out, quite loudly.

My brain somewhat out of joint, I awoke and stared at the man framing the opened doorway.

"What the bloody hell—" Sleep-sodden curses filled the room.

"Sorry! Please to… Sorry. I go!" the doorway apparition babbled, as scared as we were.

"Didn't you read the bloody sign on the door?"

"Sign, what sign?"

I got up and saw a piece of paper on the hallway floor, scotch tape still attached. I retrieved the key from the no-longer-missing Turk, nodded my thanks, then came back in and locked the door.

Kate had slept through all the commotion. We decided to take a leaf from her book. We dozed a bit, but not very much. Then Kate decided we'd all slept enough. I was sweating and uncomfortable, but surprisingly refreshed. We gathered Kate, the stroller, and the last bottle of milk, and headed down to reception. I slammed the brass table bell, and The Mouse dutifully appeared.

"Heard you got the key alright."

"We didn't get it 'alright,' but we got it," I said.

"He came in the room while we were sleeping!" Frances was still miffed.

"Oh, yes, unfortunate. Yes—" said The Mouse, adding, "He was very put out by that."

"Well, that is a shame."

My sarcasm was lost on him. We turned and headed for the door.

"Er, the key?" he murmured. "You can leave it with me. It's our policy. You know, for safety—"

I stared at him, momentarily speechless. He tried to smile and failed.

"Well, if it's for safety, there's no harm in my hanging onto it. Right? Good! See you later."

As we walked along the sidewalk, women with headscarves talked in doorways. Two old men were huddled by a tree, talking as their dogs sniffed each other and peed. An older teen was leaning into a disemboweled car with an oil can. Then we turned a corner and saw Windsor Castle's turrets and battlements in the near distance.

"Look, Kate, it's the Royal Standard!" I pointed out the gaudy flag flying atop one of the castle's towers. "The Queen must be in residence!" Not that anyone could see the Queen, of course, but everyone loves to know she's there, I added.

We looked around. The houses, the shops, the entire neighborhood within the shadow of the great castle appeared much more elegant than where we were staying.

"Why didn't we get a hotel around here? This is really nice." Frances sounded a bit crestfallen. But it was, we reminded ourselves, just for the night.

We entered a modern shopping precinct radiating around the renovated Windsor train station. A tiny gem of Victorian gothic architecture, the terminus could easily have passed for a church rather than the noisy, blustering cathedral of steam it once was. When we went in, all was quiet. The soft *swuck* of doors closing was the only train noise we heard within the station's girded, iron, green arches. The old luggage room, ticket hall, and station master's office had been turned into upscale boutiques, including a Beatrix Potter shop, coffee shops, and restaurants. Entirely cleaned up, the once derelict station now appeared as creamy yellow and bright white as an ornate Easter cake.

Keeping the looming ramparts of the castle in our sights, we pushed back up the hill. On the right was a converted pub boasting, "Windsor's best fish and chips." A lot of people were inside, so we thought we'd give it a shot. My appetite had finally outpaced my jet lag and the thought of fish and chips was appealing. We sat down next to several elderly ladies happily munching away, including a thin old bird in a flower print dress and a pink cotton coat. No question she was local. We looked at the brief menu—cod, haddock, plaice.

"Any idea what kind of fish to get?" Frances asked.

"Ask that lady what she's eating. See if it's any good."

Frances turned around, smiled, and pointed to the old bird's plate.

"Any recommendations?"

"Fish," she said, very slowly, as if we did not understand English.

"Yes, thank you. But what kind?" answered Frances, just as slowly.

"With batter." She pointed to the fish on her plate and drew semi-circles in the air with a claw-shaped finger. "All over. Crunchy. Batter." She stretched out each word interminably.

Maybe it was Frances' accent. I gave it a try. "What-are-you-having? Is-it-nice?" I asked, sounding like a badly dubbed Italian movie.

"Lovely, all lovely. With tar-tar sauce. And chips," she went on, dragging the words out, hoping I might understand. "You know, cheeps. With vin-eee-gaaar. Lovely. And peas, mushy peas. Moooosheee peas."

"Mushy peas?" Frances suddenly stopped laughing, recalling Mum's marrowfat peas. I could almost feel the smell of steamy urine rising like a green fog in her mind.

"Thank you very much," I said, as articulately as I could.

We had cod. Frances declined the peas. Kate had her freshly refilled bottle, of course, but did manage a bit of fish and a chip or two. And it was lovely. All over!

~

Later that day, we ambled back up the hill into the high street, where we found the Old Crooked House. Whether this was the original old crooked house from the nursery song, we had no clue, but the very tiny abode, warped and deformed with age, certainly deserved its name. The house looked as if it had tried to uproot itself and gotten twisted and bent in the process. We walked around to the back and saw a tiny window in the arched curved roof. A room upstairs, perhaps a tiny bedroom! Not much bigger than a child's tree house, this fabulous building had been converted into a shop for expensive pottery. The store was closed, but the house was a treat to see, even from the outside.

Climbing through a cobblestoned alleyway, we joined a small crowd watching two off-duty soldiers entertaining patrons just inside a pub. One played a snare drum and the other expertly wrestled a set of bagpipes. Obviously from a Scottish pipe band, they wore kilts, hiking boots, and green jerseys with the regimental shoulder patches of the Black Watch. The soldiers played, with power and swagger, military tunes and patriotic songs of Scotland. Their faces were red, and not just from the drinks or the warmth of the early night air. I had never seen this kind of playing close up, and I could see it required real stamina. Smiles covered the exertion they obviously felt. Perhaps this was the same staying power that helped their forebears play and march with such courage in battles past. I could understand how the pulsating insistence of the drum, the plaintive yet melodic bleat of the pipes, could have driven long ago soldiers to death or glory. The music had the power, the magic to make a man feel immortal. And with a drink inside you...

~

I stared at a brown, crinkled bacon smile with lips of fat, two jaundiced egg-yellow eyes, and a stewed tomato-tongue sticking out at me. My breakfast was being cheeky! Not the most appetizing thing to face first thing in the morning, but at least the toast wasn't rubbery.

Within half an hour of that culinary ordeal, we were on way to Winchester, King Alfred the Great's ancient Saxon capital. We found the city in a valley, pleasantly spread out in a mosaic of reds and grays, set in green. It was market day. Frances could not wait to explore.

The street market had hundreds of stalls selling everything from shoes, car parts, toys, second-hand clothes, children's books and CDs, to stacks of old, battleship-gray computers.

"You're a long way from home," said Frances to a vendor.

A Gaelic shrug of the mouth. "Wiz ze toon-el, iz no problem."

We had found a Normandy farmer's wife, with tight, curly black hair, an easy smile, and an accent as thick as Camembert. Her stall had a huge array of French cheeses and not much else. We walked on, past fruit and vegetable stalls, a poultry vendor, a pork butcher, a baker's stall with different breads as well as fruit and savory pies. I saw a knife grinder selling flatware, and thought I might even find a candlestick maker! It was fun—the noise, the banter, the odd blares from radios volumed up for sale.

The architecture in this part of town seemed to have evolved from the medieval to the Tudor, beyond the simplicity of Queen Anne to the ornate plumpness of the Victorian era, and, finally, to the ugly modern of the mid-twentieth century. At least it was changing. The city center had a vibrancy I normally would not associate with a sleepy town in the shires of England. The side street we were following narrowed, then fell away on one side to reveal a vast imposing green. And there, at the end, stood the cathedral.

But first, Frances said we must see the Great Hall of Winchester. Located just beyond the Westgate, in the city's more ancient parts, the Great Hall was a cavernous space that echoed with ancient history and housed a key piece of Camelot lore. Frances was still in the thrall of Arthurian legend, and as the building was very close to the cathedral, I did not complain. At first, we didn't see anything and thought we must be in the wrong place.

Then we found it. King Arthur's Round Table. About thirty or forty feet across, the table was painted in gold and reds and blues. Quite inexplicably, at least to us, it was hanging on a wall, like an oversized Victorian dinner plate.

The table, according to the plaque, was old, but not *that* old. It was an ancient fake created by Edward the First about seven centuries after Arthur had supposedly lived. Very disappointing. We headed for the cathedral.

Viewing old cathedrals is rather like viewing large tomes of ancient literature. It's all about obligation. But as this particular edifice took almost five hundred years to build, I agreed it warranted more than just a cursory glance. We began our slow trek down the center nave, enjoying the many medieval wall paintings. What they lacked in perspective, they made up for in dramatic and religious zeal. We walked past the inlaid grave of Jane Austen, which we'd heard attracted fans by the busload. Apparently, the novelist came to Winchester to see a doctor about an ailment, but the treatment was a failure, the ailment fatal, and so Jane Austen remained in Winchester for all time.

We continued up and down the center of the vast church, viewing with fascination, and just a little dread, the entombed kings and princes propped up forever on plinths or laid out on stone ledges. Some mortuary chests were topped with horrific, life-sized representations of their once-mortal contents. Screaming faces fixed in blackened wood, teeth bursting through rigor-set mouths. Carved skin tight about body frames like thin yet impenetrable cloth. The old souls within seemed to be struggling to escape their fate or rushing to meet it. So much for the privileges of monarchy.

Kate ran around the massive twelfth-century christening font. Hewn from a great chunk of black marble, it looked like a giant mortar without a pestle. I felt sure that if the font's size did not scare newborn mites onto the straight and narrow, the boxed princes would certainly do the trick. The cathedral was a testament to the faith and resolve of the English in the time of the Saxon kings, but not to their humor. Religion in medieval Britain was no laughing matter.

Then we were on our way, traveling from one famous cathedral towards another, this one by the sea.

We traveled southeast and, eventually, started seeing signs for our destination. Chichester. But that day, we only saw a skinny bit of spire. Swept up in a huge stream of traffic, we skirted the town, hard by a section of Roman wall. Moments later, the city was behind us.

A few miles past the scraggly bit of suburban Chichester, trees started to outnumber houses. We found the turn-off to our cottage and meandered up a small, private road for several minutes. The weather was still hot, and dust rose like steam from the gravel crunching beneath us. The hedgerows on either side finally ended where the gravel path divided. We turned, and there it was.

Situated catty-corner to neatly divided farmland was a large, eighteenth century house. A caramel-colored box of a place with very tall windows, devoid of the formal gardens I would have expected. Somehow, this small-scaled mansion seemed as out of place as it was out of time. Naturally we were not staying in the main house, but in the Terrace Cottage, a much smaller abode right next door. Perhaps our home for the week had been servant quarters or guest lodgings, or rooms for a dotty aunt who had shown up one day and never left.

The cottage was locked. No one was there to greet us or let us in. And there was no answer at the front door. Gingerly, we started walking around the mansion. We knocked on the side door. No answer. We continued to the back, where we discovered a beautifully kept garden with a great sweeping lawn and three people lolling in chairs, staring up at the sun. The air cloyed with the smell of suntan cream and freshly brewed tea. We went over and, with forced jollity, introduced ourselves.

"Go back the way you came. I'll meet you there." Madame, as we immediately dubbed our hostess, sounded a little weary. Perhaps she was tired of renting her little pebbled cottage, or perhaps she was tired of *having* to rent it. We were not sure. The other two people sunning themselves did not move or acknowledge our existence. One was an elderly lady; we were never introduced. The other, we later discovered, was The Master himself. He remained glued to his plastic garden furniture, pretending to sleep. He was a short man with spindly legs and a bald, shiny pate. His bulbous eyes were enclosed by eyelid skin, like a frog, and his mouth seemed permanently pursed.

We clomped back and found Madame outside the cottage.

She gave us the keys and showed us how to avoid getting locked out. Useful. While she gave us hints and tips, I watched Kate cross the patio onto a long narrow garden, the width of the cottage. Kate ran its entire length with a big smile on her face. High, stone-and-cement walls surrounded the garden and separated us from the larger, more opulent acreage Madame and The Master enjoyed. Even so, it was a goodly amount of space, with shrubs and a few tubs of flowers on the patio.

"There's a book of instructions. How things work, that sort of thing. And a bottle of milk and champagne in the fridge," Madame edged towards the door. She stopped and added, "No charge. I'll leave you to it, then. You'll find that book very helpful."

"Ah, where's the telephone?" I asked.

"Oh," she said, aghast, as if I had asked to borrow the Rolls.

"We understood there was a phone."

"It's just for incoming calls." She had recovered. "If you must make outgoing phone calls, we require a fifty-pound deposit. Much better to use the phone box by the newsagent. Just down the road. Only a mile away, possibly less. Yes. Much better. Well. Enjoy your holiday."

And Madame was gone. She had never entered the cottage.

"How lovely," I said, bristling. We had specifically requested a house with a phone.

Ever practical, Frances suggested we unload the car. We opened the door and went inside.

We got quite a surprise. All was white and bright and cheerful. More like a small Greek Isle villa than an English country cottage. No cozy nooks and crannies stuffed with rattan and raffia and dried flowers, but we found big windows, curving archways, open stairs, and French doors. The whole place sparkled with the warmth of the outside but, as the walls were as old and as thick as centuries, the rooms remained pleasantly cool. And with a fresh bottle of milk and complimentary champagne in the fridge, we were off to a good start.

CHAPTER 11

In the countryside of West Sussex

WE PUT KATE DOWN for a nap, found some tea, and took stock. Despite the lack of country chintz, and no phone, the cottage was fairly well-equipped with, beyond the basics, a CD player, a TV and video player, and a couple of radios. Halfway up the stairs was a small landing with a bedroom; next to it was a bathroom with a one-piece washer and dryer. We continued up the stairs to a couple more bedrooms and another bathroom. Frances had insisted on a bathroom on our level this year. We opened a closet and found big, white fluffy towels.

We took our tea to the patio. In stark contrast to the freshly minted look inside, the outside walls of our cottage looked old and strong, built with pebbles from the shore, big as fists, sea-beaten smooth and shiny, with yellowish moss clinging to the imbedded stones like shards of gold velvet.

Beyond the cottage, corn was growing, along with mud-splattered leafy green things and vivid yellow plants I did not recognize. The farmland was divided into soft, straggly squares and edged by poplar and chestnut trees. With Kate in her stroller, we walked along a grassy path, then looked back. The land dipped and rose and seemed to shimmer like a damask tablecloth haphazardly thrown into place. It was a pretty sight and, despite the drawbacks of having to drive everywhere, we started to relax.

~

Around six that evening, we stirred from a restful nap. The day was still bright, the sun reluctant to leave. And so were we. We were all quite content to do nothing except enjoy the long summer eve. But, apart from a diminishing bottle of milk and a bottle of champagne, we had little in the way of edibles. Jessie and Lew were arriving the next day, driven down by my cousin Pam and her mum, Aunt Flo. We had invited them to stay overnight. So we headed to Chichester on a grocery run.

We swooped back around the Roman wall, then inexplicably found ourselves heading out of town. We had missed the city center completely. By chance, we saw a turnoff for a supermarket, so we swirled around a couple of spurs and ended up in the parking lot of a very new, very large Tesco, quite unlike the Dagenham Tesco, with its meager selection of bangers and bacon and the odd side of beef. We even found fresh duck breast, partridge, and quail. Quail! Individually wrapped. A money area indeed, as Jessie might have said.

"What's green-back bacon?" Frances seemed mildly alarmed.

I assured her it was not off despite its off-putting name, but Frances remained unconvinced. Neither was she impressed by a large slice of Mowbray pie, encased with golden pastry. Pink pork, speckled with fat like polished marble, with a hard-boiled egg in the center that gleamed like a cyclops' eye. I assured Frances it all tasted better than it looked.

We stocked up on sherry for Mum, Guinness for Lew, and wine for us. After considering the different kinds of milk available, silvertop, sterilized, and gold-top, we abandoned health and chose the gold-top, with its two-inch rim of thick cream and familiar gold foil cap. As a boy, I drank gold-top milk for a treat. We always tried to get the milk in as soon as the milkman delivered it. Left on the doorstep, the bottles' shiny gold cap would invariably get pecked off and the top of the milk would be slurped up by birds as hooked on the stuff as I was.

"Look at this! I love these," Frances said, holding up some toys and brightly-colored, Kate-sized tee-shirts. This store seemingly sold everything. And, it seemed, we bought everything! We piled up our culinary and sartorial treasures on the checkout counter. The cashier rang us up. I paid and waited. I looked at my unbagged groceries, then smiled. The checker stared at me. Nobody blinked. She finally said plastic bags were at the end of the counter. We hastily bagged. Oh, well, when in England…

~

Sunday morning was bright and sunny. We put bread in the toaster and switched on the electric kettle for coffee. I turned on the radio to catch *The Archers* and Alistair Cooke's *Letter From America*, started the coffee grinder. Then everything stopped. The entire side of the cottage was without power. "Marvelous," I fumed. "Haven't even had any bloody coffee yet. Just marvelous!"

I waded across the gravel, kicking up pebbles in the wake of my anger. I knocked on the door. No answer. I went around the back and rattled on the kitchen door.

"Yes? What do you want? Please?" A young, nervous French girl peered out at me.

"I want The Master, or Madame. We have no power. *Sans* illumination!" I spoke slowly, in English and fractured French.

"Zay are not—'ere! I, 'ow you say—I am ze nanny. Zay, ah, do zee djog to-gez-zair."

"C'est parfait! Well, tell them! Pro-blem dans le petit bleedin' maison!"

My French was appalling, and the Cockney accent I usually disguised had clawed its way over my vocal chords and reasserted itself. Most disconcerting. I marched back to the cottage, where I found Frances talking to our hosts. The Master smiled at me as he jogged in place, baseball cap over shiny pate. I glared. He jogged off. Madame stayed on, puffy and red, talking breathlessly.

"Fuses. Does that. Not a problem."

"Not for you," I said, flatly.

"Be right back. Not to worry." She incanted the words like a spell as she jogged away. A few minutes later, she returned, went straight to the small fuse box, and put in a new fuse. Obviously not a new problem. She mumbled something about doing the best she could, then left, no doubt hoping that was the last she'd see of us.

"I missed *The Archers!*" I whined as I munched toast and slurped coffee.

But Frances wasn't listening. She was happily plotting out the next few days, finding sights to see and places to visit. All, she promised, within easy traveling distance.

Then gravel crunched under tires. Car doors opened. Through the window, I saw Lew clambering around the back of the car, prying Mum out of her seat like a cork from a bottle. Pam was helping Aunt Flo, who looked rather poorly but was smiling. We emerged with Kate. Lew's weathered face cracked into a wide grin.

"Hello, hello! Welcome to Chichester!" I said.

"Welcome home, son," said Lew. "Welcome home."

~

Lew and Jessie looked remarkably well. Lew was getting around and squiring Mum as well as I remembered, although he was using his cane more forcefully, relying on it more than before. Not that Jessie noticed, and he would never want her to. They were a team, argumentative and solicitous by turns, independent and cantankerous, but still together. Jessie was, as always, rosy-cheeked, only now she looked tanned and appeared to have lost a bit of weight. Large, framed glasses sat squarely on the bridge of her Roman nose. Her broad, open smile, set within a wavy mouth, still made her face glow so distinctively. Only now, age and encroaching vagueness and uncertainty periodically clouded the bright, milky translucence of her eyes and shadowed her cheerfulness.

Lew was also tanned and, despite the cane, quite spry. Not bad for eighty-seven, I thought. Standing as upright as the sergeant major he once was, skinny chest thrown out defiantly, he surveyed the cottage and its surroundings slowly and carefully. He had lost a little weight, but then he had always been thin.

Kate ran around her aged relatives as we helped them over the gravel, down a few steps, and across the flagstones into the house. They tottered about, viewing the cottage as if it were a museum. They were impressed and spoke in almost reverential whispers.

"Very nice. Very comfy. You've done alright here, Denis." Flo approved.

"Hasn't she grown? Oh, look! Look! Oh, bless her!" Mum tooted enthusiastically, one hand grasping a chair for support.

"Hello, Katie, hello, darling," said Pam, quietly. In England, Kate was always "Katie."

"Ah, a nice drop of the rosie lee. Lovely! I'm gasping," said Lew, hearing the kettle whistling.

"Rosie Lee?" asked Frances discreetly.

"Tea," I whispered, then turned to Lew. "Had a haircut, Dad?"

"Yeah. Yeah, well, at least I still got hair to cut!" he said happily.

"He has it cut so you can't see the gray at the sides of his head," said Jessie, quite aware that her own hair was the color of frayed silver wire, curled and teased into submission, while Lew's was still virtually nut brown. For a while Mum had worn a large, brown wig that would have looked better on a seventeenth century dandy than a twentieth century Cockney. Now the wig was gone but the resentment over Lew's head of hair remained.

"I've got bleeding gray hair everywhere else," said Lew, chuckling with amazement.

Frances looked up, startled.

"I could have told you that!" Jessie gave a slight hoot, then trotted off to the loo.

"Rather you didn't, though, Mum!" I said nervously. I shrugged apologetically at Frances.

"Alright, alright." Lew suppressed a hint of a smile. He tried to look innocent, but failed. "Where's that cup of tea, then?"

Where indeed! I bolted and started pouring.

⁓

Mum appeared on the landing, clutching the handbag that went everywhere with her. She made it downstairs very easily. Unlike our little nest in Rattlesden, the steps were not steep. Another plus for our little cottage.

"Did you miss me? Lovely bathroom," she said. Lew sidled up to me as Jessie made her way into the dining area.

"She likes it," said Lew. "Thank Gawd for that!"

Kate made happy yelping noises at Lew, who immediately leaned over and started making wah-wah noises at her. Jessie soon joined in with, "Where's the baby? Where's the baby?" covering and uncovering her face while blowing raspberries and laughing. Kate toddled towards her grandmother, fascinated by this English version of Peek-a-boo. Kate giggled, grabbed Mum's necklace, and started tugging rather sharply.

"Where's your mother?" Mum looked around, suddenly nervous. "Where your mother?"

Frances joined us momentarily to disentangle Kate from Jessie's jewelry.

"Got a grip, hasn't she? A strong grip," said Jessie, gingerly touching her neck.

"How was the trip down?" Frances was asking.

"No trouble, really," said Pam. "I know this part of the world. Spent some time down here, haven't we, Mum? With the other branch of the family." Pam looked at Flo for confirmation.

"His family. In Hastings," Flo agreed. "Not that he ever sees them."

"His" name remained unspoken, but Flo meant her reclusive husband, my Uncle Tom.

"Can't remember last time I saw Tom," said Lew. "Hastings. He loved going down there."

"A bit ramshackle now, of course. Just like the rest of us!" Pam laughed nervously.

Pam was wrong—she still had her looks. The long blond hair, the freckles across the nose, the impish grin were all still in place. Only now, her voice reverberated with a certain wistfulness.

"It's good to see you, Pam. And thanks for bringing Mum and Dad down." I smiled.

"Not a problem Denis, glad we could all make it. Nice to get away, isn't it?" Pam said in her quiet way.

Better than any of us, Pam understood about having elderly relatives set in grooves as deep as ravines. Fortunately for me, her love of family included my parents as well as her own. Pam often drove Jessie and Lew out for a trip, to a pub, the seaside, or the countryside. As she had on this occasion.

After a cup of tea, we headed to the local pub for Sunday lunch. We were on the main road for just a minute before turning down a country lane roofed by arching trees. We quickly emerged from this canopy of greenery to find ourselves on a slight incline overlooking farm fields and woodland. And there was our "local," The Royal Oak, made of plaster and wattle and tiny red bricks, sagging with age.

The public bar was clustered with nooks and crannies, with an irregularly shaped wood floor and flagstones set on different levels. Big doors and large French windows were flung wide open, embracing the surrounding countryside. The bright sun made the inside of the pub seem darker, as if it were glowing in the warm, muted light of a good pale ale. The bar was shiny with elbow polish, propped up by patrons who, drinks in hand, stared out at the sunshine and smiled.

They gave us a long table positioned half in the pub and half on the patio. Lew was first up to the bar and got in the first two rounds. Soon after, one of the barmaids took our orders for lunch. We relaxed with our drinks and watched Kate as she toddled around her elderly relatives, who seemed bemused by her antics. Then Mum reached across to me.

"What you having for lunch, son?" asked Jessie. She appeared distressed.

"I'm having the beef, Mum." It was the usual selection of Sunday roast meats.

"What am I having?"

"The lamb," I said.

"Did I order that?"

"We both did," said Lew, returning with another trayful of drinks.

"What you having again? For your lunch. What you having?" Mum pointed a finger at Lew.

"Lamb. Same as you. You already asked me that."

"And I'll probably ask you again in a minute." Mum said with unexpected insight.

"Yeah, I suppose you will." Lew swiveled around in his chair and stared at me. "Drives me up the wall, she does, really."

"Come on, Mum, drink up. Lunch will be along in a minute. I've ordered lots of red wine."

"So, what are you having for lunch, then?"

Eventually, lunch and wine arrived. Kate sucked happily on her bottle while we drank ours and tucked into the traditional Sunday fare.

"That's it! That's it! Last time I saw Tom was at May's funeral" said Lew suddenly. "It's about the only time we see anyone these days, when someone wraps up."

"Wraps up?" Frances asked.

"Wraps up, my girl," said Lew. "When someone dies, they wrap up. Finish."

"Tom! I remember. He dropped Mum." Jessie was suddenly recalling an event from half a century before, as clear as day. "It was outside the Vic."

"He did what?" asked Frances, confused.

"He was in drink," said Flo, as if sharing the same memory, the same thoughts, as her sister.

"Your mother was three parts to the wind, an' all!" said Lew, another eye witness.

"No, she wasn't!" insisted Jessie, knocking back her wine. "Tom was swinging Mum around, and she jumped on his back to steady herself. Then he dropped her!"

I tried to picture the scene. It sounded like a fight to me, but Jessie made it sound like they were under starter's orders at the Derby. Lew rolled his eyes and filled in the background when Mum was out of earshot.

My nanny, Jessie's mother, had six daughters, and they all had boyfriends, most of whom became my uncles. Their big night out was always Friday, because Friday was payday. The Vic was the place to go, and Nanny Evans always came along. According to Lew, my old grandmother would sit in the corner nursing a Guinness, and, whenever a boyfriend would buy a drink for his girl, he was obliged to ask Nanny Evans if she would like one, too. Nanny Evans never said no.

"Your Nan would sit there drinking and then, for no reason, she'd start in on one of us lads. For no reason at all—" continued Lew. "And God help us when she did."

"She was probably jealous," I shrugged.

"Our Mum wasn't jealous." Jessie plonked down her empty glass rather forcefully.

"Well, you know, you all had boyfriends, and she had no one," I said, reasonably.

"I wouldn't have got jealous about what we had, would you, Jessie?" Flo snorted.

"Never!" Jessie answered, in defense of her mother and, possibly, womankind in general.

Lew slowly lifted himself out of his chair and smiled at me as he went up to the bar. Rather indulgently, he bought another round of drinks. More oil for the flames.

"She'd finished with men, our mum had!" said Jessie suddenly.

"Remember what Mum said, Jess?" Flo went on, not waiting for a response, "'I would not have another man if his arsehole was hung with diamonds!' That's what she said!"

Lew gripped the rail at the bar, waiting for another order. He was trying not to listen, but I knew he was well within range. Poor sod.

"The things we have to put up with, eh, Jess? At least now Tom leaves me alone. Done my bit. Mind you, there was nothing much there to begin with!"

Harsh cackles burst forth from both sisters.

"Every Saturday night!" Jessie roared like a town crier. "That's what I had to put up with. Sex! Every Saturday night! Sex!"

"Alright, alright—" Lew had returned with drinks.

"When he retired, I retired. 'No more sex,' I said! That was it for me!" said a jubilant Jessie, her face now fire-engine red, her smile a harsh gash. "I put my foot down, I did!"

Pam rolled her eyes; she'd heard it all before. Frances, who had not heard any of it before, started to look concerned. With some foresight, she took Kate out to the patio. I just sat there, pretending to be shocked as my mum and aunt blistered with laughter.

"That's enough!" Lew was now angry.

Both sisters ignored him. They continued hooting like giant, blood-shot owls, tears of laughter streaming down talcumed tracks in their faces. Eventually their merriment ended, and both women fell into a vengeful silence when Lew, rather bravely, said he would not buy Jessie any more drinks. Fortunately, Kate sped back towards them, ending the tension. Jessie blew raspberries and made wild mouth gestures that disturbed me but amused Kate greatly.

We all made it back to the cottage in one piece. No harm done. My folks and Flo settled themselves in the living room for a natter. Frances and I put Kate down for a nap, then we joined Pam for a walk around the countryside.

Thanks to ancient right-of-way laws, pathways and footpaths wove their way through the countryside tapestry. We could walk anywhere from our cottage without fear of being chased off, or shot at, by irate landowners and farmers with yapping dogs. The weather had turned a little cooler but, for a country stroll, it could not have been better.

We walked along the side of the cottage, keeping the farmland to our right. On our left and beyond, open fields gently sloped down to a tiny brook in a deep gully. We carried on until we found a footbridge, then ambled towards a cluster of beech trees.

The afternoon sun was gently being anchored onto a near horizon created by a vast row of poplar trees. We jumped back across the stream to the trees and saw new houses clustered together in a suburban setting. We had peeked behind a bucolic façade, and the rolling countryside had rolled to a complete stop. We turned back, trying to ignore the housing development.

We followed the hedgerows through ploughed fields of that unnaturally bright yellow crop I'd noticed earlier. The path widened, and we followed embossed, red-clay tracks left by a tractor.

As we approached the cottage, the intermittent bird song and the methodical drone of distant farm equipment were cut short by the rasping but welcome whistle of a tea kettle. Lew must have been waiting for us. As we walked in, he was putting out cups and saucers.

"Have a nice walk, then?" asked Lew. "Everyone else is having a kip!"

"It was fun," said Frances. "The weather's lovely!"

"You're lucky, lucky you are, with the weather. Only last week—"

"Yes, Dad, I know, I'm sure it was bad. So, Pam tells me—"

"Did someone mention tea? I'd like a nice cup." Flo woke up, looked around, "Pam! I've got to go."

"Do you want your stick, Mum?"

"Don't fuss, Pam. Don't fuss! Just help me up!"

"You okay, Pam?" asked Frances. Pam smiled, gently shaking her head as she maneuvered her mother towards the stairs.

Frances and I made sandwiches and laid the table. We had found just six of everything and no dishwasher, so we did not have enough plates and cups and had to wash up as we went along. I was not handling this too well.

"We've got all this salad stuff! And the pies, the sausage rolls—"

"We should have bought paper plates." Frances shrugged. "Why you buttering the bread?"

"Bread is always put out buttered over here," I said snappishly. "Haven't you noticed?"

We put out cold cuts, cheeses, sausage rolls, salad augmented with coleslaw, anchovies, and lots and lots of buttered sliced bread. We held back on dessert, as there was no room on the table. And we had no plates. After the initial oohs and aahs, and a general consensus that we had made "far too much," my relatives proceeded to eat everything in sight. Not to eat it all, I was told, would be a wicked waste.

For dessert, or sweet as my family called it, we put out freshly washed plates with apple and blackberry pies, tiny iced sponged cakes, and individual Swiss rolls covered in chocolate. We also had a Bakewell tart, a sort of pecan pie without the nuts. Jessie tried to make it once, without the benefit of a cookbook. Mum was convinced cookbooks were for people who could not cook and, therefore, not for her. Blaming the instability of her oven, she had announced that the pie "had caught." I had no idea what she meant until she brought it out. The crust had the look of burnt paper, and the filling had the consistency of freshly laid tarmac. Mum had baked her Bakewell tart from memory but, as she had never baked a treacle tart before, there was not much to remember. But at least she had tried.

Everyone said how lovely tea had been, they could not possibly eat another thing. Just as well, because we had nothing left. I had thought we had enough food for a siege. We cleared the table and decided to get an early night. We'd been sitting and talking for hours. Jessie gave Frances and me a kiss, then trotted upstairs. Frances checked on Kate just before she turned in. Pam helped get Flo settled, then came back down just to say goodnight. I remained up with Lew.

We sat in the lounge, sipping Jack, just the two of us in the quiet of the late evening. A favorite time. So, Dad, how are you doing?

Pam says you get a bit down. How has Mum been? Is her memory worse? How are you both managing? But all the things I wanted to say remained unspoken. Lew drained his drink, smacked his lips, and contentedly breathed in the last of its strong aromas.

"Good drop of stuff that, my son. Good drop of stuff."

I could not agree more.

CHAPTER 12

To Weald and back

FRESHLY BREWED TEA was being handed around as I stumbled downstairs for breakfast. I blinked. My relatives were smartly dressed, almost formal. They looked as if they had been up for hours. I glided through bits of laughter and the odd mutter of conversation. I gulped down some tea, turned on the coffee, then chopped up and passed around some Danish pastry that had somehow survived last night's tea. Frances entered the scene with Kate.

"Come on, Jessie, come say good-bye to your skin and blister!" yelled Lew.

"I'm coming, I'm coming," said Jessie as she shuffled out of the bathroom.

"Skin and blister?" Frances asked.

"Sister," I explained. "More rhyming slang. He's only doing it for your benefit."

"That's sweet," said Frances.

"Come on, Mum, best be going," said Pam, hooking an arm around her mother's shoulders.

"Thanks for letting us come down, Denis," said Aunt Flo with a radiant smile. "It's been very nice. Lovely weather for you. Enjoy it. You, Frances, and Kate. Make the most of it."

"Time to go, then," said Jessie.

"You take care of yourself, Jess," said Flo.

Jessie and Flo did not hug or kiss but held each other's hands in the tightest of clasps. Their silent exchange spoke volumes.

"I'll be over to see them," Pam told me as she helped her mother into the car. "And you, enjoy your visitors, Aunt Jess."

"Don't you worry about that, Pam! I will. Go on with you!" said Jessie with a tinkling laugh.

As they drove away, Lew turned to me. "So, where are you going today then? You got plans?"

"Well, yes," I said. "Frances has plans, actually—for all of us."

"Oh? Well, you bring up the jam jar and we'll be ready to go."

"Jam jar?" asked Frances.

"Car!" said Lew, chuckling.

Half an hour later we were motoring down a winding lane that rose and dipped with pleasant regularity. Occasional shafts of golden sunlight hit the windshield with blinding intensity. I blinked, reached for my sunglasses, and slowed down. Just as well, as I almost missed the turning. We drove into a broad valley where green and yellow crop fields checkered the landscape.

And there it was. The Weald and Downland Outdoor Museum, a sprawling exhibit of centuries-old buildings and houses. Each property had been lovingly saved from demolition, transported, and rebuilt on fifty acres of meadowlands bordered by copse and hedgerows. The place looked like an ancient village.

"What's the point of any of this?" Lew shook his head, smiling at our obvious naiveté.

"You can see how people lived in the olden days," I said, reasonably.

"I know how they lived in the olden days." Lew's voice filled with conviction. "Life was hard. Bloody hard. Cold. Not enough work. Never enough to eat. And always behind with the rent. I know what it was like." He was describing his own childhood, but he was not far off the mark. For some, nothing much had changed over the centuries.

We walked to a field surrounded by an intricate fence seemingly made of ancient, stretched-out wicker furniture. Next to this was another fence, this one made of logs, rough-hewn with pointy ends. I read the sign.

"It's an exhibit, Mum, it shows the kinds of fences they used in the country. Way back when! And I thought it was all hedgerows and stones. Who knew it was like this?" I said, trying to generate interest in what I thought was the most boring display I had ever seen in my life.

"Right then, we've seen enough," said Lew firmly. "Where's the caff?"

And with that, my parents toddled up the hill to find the tea-room. With Kate in tow, we flitted from house to barn to building. Nothing was behind glass, we could walk into any exhibit and feel a sense of place and get a sense of the people who once lived or worked there.

We entered a farm laborer's cottage. It was dark inside. We were struck by the rawness of the place. The walls were rough and spiteful looking. The floor was uneven and strewn with straw. Nothing looked comfortable. Even the hearth looked cold and meager. It made my parents' house in Dagenham look like a palace. A grisly but fascinating reminder of how peasants once lived. We saw other houses that were far more splendid and quite beautiful, but the image of the peasant's cottage was snagged in my mind like a splinter from its rough-hewn door frame.

Along one of the grassy thoroughfares, we came to another "street" with rescued houses from the Georgian, Regency, and Victorian periods. We also found a re-assembled school house, almost two hundred years old. The furnishings were sparse and rendered in dark, almost black, wood—a couple of cabinets, a teacher's table complete with bible, a hand bell, a day ledger for taking school attendance, and a quill pen and pewter inkwell. In one corner was a small stool, a conical dunce cap, and the schoolmaster's Malacca cane ready to quell the naughty, the unruly, or the tardy. There was a blackboard, of course, and in another corner of this austere room was a large globe showing filigree outlines of discovered lands, replete with pink cherubs blowing favorable winds.

The globe's romantic view of the world did not extend to this school, which reminded me of my own primary school classroom. The rows of tiny desks with flip-up seats were just as I remembered. On each desk, at the top right-hand side, was an inkwell hole and a groove for a pen. Those old ink pen sets never favored left-handers like me; as I wrote, I usually smudged whatever I had already written. Across one desk I saw the telltale ink stains, smudged from right to left, and felt an immediate kinship with the long-dead, long-forgotten student.

"My primary school wasn't much different—like something out of Dickens," I lamented.

"Oh, please! Even you're not that old." Frances grinned.

Of course, I was stretching a bit with the Dickens reference, but the blackboard schoolroom, with its rows of inkwell desks, was not just a museum relic. Just add a bit of grime and a sandpit and most schools were good to go for about a hundred and fifty years. Until the nineteen sixties, similar temples of rote learning were easy to find throughout an entire strata of English society.

On the way back to the teashop, we passed an old toll booth, a tiny shack of a place hard by a tiny footbridge. I started to trudge up the hill with Kate in the stroller. Frances went inside. A moment later, she came running out and yelled at me to come back.

"You've got to see this, you've got to! Come on, I'll stay with Kate."

Reluctantly, I retraced my steps back down the hill. Frances waved me on, still smiling. I entered the dank and gloomy toll house. Through the empty toll office I walked into the tiny bedroom beyond. Then, against my will, I stopped. There, in the bed, was a wax model of an old woman, red of face, a bit plump, mouth open, and, despite the lace cap, her hair was silvery and curly and quite recognizable. She even had a Roman nose. Beside the distinct likeness of my mother, a cadaverous waxwork was attempting to get out of bed.

"AAAAAAAAH!"

It was Lew. Apart from the nightshirt and nightcap, it was him. Right down to the tenacious crook of his frame and the deep scowl he used to focus the anger that could stare down a blizzard. I could almost hear the figure mutter "Ghrrr." I fled the toll house and raced up the muddy track, where Frances was waiting for me with a told-you-so grin on her face.

～

Back at the cottage, we did some laundry. After an hour in the dryer, the clothes were still sopping wet. We fiddled with knobs and dials, and tried again. Same result. All spin, no heat. We found a clotheshorse, a big, wooden, concertina-like contraption that we erected

on the patio. We draped our wet items on it, then I went to the big
house to lodge yet another complaint.

I had been relegated to performing menial tasks in the shadow of
The Master's abode. The clotheshorse was a symbol, a class hurdle
I thought I had leaped years ago. I walked around to the back and
knocked on the door. As ever, no one was around except the French
au pair.

"Oooh ay The Master?" I asked, rather too loudly. She cringed
a bit.

"Pee-tair, 'ee iz in Lhon-dhon."

"Oooh ay Madame? Doing the jog-jog again, is she?"

"Oui!"

An hour or so later, a sweat-suited Madame showed up on our
doorstep.

"I'll tell my husband. I had no idea. We try and maintain this
cottage to the best standards." She flitted about and then was
gone.

Duck was on the menu that night. I set to. A knife in the drawer
looked like a chef's knife, but it was as blunt as a spoon. Tomatoes
folded beneath my blade and squirted in all directions. Duck breast
slid on the cutting board as trimming turned to hacking. Then, as
Frances turned on a light, the power failed. Along with my patience,
the fuses had blown. Again! Once more, I stormed across the gravel
walkway and left another message. Madame was in-deez-posed, the
au pair said.

"Now it's the fuses. Again. And the dryer, don't forget le dryer.
And the knives. The knives in the kitchen. Blunt. Useless. You could
not cut oeufs with them. Tell them!" I spoke in the time-honored
way we English speak to foreigners, slowly and loudly. The au-pair
had a bewildered look on her face. But I knew she was being delib-
erately obtuse and obstructive and, well, foreign. I turned away,
growled my version of Ghrrr, and headed back to the cottage.

Somerset Maugham once said that money is the sixth sense that
enhances the other five. My senses, like the knives in our cottage,
remained blunted, despite the money we had shelled out for the
place. Frances tried to reason with me, encourage me not to make
too much of it. No one else seemed concerned. Jessie leafed through

a magazine and sporadically rolled plastic blocks towards Kate. And Lew was happily rabbiting on to Frances.

"Everything alright, is it?" The Master had shown up, out of breath and jolly, about half an hour later. He sounded almost friendly.

I told him everything was not alright. I caught myself sounding ominously like Lew. The Master again replaced the old-fashioned fuses in the huge wall sockets. He then produced a tiny, obviously cheap knife sharpener and set to on our blunt cutlery.

"Eddie. Our fix-it man. He'll be stopping by. Tomorrow. He'll get the dryer going."

"When?" I asked. "We want to go out tomorrow. I don't want to wait around."

"Don't worry, I'll give him a key. He'll let himself in." The Master caught the look on my face as he made for the door. "Oh, don't worry, he won't nick anything."

Then he was gone. I stood there for a moment, perplexed. To "nick" was to steal, a working class expression, definitely East End lingo and hardly part of The Master's vocabulary. Or was it? Was he dropping his guard? Or was he just being patronizing? I wasn't sure, then I realized that, with two Cockney parents in tow, no amount of honey-spun words or soft tones were going to lull his protruding ears into thinking I was anything but an East End kid with a poshed-up accent.

"Hey, where's my trouble and strife, then?" Lew asked as he scanned the inside of the fridge.

"Trouble and strife?" asked Frances, entering the kitchen.

"'Wife.' Trouble and strife is wife." Lew chuckled, grabbing a cold can of Guinness.

"That's not very nice," said Frances primly.

"It rhymes, gel," said Lew, somewhat condescendingly.

"So does 'love of my life'! Why not use that?" Frances was quick.

Lew was momentarily taken aback, then he started to laugh loudly.

"Oh, yeah. Oh, yes. And so it should be," said Lew, still chuckling. "So it should be!"

~

The electrics worked, the knives cut, and we proceeded to prepare dinner. I sautéed the duck breasts, deglazed the pan with some red wine, then mixed in some blackcurrant jam and made it into a sauce. I sliced the meat with a newly sharpened knife and served up the duck with some tiny, buttered new potatoes and freshly shelled peas. Mum and Lew seemed wary about eating duck, but quickly overcame their timidity and tucked in with great gusto. Even Kate liked it.

While we cleared, Jessie and Lew took Kate and settled into the lounge. By the time we joined them, we were both feeling more relaxed, although a little tired.

"Oh, beautiful Katie, oh, beautiful Katie, you're the only little girl that we adore—" Lew serenaded his granddaughter with great verve. Then Jessie joined in. "And when the moon shines over the mountain, we'll be waiting for you at the k-k-k-k-k-k-kitchen door!"

My first reaction was, oh, God, they're choking. Lew's swallowed his teeth. Then they both started laughing, gently prodding Kate in the ribs as if she were a giggly pincushion.

"You haven't swallowed your teeth, have you, Dad?" I asked.

"Naaaw, I've got 'em right here!" He took his teeth out of his trouser pocket, wrapped in a handkerchief. "I 'ad 'em in at dinner—then I took 'em out. Give me gums a rest."

"Lovely!" I said laughingly. "Just lovely—"

"What was all that ker, ker, ker stuff?" Frances asked.

"It's a stutter song," explained Lew. "From when we were kids."

They had both remembered a stutter song from nineteen seventeen! So physical impediments were fair game in their day. Before I started feeling too superior, I recalled a big hit from "my" day, "Bridget the Midget." Their song was nicer.

Later that evening, when the ladies had retired, Lew remained in place eyeing the Jack Daniels. I took the hint and poured the drinks, putting less in mine and hiding the difference with ice. Lew took his straight. We sat for a moment. I told him about the schoolhouse we had seen that day.

"Brought back some memories—not that my school was that bad. But still—" I said.

"You weren't much for school," said Lew.

"Out when I was fifteen. I think I wanted to stay on," I said, without certainty.

"Well, you weren't much for it. You weren't good at maths." Lew always said "maths." He wasn't really listening to me, but I must have snagged another memory from the shadows. And it was a revelation.

"I was good at maths," he said, casually.

"You what?" I was surprised.

"When I was in the artillery, I calculated gun angles. Six guns, I had. Different elevations, different targets. Distances. We had a contest. I had my guns set up and ready to fire when everyone else was still farting about trying to calculate the range. You see, I could do logarithms in me head. Monty himself came up to me, personally. Congratulated me, he did."

"You never told me."

"About Montgomery?"

"About the math."

"You got a prize though, didn't you?"

"History," I reminded him.

"Well, there you are, then! More than I ever got from school!"

I stared at Lew for a moment, not knowing what to say. Then he asked for a refill, and I joined him. For that round I did not dilute my drink with ice.

CHAPTER 13

Chichester to Fishbourne

WITH GREAT FORESIGHT, we decided to start another load of laundry first thing the next morning. We cranked the clotheshorse back up and corralled it outside. Then we laced up the garden with a clothesline Lew had found under the sink. Laundry soon flapped in the wind like misshapen bunting, all within view of The Master's House. I liked that.

Before we left, Eddie, The Master's fix-it man and gardener, showed up. He had a lilting, almost shuffling gait, and when he walked, he looked as if he was wading through a great body of water. He wore a thick, Sherwood-green shirt, light brown trousers with corduroy bumps as thick as spaghetti strands, and a belt as wide as a two-by-four. He could have been a ruddy-faced gamekeeper but, whatever his provenance, he looked every inch the image of a countryman. Only his voice betrayed different origins.

"'Allo mate," he said.

Eddie was a Cockney. He had grown up in the East End and lived for many years in East Ham, not too far from Dagenham. I asked what brought him to Chichester.

"I was on me 'olidays, at Bognor. I was a Master Gardener. In East Ham, I just worked for the council, mostly privet cutting. Boring, it was. I thought, I could be a gardener 'ere as well as there. So I moved down. Never regretted it. New life, better. Work for the parish council, mostly."

"Do you miss London?" ask Frances.

"Not on your life, darling. The country hereabouts is lovely. Get the sea breezes. You won't get me back to East Ham! Anyway," he turned to me and got down to business. "I got a word from the missus, in the 'ouse. Dryer acting up, is it? Let's take a look."

He took a look, ran it, poked around. Then he said the whole thing would have to be replaced.

"But when?"

"Well, I dunno. At least you've got the sun. That'll get your clothes dry!"

I muttered under my breath, but he just smiled and wished us all a good stay. I waved Eddie away, somewhat annoyed by his breezy cheerfulness as if he was the one on vacation, not me.

Frances had planned a post-laundry trip to the Roman Palace at Fishbourne. Looking around an archeological dig did not sound too appealing to my parents. Lew announced that he and Jessie would be far happier in the garden with the racing page.

"We'll keep an eye on the laundry, son."

"Make sure it doesn't fly away?" I smiled.

"The weather, son, can't rely on it. Sunny one minute, pissing down the next—"

Lew was as gloriously pessimistic as ever and could not have been happier. I envied him. While Frances and I were traipsing around exposed bits of foundation stone, Lew would be relaxing in the garden, a cup of tea by his side, happily scanning the picture-perfect blue sky for errant clouds. My parents loved the cottage, that was obvious. And I suddenly realized it wasn't too bad, in spite of the odd problems and hassles. I was beginning to like it. A bit.

In short order, we packed Kate into the car, said our ta-tas, and were happily shooed away.

Within fifteen minutes, we had traveled back almost two thousand years. And what a journey it was. The excavated part of Fishbourne Palace turned out to be just one wing of one of the largest Roman homes ever built. Bigger than Nero's palace, the one that burned down in the Great Fire of Rome. An enormous find, with many artifacts in copper, gold, and silver. The greatest artistic treasure on display was a colorful mosaic of a slightly stout, winged boy riding a dolphin. Not surprisingly, he looked rather breathless. We pushed Kate slowly around the wooden walkway, impressed by the intricate beauty of the inlaid mosaic floors. We were just as impressed by what lay beneath them.

Vestiges of indoor plumbing and floor-warmed central heating had been found, with hot and cold running water concealed behind walls and connected by tile work of elegant simplicity. The palace offered more modern conveniences than I had grown up with in Dagenham! My retroactive envy was tempered by real interest and, despite myself, I suddenly wanted to explore more.

Fishbourne Palace was given in the first century to Cogidubnus, a despicable local princeling who collaborated with an invading Roman legate called Vespasian. His information led to the success-ful conquest of Southern England, part of the Claudian invasion of Britain. A grateful Vespasian, who much later became Emperor, made the traitorous Cogidubnus king of the surrounding lands and built him the palace of Fishbourne.

The palace gardens had been laid out in an educated approxima-tion of their original design. Not exactly pretty, but functional and orderly. Very Roman. We strode around the herb garden and along pathways bordered with flowers and plants apparently extant dur-ing the Roman era.

A long block of ancient, concrete foundation seemed to peter out just before a hedgerow. Beyond this clumping mishmash of bushes was a row of late Victorian, terraced houses. Did the site end there? I asked a gardener working nearby. Apparently, one wing of the villa extended beneath the Victorian houses, but they could not excavate further.

"Grade Two. Historic, ain't they?" he said. I could see nothing special about them. I'd seen endless rows of similar houses, but only one Roman palace of this magnitude. It was a shame, I said.

"Why did they build the houses so close to the palace?" Frances asked.

"Didn't know it was there. They only discovered the palace around nineteen sixty, when they were laying a foundation for a new lot of houses. Funny what you find when you're not looking."

"I bet those houses didn't have central heating." I pointed to the Grade Two houses.

"Still don't!" The gardener chuckled. "The Romans had it better! All mod cons!"

"But the Romans didn't have electricity!" said Frances, as he walked away.

"Nor did we. Well, we did, until it ran out—" I said dramatically.

We had electricity, but the supply to our little house in Dagenham was metered. The electric meter was situated in the hallway, and attached to it was a coin box that took two-shilling pieces. If we didn't feed the meter, the electric power switched off. This happened many a night, and if no one had coins handy, one of us would careen into furniture, groping a way through the dark until the "light money" was found. The light money was kept in an old Rowntrees pastille box, on the ledge on the farthest wall of the kitchen. Coin in hand, the person sent to "do the light" would feel the way back, patting the narrow passageway until it turned, then shuffling across the hall before colliding with the chair that was always there.

The meter was out of reach to everyone except Lew, who was just over six feet tall, and even he had to stretch up on tippy toes to insert the light-giving florin. Jessie, Tony, and I had to stand on the chair in the pitch blackness, grab the exposed electrical cable for balance, insert the money, and turn the handle. Once again, light would bathe our little house and, most importantly, the telly would come back to life. Mum tried to keep a two-bob bit handy, especially if she was watching a favorite show. But if we stuffed the meter before settling down for the evening, Jessie would scream bloody murder. Plying the "electric" before the "juice ran out" was a wicked waste, she would say, convinced the "juice" would simply evaporate if money was fed into the box too soon.

"Didn't you have a flashlight?" asked Frances.

What a beautifully simple idea, I thought, and smiled. So practical. So American. A flashlight might have made living in Dagenham a little easier; that's probably why we had never thought of it.

On the way back from Fishbourne Palace, we came across an old weather-beaten butcher's shop with a large blackboard sign promising fresh, homemade sausages. We pulled into a small car park. The butcher sold all manner of meats, but one refrigerated case was solely dedicated to sausage. He sold at least twenty different kinds, from white to black and everything in between, including sage and thyme, apple, lamb and mint, game, duck, even beef chipolatas. We bought my favorites, the very meaty and savory Cumberland sausages.

~

"These are really lovely, these are," said Lew, cutting into his second sausage. "You can't get sausages like this anymore. Not for love or money. This is how they used to be, didn't they, Jessie?" Lew managed to find the cloud's lead lining.

"Mmmmmm," murmured Jessie.

"We found the shop by accident. We were just driving by and there it was," said Frances.

"The things you find! I couldn't find a tunnel with a ferret," said Lew, shaking his head.

"'Cos' he's got a car, so he gets around," Jessie chimed in provocatively.

"Don't start that again!" said Lew, packing his thin cheeks with sausage.

Frances buttered more bread while I made tea.

"Who do you think she takes after, then? Little Katie?" asked Mum.

"I think she looks like Frances," I said, not trying to be provocative.

"She has my eyes and my hair, she does. A proper English rose, she is. Bless her! Has Katie been christened yet?"

Frances braced herself. We'd had this conversation before.

"No, Mum. We're not religious, Mum, I told you that, darling. And anyway, Frances is Jewish. Remember? I told you that, too."

"Jewish?" She looked surprised.

"Yes, Mum," I intoned the words, almost knowing what was coming next.

"On both sides?" Jessie asked.

"Yes, Mum," I said.

"But Katie is English," said Jessie, hope in her voice.

"Well, actually, Kate is American. Born in Washington, D.C." Frances sounded a bit peeved.

"She is also a British citizen, though, Mum. She has a British passport." I wasn't helping.

"Well, of course she is, you've only to look at her to know she's English! Bless her! You were christened!" Mum looked across at Frances and added, "Denis was christened—"

Frances and I got up and started clearing the table. Frances was picking up napkins when Mum gathered up some crumbs and tossed them at her.

"Could you please not throw garbage at me?" asked Frances, with brittle cheeriness.

"I was trying to help, wasn't I? I always do that, don't I, Lew?"

"Well, please don't do that any more."

"Well, I've done it now," Mum twittered nervously.

Frances fisted the napkins and went into the kitchen in silence. I said what any Englishman would say under such circumstances.

"Make some tea, shall I?"

Without waiting for a response, I moved quickly into the kitchen. I tried to apologize, mumbled a few soothing platitudes, but I could see Frances was annoyed.

"I've just about had enough," Frances said, not unreasonably.

"I know, I know. They're...what they are. A couple of old funnies. Well, you know..."

Frances sighed and tried to smile. "I'll put Kate to bed."

"Yes, yes, good idea," I said, floundering. "You go. I'll finish cleaning up here."

It was another warm night. Lew and Jessie settled down just outside on the patio, quite unaware of Frances' anger or my frustration. No point in making a scene, I thought. I poured tea and took it out to them, as though nothing had happened. In a way, nothing really had. Then Frances joined us, guidebook in hand. The warmth of the early evening melted the frostiness that had lingered at the end of dinner. We all drank our tea and lounged around the patio as if we were in a light-filled sitting room. All we could hear were the trees as they rustled in a faint, occasional night breeze, like so many hands being rubbed together in front of a crackling fire. And all we could smell was the honeysuckle that clung to a corner of the patio and perfumed the air.

CHAPTER 14

Arundel Castle to Bosham

ABOUT HALFWAY BETWEEN Chichester and Brighton, we reached the ancient town of Arundel, which encircled the soaring castle like a brickwork-layered petticoat. We swung by the river Arun and entered the lower castle precincts.

"Don't pay for us, son, we'll wait in the car!" said Lew when he saw the admission rates.

"It's cheaper by the car anyway," said the attendant, who had overheard.

We hurriedly paid and drove into the car park. Frances told us the castle owners, the various Dukes of Norfolk, had been clued into the tourist trade for almost two hundred years.

"Perhaps early visitors were charged by the cart," I said. "Up for a tour?"

"Lead on," said Lew. "Lead on!"

We walked through an entranceway covered in smooth yellowed flagstones. High above the Great Hall, the innards of a blackened timbered roof lay exposed. The dark, wooden walls were covered with tapestries and paintings, some of which were as big as cricket pitches.

"Oooh, look at those paintings. Lovely, just lovely, they are!" said Mum.

Mum was looking at one of the many large hunting scenes. Interspersed with ravenous dogs and fleeing deer were lots of heavy-framed portraits of the ducal family, present and past. Why the Dukes of Norfolk, whose family name was Howard, lived in Sussex for hundreds of years and not in Norfolk remained a mystery to me. If the portraits were anything to go by, the Howards were not a very attractive bunch, but there were certainly a lot of them. The most famous Duke of Norfolk was an adviser to Henry the Eighth who tried to further his career by arranging for two of his relatives to marry the King. The first one was Ann Boleyn. After that spectacular failure, the Duke again tried his hand at matchmaking, this time with his free-spirited niece, Catherine Howard. This too, proved less than successful. Not surprisingly, after two royal marital blunders, Norfolk fell from favor and wound up in the Tower of London with an ax hanging over his own head. Fortunately for him, Henry died before the death sentence was carried out.

And here we were, centuries later, ogling the present Duke's paintings, gold-encrusted teapots, and a whole array of baronial baubles and richly decorated knickknacks.

"Lovely paintings," said Jessie again, nodding to Lew. "Looks so real, doesn't it?"

"This is what you call paintings," agreed Lew. "Remember that place Denny took us to, in the West End?" Lew gently shook Jessie's arm, as if trying to nudge a memory.

Jessie didn't seem to remember, but I did. My parents' loud belligerence had created a mild ripple of disturbance within the gallery. They had attracted a small group of students who followed them from one Jasper Johns painting to another, delighting in every utterance, every critique. "Oooh, look at this one, Lew," Jessie had called out. "Look at it, just look at it. Like squitters!" "I wouldn't give it house room, I wouldn't! Not if you paid me!" Lew had sniffed and snarled.

Ghrrr.

While I enjoyed my parents' state of shock at the state of the arts, I had eventually left them to their gaggle of followers. But, as I counted yet another stripe on yet another painting of yet another American flag, I secretly admired their forthrightness and blatant honesty.

～

Arundel Castle was a different story. The walls appeared to be tiled with paintings of aristocrats and romantic landscapes by Van Dyke, Reynolds, and Gainsborough. My parents were impressed and, I must admit, so was I. We walked past an old fireplace big enough for a small study, certainly big enough to stand up in. Everything about the castle's public spaces seemed enormous. The ceilings were high, the stairs wide, the wall panels as big as doors, the braziers man-height, the wooden chairs plus-sized. The carpets could easily have covered a modern squash court, and we could have used a couple of the paintings as room dividers back in Dagenham.

We followed thick red ropes in and out of the rooms open to the public. Strangely, and most pleasantly, we saw fewer guards and attendants in Arundel than we had at other, far less regal mansions. That made our tour more relaxed, especially with an unreined child in attendance.

We entered a suite built for a three-day visit by Queen Victoria and Prince Albert. The bedroom had tall ceilings and velvet wall coverings. A library casement was thoughtfully filled with ancient tomes in hand-tooled bindings. The massive fireplace could easily have accommodated Santa and a reindeer or two. The ornate canopy bed was something out of a fairy tale. According to legend, after the royal couple's visit in 1846, the bed was never used again.

Until Kate climbed on it.

Thankfully, no alarm bells sounded and the bed, after we straightened out the coverlet, did not look any worse for wear.

"Gasping for a cuppa tea, son," said Lew.

My folks had been deprived of the local brew for at least two hours. The cafeteria was in the old servant's hall, with a hearth large enough to roast a herd of sheep. Tapered leaded windows and a broad flagstone floor gave it a monastic appearance. We sat on high-backed chairs that looked like thrones and munched on teacakes in an appropriately regal manner. Out of the blue, Lew announced that all this touring business wasn't 'alf bad, and the castle had been worth the visit. I had to agree.

"Bleeding glad we're sitting down though, me pins ache something rotten," he added.

～

That afternoon, while Kate napped and Lew and Jessie dozed, Frances and I went back to the butcher's shop near the Roman palace to stock up on the sausages we all loved. On the way home, we stopped at the gourmet Tesco's and picked up some fresh brown bread, creamy Danish butter, cold cuts, and hand-sliced smoked salmon, along with an assortment of locally grown lettuce, cucumber, and tomatoes.

As evening approached, I served drinks on the patio. It was all most relaxing. After playing with her grandad, who was always a good sport, Kate decided to throw soft round objects at Jessie, which threw her into a mild panic and evoked the usual response.

"Where's your mother?" she asked, looking around anxiously. "Where's your mother?"

We put out food and the family gathered. Lew was impressed with the smoked salmon Frances was artfully arranging. Meanwhile, I was putting out bread. Buttered, of course.

"Sorry, Dad, couldn't find any bagels to go with the salmon," I said.

"I haven't seen any here," said Frances. "Didn't know you had bagels in England."

"No bagels in England? Cor strewth! Remember the bagels we got down Club Row, son?" asked Lew. "Hot, they were. Do you remember? We got them in the Jews' market on Sunday, just off Petticoat Lane."

I remembered. Huge tourist crowds flocked around Aldgate every Sunday and descended on Petticoat Lane, the famous street market in London's East End. With so many shops, restaurants, and theaters closed on Sunday, Petticoat Lane market was a magnet for tourists with nothing to do on that most desolate of days. Yet beyond the crowds, the buskers, the Pearly Kings and Queens, and the market pitchmen selling everything from clothing to cutlery to tourist swag, was a different part of the market, a place for the locals, at the farthest end of Wentworth Street. It was called Club Row.

Club Row was vibrant, alive, and very noisy with fishmongers, kosher butchers, and delis with vast wooden vats filled with salted fish, cardboard-stiff herrings, and big wooden slabs covered with sides of smoked salmon. Here, like in the street market, everything and everyone seemed open for business, conversation, argument, or all three. And the smells—the human gaminess, the metallic steamy hot water exploding in tea urns, warm pies seeping gravy, the musty animals and birds, the wafting pong of pickles and waste—all mingled under one roofless emporium.

I particularly loved the bakeries, with their weirdly shaped loaves, twisted and plaited and covered with what I thought was bird seed. And rolls with holes, threaded onto long sticks! Amazing. No bread was sliced, or pre-wrapped in printed waxed paper. Fresh. Lew once bought us a bag of small, hot breads that were soft on the inside and crusty on the outside. Steam filled the bag and a yeasty, sweet aroma filled the air. My first bagels. What a treat. We ate most of them as we mooched around, looking at budgies and songbirds and kittens and puppies for sale. For a few hours, I had become a part of Lew's polyglot, unpredictable, and distant past.

~

"I never liked it much there, in Club Row," said Jessie. "I worked for a tailor down Brick Lane, he was Jewish. Well, it was all Jews in that area, wasn't it? I made shirts for Austin Reed's. Collars and cuffs. Very particular about the work we did, the man from Austin Reed's."

"I used to work down the Jews' market when I was a kid, portering for pennies." Lew smiled at this happy memory. "That's where I learned to speak Yiddish. Then I got a proper job in the fish market. My guv'nor had a stall there. Up to his elbows in fish and eel guts from early in the morning till late at night, he was. Cor, what a job! He made money, and he threw it around like a man with no arms! But he was good to me, though. And could he cut smoked salmon! He cut salmon so thin you could read a newspaper through it. Things you remember—"

"I didn't know you spoke Yiddish," said Frances, fascinated.

"You're Jewish, aren't you?" said Mum, looking at Frances.

"Yes," said Frances, sighing.

"Well, I'm Christian, I am," said Jessie, as though scoring a point.

"Don't start that again, Mum," I said.

"Alright, Jessie, steady on, girl," said Lew, patting the air with his hand. "Steady on."

"They were all Jews, in Brick Lane," said Jessie, as though Lew hadn't spoken. "Never spent on themselves, but made of money! Wouldn't believe it to look at them. They kept themselves looking dirt poor, they did. Wore rags, like tramps! But when they had functions, weddings, no expense was spared. My grandfather knew; he was a headwaiter. Did all the big dos. Silver service. He knew."

"Can we drop it now, Mum, okay?" I said. "How about another drink?"

"No, no, I'll wait, I better get some food inside me to soak it up."

"Good idea. Let's eat," Frances said, wearily. She gave Kate some salmon.

Lew tried to fill the awkward silence with a story about brown schmaltz herrings and the smoked salmon he used to bring home from the market. But Mum wasn't done yet.

"You should have seen the salmon my grandfather brought back from those Jewish weddings! They had the best! Those Jews. The best of everything!"

"My grandfather was Jewish, and he did not have the best of everything," said Frances, her anger barely controlled. "He was in a concentration camp. So I don't want to hear any more about the Jews having the best of everything, okay?"

Mum seemed genuinely shocked, but she was not one to be stunned into silence. Alas.

"What did I say?" she asked innocently, "I didn't mean anything by it!"

"You always make these comments. Every year you have to say something about the Jews and how you hate them." Frances spoke forcefully.

"I don't hate the Jews!" she said, then added, "Denis is a bit Jewish, and I love him!"

"For God's sake, Jessie, put a lid on it." Lew growled at her.

"And look at Lew! He's even more Jewish than Denis, and I married him!" Mum tried to laugh it off.

Frances picked up some plates and went into the kitchen without another word.

Lew scrambled to his feet and padded after Frances. I shot Mum a look, then followed him.

"I'm sorry, girl," I heard Lew say. "She gets a drink inside her and you don't know what's going to happen next. One minute she's happy as a clam and the next minute she's a right cow—her mother was just the same. I'm sorry, darling, she doesn't mean any harm. She's not as bad as she sounds, she really isn't." He sounded sincere. When he saw me, he just shook his head, out of words.

"Cup of tea?" Frances smiled feebly.

~

The following morning, I suggested we should all be tourists together. I thought spending the day as a family might help clear the air of any lingering sourness. Our new destination was not far away and the countryside was pretty, even from the roadside. For some reason, the hedgerows in Sussex were a lot lower than the ones we had seen in Suffolk the previous year. So there were sights to see, a vast, slightly mysterious landscape speckled with giant shadows of clouds and snapshots of animals as rooted to the earth as the trees and the ancient milestones.

"What's in Bosham?" asked Lew.

"It's pronounced 'Boss-em' apparently," said Frances.

According to her guidebook, the coastal village of Bosham dated back to pre-medieval England. It's where batty King Canute—more pickled than a herring—commanded the tide to turn. The tide did not oblige and Canute got a well-deserved soaking. Like all English schoolboys, I knew that story instinctively, rather like 1066 and the Battle of Hastings.

"It's from Bosham that Harold set off to fight William the Conqueror," Frances added.

"Now that, I didn't know," I said.

"Just so long as we get a bleedin' cuppa tea when we get there."

"Don't mind him, we'll fall in with whatever you want to do," said Jessie. "Mind you, if you want a cup of tea, I'll go along with it."

We parked quite near the harbor teashop. As we entered, I noticed a rather unusual road sign showing a car floating above wavy lines.

Amphibious cars crossing, I mused. But no. Our friendly waitress told us the road beside the tearoom was regularly submerged by the tide. Many a car had been caught by the rising waters. We found that hard to believe.

After a cup of tea and a slice of cake, we were ready to explore. We discovered a pleasant little village with pubs and teashops and craft shops huddled close to the water's edge and surrounded by the masts of dozens of yachts, anchored like a waterborne forest of silvered trees rattling and clacking in the breeze.

Farming, fishing, and boat building were flourishing in Bosham three hundred years before the Battle of Hastings was fought, and these traditional occupations remained intact until recent times. Now they were all but gone. We found a burgeoning commuter town peppered with well-heeled boating types and landlocked tourists. And yet, surprisingly, Bosham's skyline remained similar to the outline stitched into history so many centuries before in the Bayeaux Tapestry.

Lew and Jessie wanted to buy us a belated anniversary present, so we walked around a converted barn filled with artisans of every description. We found a blacksmith who used his age-old skill to hew iron into contemporary craftwork and, from his selection of birdbaths, ornately shaped hooks, and lamp fixtures, we selected a couple of large candlesticks with big enough points on them to pierce a suit of armor. They looked as if they had been ransacked from an abandoned abbey, and we loved them immediately.

"Think of us when you use them," said Lew.

When we picked up the car, we looked towards the tearoom and, sure enough, the road was gone, along with most of the pole and its strange street sign. And yet less than an hour had passed. The Bosham tide must have snapped back with alarming speed. No wonder the befuddled Canute had gotten such an unexpected soaking!

~

On the way home, Frances said we had been so close to Chichester all week, yet it seemed we might miss its cathedral entirely. So we decided to be a little spontaneous, and off we went.

Unlike Winchester or Canterbury, Chichester's cathedral was small. The huge spire and tower, almost three hundred feet tall, would, on reflection, have looked more appropriate on a bigger church. Yet inside, the cathedral's smaller size gave it an intimate charm not normally associated with such edifices. And, of course, Lew and Jessie were delighted to find they could walk around the entire place in a couple of minutes.

Although the cathedral was almost a thousand years old, its lack of relics or walled-up VIPs kept it off the tourist path. During our visit, we only saw one other person, a woman down on her knees, hands locked in earnest prayer. The lack of people, living and dead, rendered the place blissfully tranquil. Quiet flowed beyond the ancient walls into the cathedral precincts and gracefully arched cloisters. We peered across manicured lawn to the flowerbeds, then ambled along Saint Richard's Walk, where Jessie and Lew admired the roses. A wonderful herb garden overflowed with medicinal and culinary plants. We were lucky to have found, so close to a bustling city center, a sequestered, peaceful haven we could all enjoy together.

When we got back, Kate went down for a nap, and we sat out on the patio. The only sound was our laundry on the clotheshorse, now snapping to attention in the cooling summer breeze. Along with a pot of tea and a plate of cookies, Frances brought out photos we had brought over from America. She passed them around and, like the cookies, the pictures were devoured with great pleasure.

"Has he been fixed yet?" asked Jessie, waving a picture of our black cat, Oscar. She used the photo as a pointer. "You have him fixed, and he'll grow intro a big lovely cat."

"Mum, he's been taken care of," I said, quickly. Frances didn't want to hear this.

"Good," Jessie continued, then, "I had my Tony done."

"Tony?" I asked. The only Tony I knew was my brother.

"My cat, Tony. A big ginger tom, lovely cat. Settled down, he did, once he was done."

"What did Tony think about that?" asked Frances. Mum looked confused.

"Your son, Mum! She means, did Tony mind that you called the cat after him?"

"Oh, no. I didn't call the cat after Tony; I named our Tony after the cat! Lovely, he was, once he was fixed."

"Tony wasn't named for the cat," growled Lew. "Named for Anthony Eden, he was."

Ignoring him, Jessie looked again at the photograph of Oscar. "I never thought our Denis would end up with a pussy."

So that was that conversation. Frances picked up the empty cookie plate and went back inside for refills. But as she turned, I saw her look of disbelief ripple into a good-natured smile.

"I'm all for staying in tonight. How about a curry?" I suggested.

"A bit of take away? I'm all for that!" said Lew, rubbing his gnarly old hands in anticipation.

$\sim$

Later that night, Lew handed me a drop of Jack and sat down with me.

"Well?" I said. Lew had promised to tell me about Mum's grandfather, the headwaiter. He had hinted at a skeleton in Mum's closet, and, I suppose, I wanted to rattle it.

He looked this way and that, like a stage magician about to let kids in on a secret, but really making sure Mum was not about.

"He was a waiter alright, but he was in charge of nothing." Lew's words bubbled with contempt. "He wasn't even your mother's grandfather. It was just what the kids called him, because he was older than Jessie's father." I was rapt; this was all new to me. Lew went on, "You see, when your mother's father, *your* grandfather, went off to fight in the Great War, her mother took up with this waiter. Bill, his name was. The old woman got pregnant, then Jessie's father came back from the war, saw what was going on, walked over to Wanstead Flats, and drowned himself in the ponds there. The old woman said he was drunk and fell in. Lot of bollocks, that was. You can't fall in Wanstead Flats and drown. Too shallow. The only way you could drown was to go in from the edge and keep walking. And that's what he must've done. Just kept walking. Poor bastard."

Almost a century separated me from my grandfather. He had survived Passchendaele, one of the great battles of the First World War, only to discover that the home fires had been kept burning for someone else. Lew was right. Poor bastard.

CHAPTER 15

On to Brighton

FRANCES AND KATE and I decided to spend our last day in the area visiting "London by the Sea," the famous coastal town of Brighton. My parents had had enough of touring and, as usual, were quite happy to see us on our way. Brighton used to be *the* place for a naughty weekend. It changed a bit in the sixties. Tabloid newspapers were then filled with gritty pictures of Mods and Rockers having punch-ups on the front. The Brighton we found was much calmer.

Seaside slums and reeking pubs cozied up to posh homes and expensive restaurants. This odd mix of dilapidation and sophistication extended to the local populace. We saw well-dressed young blades with tousled hair and angry kids with nose rings, all in shades of black, as if they had just attended a funeral with a casual dress code. Families like us were also out and about, as were old ladies in faded print dresses and threadbare cardigans, heads and smiles turned to the sun.

Apart from Brighton's promenade, with its ornately decorated piers, the main attraction was The Royal Pavilion. Resembling an Indian palace with white domes like upturned jelly molds, Brighton's Royal Pavilion was built as a seaside retreat by the architect John Nash for the Prince Regent, later George the Fourth. It was quite a sight. The Pavilion was a vast, Taj Mahal-like building plonked on a very ordinary looking street, flanked by a municipal library on one side and a gentleman's urinal on the other. Queen Victoria graced the place with her presence at the start of her reign, but she did not like it too much, and found a far less exotic but equally grand hideaway on the Isle of Wight.

Inside, the Pavilion was decked out with sideboards supporting giant gilded tureens. We shuffled by oversized red chairs that looked like plump, gaudy courtesans awaiting an audience, and bulbous floor vases that could have accommodated bunches of freshly cut trees. We felt quite out of scale, like diminutive grandees. The kitchen was enormous, too, and great fun with its life-sized plastic animals skewered on giant spits to create an ambiance of days gone by for even the most unimaginative.

Upstairs, the large banqueting hall had a kind of rococo, curry-house style. The colossal dining table groaned beneath the gilded cutlery and ornate plates awaiting their plastic roasts. The excess continued in the Chinese room, with black-lacquered walls and furniture adorned with painted birds and flowers. The expensive fakery was exemplified by the bamboo furniture, which, on closer inspection, turned out to be gold-painted metal tubing. The whole place seemed like a Cook's tour of the exotic East, the oriental glam and sham of two hundred years ago. But it was fun and quite breathtaking, in a strange kind of way. We had tea among the fake metal fronds and golden bamboo and pretended we were Maharajahs!

~

Jessie and Lew were so pleased to see us, they cheered when we got back. They clambered out of their seats on the patio, all smiles. Kate loved it, and so did we. Did we like Brighton? Yes, and we did see the Pavilion. Did we get on the beach? No. Did we go on the famous pier? No, but we saw it, from the prom. Never mind, ay. But you all had a good time? Yes? Yes, we had. And you got to see all you wanted to see? Yes, Dad, we did.

We all sat out on the patio, where Frances plopped some ice cubes in her tea and tried her best to chill it down. My parents thought icing tea was even stranger than drinking it without milk. Conversely, Frances could never understand why we drank hot tea in the heat of summer.

"It keeps you as warm on the inside as you are on the outside," said Lew knowingly. "Keeps you less thirsty. Do you know, my girl, we even drank tea in the desert, during the war?"

Unconvinced, Frances happily sipped her ice tea. With our own tea in hand, Lew and I kept a watchful eye on Kate as she ran around the garden, plunking herself down whenever she felt like it, then, with great effort, pulling herself back up, never dropping her ball. She was wreathed in smiles.

It no longer bothered me that The Master had a bigger yard, as we all shared the same view. And what a view it was! Farmland gave way to the soft roll of the hills studded with poplars and oaks and ruffled clumps of hedgerow, and it was all at the end of our garden. On the far horizon, I pointed out the roof of the grandstand at Goodwood, seemingly the only building for miles around.

"Glorious Goodwood!" Lew turned to me. "You like it over there, don't you? The States."

"Yes."

He nodded and smiled. We both looked into the near distance.

"I had forgotten how beautiful all this was," I said. "Or maybe I never realized it before. Not sure. But these trips back here, you know, seeing things, I've liked it all. Most of it, anyway."

"Well, of course you do!" said Lew, expansively, "It's your home!"

My home. He was right, in a way. Perhaps this explained why I flew into rages over the smallest things, why I had no patience for people's eccentricities or the petty inconveniences we had to put up with. Because a part of me still considered England home, and that part of me wanted home to be something it could never be. Perfect.

∼

We decided to use up the remaining vittles in the fridge. So, dinner that night consisted of a happy mishmash of savory dishes. Eggs, tomatoes, salad, baked beans, and, of course, sausages. I also melted down some bacon and fried up some leftover spuds and greens in the rendered fat, and ended up with another cornerstone of English cuisine: Bubble and Squeak. It all went down very well with everyone except Kate, who would eat nothing but sausage! All in all, it was quite a feast, like having breakfast for supper, but instead of tea and coffee, we polished off the remaining beers and the last bottle of wine. Then we made tea.

While Frances and I cleared, we heard Lew and Mum serenading Kate again, with a song called "Two lovely blue eyes." They sang and swayed, then la-la-lahed and hummed forgotten words. Frances and I joined in, singing not much better than my parents, but it didn't matter. Kate was enjoying the attention as much as we were all enjoying that moment together.

"Well, I'm going up now. And I don't want you disturbing me when you come up," said Jessie, with some resolve.

Ghrrr.

Mum beamed her huge winning smile and went off to bed. Kate was already asleep. Frances turned in next, and I was left downstairs with Lew and our usual glasses of Jack.

"So, you both doing alright?" I asked.

"Oh, yes! It's just that we can't do what we once did. Gadding about in castles, and Gawd knows what else—"

"You didn't do too badly, Dad."

"No, I suppose we didn't do too badly at all, my son!"

"Here's to you, mate. Been a good trip, all in all." I raised my glass.

"You know, it's hard to believe, but your mum...funny cow, she is." He sipped on his whiskey before continuing, "Do you know, before the war, she'd have nothing to do with Mosley and his Black Shirts. Nothing. 'We kicked them out the East End,' she told me once. 'Didn't want the likes of his lot around.' That's what she said— straight up! And you know, Mosley and all those other bastards were only in the East End to stir up the shit, because they knew Jews lived amongst us. So they thought, they'd get support, like—well, I tell you, Jessie and a lot like her shot him right up the arse! Tell Frances sometime, you know, not now, but sometime..."

"I will, Dad, I will tell her."

"Means the world to see you, son. Your little family, does really. Been grand. Lovely lodge, this. And the weather! You couldn't have asked for better weather than you've had here. Now, mind you—last week. If you'd had come last week—"

~

Sequestered on a quiet suburban street, our hotel in Windsor was replete with bow-tied French staff who were not only competent but actually liked children. We were tired and did not feel like moving.

After dinner, we strolled around the charming garden. Kate made a bee-line for the pond like a human divining rod, startling the fat goldfish and startling us with her newfound speed. Thankfully, that was the only excitement in store for us that evening.

The following morning, as always, I called my parents from the airport.

"You're a wooden 'ead, you are. You forgot your pickled walnuts!" Lew chuckled.

Pickled walnuts. Those big, soft, black blobs that taste like intensely flavored mushrooms were hard to come by in Maryland. Even so, I could not remember being told to take them.

"Don't worry! They'll keep 'til next year," said Lew.

"That long? They'll keep that long?"

"These walnuts? They'll last longer than me, they will!"

Hackle. Hackle. Hackle.

"That's good then, I'll pick them up next year! Now, put Mum on and let me say good-bye."

We said our good-byes. Our promise to return, like the walnuts, would keep well.

YEAR FOUR

*A Carriage House
on the Saxon Shore*

CHAPTER 16

To Romney Marsh and Rye

I SAT BEHIND THE WHEEL, stitched with real leather. I ran my fingers over the smooth wood dashboard. The engine purred. I was behind the wheel of an Alfa Romeo. Me. And I wanted that car, if only for a week. It was rather like destiny.

We had brought sing-along tapes for Kate but, since our last visit, CD players had been installed in virtually every make of car. So, while the obliging lady at the rental place searched the lot, I happily remained in the only vehicle she had found that still played cassettes. Perfect! Kate would hear her songs, and I would hear the hum of a glorious Alfa at no extra change. I had that enchanted look in my eye. Frances broke the spell.

"What about your parents?" she asked. "Where are they going to sit?"

"In the back. With Kate. The leather—did you smell the leather?"

"There's not enough room. Where are we going to put their luggage?" Frances asked, slowly.

"I don't care! They can put their suitcases on their laps. I love this car. I want this car—"

"This car is totally impractical!"

"Exactly!" I said, deliriously.

"The lady has found one other, a station wagon. We can all sit in that one, and the luggage will fit," said Frances, encouragingly.

"Don't care!" I cried happily. "We can make the Alfa work!"

"Weirdo!"

~

It was still early when we left in the station wagon, built like a tank but with the requisite tape deck, heading for the Cinque Port of

Rye. I explained to Frances that the "Cinque Ports" were, originally, a cluster of five ports established and reinforced by the Plantagenet kings in the thirteenth century to protect the realm from sneaky and persistent French attacks. The ruling class in those days, descended from William the Conqueror, spoke mostly French, and "cinque" had been derived from the French word for "five."

"So 'cinque' is pronounced 'sink'? That's odd," said Frances.

"Odd? Doesn't sound odd to me! English pronunciation of French—get it?"

Eventually, we found a coastal highway. The sea was on our left and the vast expanse of Romney Marsh on our right. I smiled as I pulled up in the town of Dymchurch.

"Why are we stopping here?" asked Frances.

"Doctor Syn, alias—The Scarecrow! Remember? Never read the books? No? Of course not. Boy stuff. Anyway, this, this is the place. He was the vicar here. Of Dymchurch. Doctor Syn!"

I tried to share some of the mystery and romance Russell Thorndike had so vividly evoked. He depicted Dymchurch as a quaint and ancient seafaring village brimming with intrigue and smugglers. The town was known for its famous seawall, where we were now parked. In times gone by, this famous landmark was viewed with dread and hope. If the wall collapsed, much of the surrounding countryside would disappear beneath the sea. "Maintain the wall" was the Dymchurch motto. And so the wall was maintained.

The present-day edifice was neither romantic nor mysterious, just a vast concrete slab that looked like a gray, beached whale washed up on a huge car park. To one side were caravans, vacation trailers in pinks and greens and yellows, strung out along the coast like cheap strands of jewelry. We stood atop the massive wall. The wind howled and gushed with such force it could have creased a brick. Yo, ho, ho. This was no place for smugglers or imagined memories of derring-do.

From Dymchurch, we traveled into the marsh proper. Here and there, we saw an occasional church spire or a windburnt tree, but not much else. Romney Marsh was divided by small roads and tracks, like lines of lead separating stained glass panels in church windows, secure yet always vulnerable. Huge tufts of grass appeared haphazardly out of tiny islands of sludge. Yellowed, brittle-looking reeds poked out of black water pools like nicotined fingers. A vision of verdant chaos. So flat and so open and yet, somehow, it also appeared to be shadow-fisted, as if it held within its grasp the secrets of centuries. I thought, maybe this is what Dagenham looked like before concrete and tarmac filled in its watery veins and squeezed the land dry. Half an hour later we saw Rye, rising from the flatness like the fossil of a friendly sea monster.

We pulled up on a small square, just off the high street. We had reserved a room at an old Georgian home converted into a small, cozy hotel with, importantly, guest parking. We ventured inside and found a small lobby festooned with antiques, thick pile carpet, and pastel walls.

Our room had a view of the Rother. The tide was low, and the river's banks looked as if they had been sponged almost dry. From another window, Rye's ornate and picturesque hilltop swept down in rows of red-bricked houses to the marsh level.

After a brief nap, we headed out. Now two and a half, Kate was still happy to be chauffeured around in her stroller. We were happy about that too, for we could more easily—as her conveyance implied—stroll.

The Gun Garden, a rather large apron of grass and flowers with a spiked cannon, jutted out from Rye like the prow of a ship and provided an unparalleled view of the surrounding landscape. Across the river, we could see the marshy flats and the sea beyond. Rye Harbor was a couple of miles away, with a few yachts bobbing in attendance.

The sea that had encircled the town in the Middle Ages had long since receded, leaving the town marooned on the marsh. However, from what we could see, the changing coastline and the marsh seemed to have preserved the town's eccentric, old world ambiance.

We followed a steep and winding road down to the old harbor quay. A tiny flotilla of rowboats and sailboats were precariously angled in tiny rivulets that surged with the tide, enabling smaller craft to thread their way to the open sea. The old harbor chandler shops and warehouse buildings, now bereft of nautical tackle, sold antiques instead. We bought a large platter dating back to the turn of the nineteenth century, and a silk waistcoat. It was now just past lunchtime, and we were all famished.

At the nearest pub, the only menu item not withering away under hot glass was fish and chips. We ordered some before getting a round of drinks. Half an hour passed and so did another round of drinks. We still had no food. We talked and tried to amuse and distract Kate, and ourselves, from pangs of hunger. I finished my second glass of cider. Still no food. I walked up to the bar and, as politely as I could, inquired about our lunch. By now, Kate was not the only one feeling cranky.

"It's not McDonald's, sir," the barmaid-cum-server said, hanging on the words like a double-barreled insult. She thought I was an impatient American! Then her jaw dropped as she watched us get up to leave.

"But I've just taken the fish out!" She sounded distraught. "Fresh out the freezer!"

"Fresh out the freezer?" asked Frances, close to speechless.

"Yeah! It's in the fryer now. Ready in a minute."

Sighing, we sat back down. The server was right. This was not a bit like McDonald's. The prefabricated squares of fish covered in bread crumbs that eventually showed up looked like mahogany sandpaper. Beneath the breaded casing were hospital smears of mysterious white fish. Kate wouldn't even try it.

We left the pub in search of somewhere to wash the taste of lunch away. We turned onto Mermaid Street, steep and cobbled and imbued with history, literature, and romance, perfectly exemplified by the renowned Mermaid Inn. This ancient Tudor hostelry, with its uneven floors and walls, seemed to glow with the soft gold of well-worn leather. In one room we found exposed rafter beams hundreds of years old, a huge fireplace, and a gently propped-up bar offering warmth and friendly reassurance. And more besides.

The Mermaid was replete with secret passageways, a hide-out for contraband and a meeting place for smugglers! According to the walking guide Frances had picked up at the hotel, as Rye's importance as a seafaring port diminished, its importance as a smuggler's haven increased. The notorious Hawkhurst Gang used to hang out at the Inn, no doubt sipping their illicit contraband while keeping a watchful eye out for revenue officers. However, the hostelry's most famous smuggler was fictional, Thorndike's Doctor Syn, the vicar of Dymchurch! Frances rolled her eyes as I again rambled on about all his yarns, many of which featured Rye's Mermaid Inn. For me, those fictional memories were suddenly anchored in reality.

Of course, the other notable writer who set his novels in Rye was E. F. Benson. He lived just at the top of Mermaid Street, in Lamb House, renamed Mallards in his Mapp and Lucia novels. Here, Queen Lucia held reign. The streets and settings were all unchanged by time, just as Benson described them. I counted houses to where Georgie Pillson would have lived before he became—in name only—Lucia's husband. I picked out the places where my favorite characters had done their marketing. The street corners where they sniped and spied and gently but cruelly admonished one another, scoring points where they could, forming alliances and fighting social battles much to the delight of generations of fans.

Before Fred Benson, Lamb House belonged to Henry James, the ultimate American Anglophile. During his tenure, James entertained a gallery of literary types, including H. G. Wells and George Bernard Shaw. He also managed to write several books there, including *The Ambassadors* and *The Wings of a Dove*.

For no apparent reason, and much to my disappointment, the house was closed that day. I gazed longingly at the tall mounted windows and curving brick wall, too high to see beyond. Lucia's window, which offered such a commanding vantage, her piano room, and her *giardino segreto* remained confined to my imagination. And perhaps that's how it should have been. I smiled, undaunted. "*Molto bello!*" as Lucia might have said. I was enjoying myself and wanted to see more.

Rye bustled with life. We found ancient bits of castle stretching back to the medieval period, as well as higgledy-piggledy Tudor cottages and elegant Queen Anne houses. Quaint cobblestone streets led us through a maze of little alleyways, down hilly streets, and around unexpected turns that added to the town's chaotic layout and fussy charm.

We walked back through a medieval gatehouse named the Landgate. The castle-like structure had two forty-foot towers with arrow slits and gullies, down which boiling oil was once poured upon marauders from across the Channel. Good show! I'm glad Frances stopped to look, for within the Landgate's shadow we found a tiny restaurant. It looked unpretentious, rather like a converted shop.

The menu was small and surprisingly expensive, but we reckoned we could manage the prix fixe, so we went inside. Memories of our faux fish luncheon fled from our minds as soon as the first course arrived. Frances and I eagerly shared and savored everything, especially the pan-seared cod in a ginger cream sauce and the wild duck in red wine. Kate loved her ravioli. We finished with an ethereal fruit tart and honey ice cream.

On the way back to our hotel we walked through Church Square. Frances wanted to see the Cathedral of the Marsh, the eleventh century parish church of St. Mary's; I wanted to see its Benson window. The Tudor-framed houses bordering the square in the daylight hours were now barely visible, lit only by gas street lighting seeping onto our path. The haphazard-shaped roofs and askew chimneys were just silhouettes. Clusters of TV antennas were now quite visible, like straight lines of meaningless graffiti scratched into an azure blue sky. We entered the churchyard.

"Looking for the Benson window? It's over there! See it? There! Just there!"

The slightly elderly man calling out to us had red cheeks glowing from a large Mister Potato head. A pipe was clenched between large teeth, making him speak like a ventriloquist. Decked out like a typical county squire, he wore a shirt with small green checks, a woolen necktie, tweed jacket, corduroy trousers, and a kind of Tyrolean hat.

"The name is Raynes. Leonard Raynes. And this is Sophie and Rosie." He waved his pipe in a downward circular motion towards the middle-aged woman and dog who stood obediently beside him. He didn't actually tell us who was who. We greeted both canine and human with equal politeness. I introduced Frances and Kate, who was fast asleep in her stroller.

"Ah, there's three of you, you see—and three of us. The Trinity. The Trinity!"

"Why do they call this the Benson window?" asked Frances.

"There's two of them. One for his brother, Alec Benson. Wrote 'Land of Hope and Glory.' And this one is dedicated to his parents. It's called the West window."

"This one's a bit whimsical, so like many of his books, I would say," Rosie or Sophie added, her drawn face tinged with wind-red cheeks nestled above a big wool muffler.

"I was talking—" Mister Raynes smiled rather ominously. "Whimsy aside, it depicts the Nativity. And it may interest you—" Mister Raynes was again cut short, this time by Frances.

"But why is it called the Benson window?"

"I was talking, I was talking!" Mister Raynes yelled, then continued, "But no matter, no matter. Go on, my dear. Tell them when the window was installed."

"Well, it must have been at least forty years ago." Rosie or Sophie looked uncertain.

"How many years? How many years?" Mister Raynes intoned with the impatience of a Dickensian schoolmaster. He rocked back and forth on his feet and bit into his pipe. His eyes shone with the dull gleam of incredulity.

"Fifty, I should say? Yes, I'd say fifty," said Mrs. Raynes.

"How many years?"

"As I said, I think it was fifty years ago." Rosie or Sophie smiled meekly.

"She thinks! She thinks! It was close to sixty years ago when those windows were installed. Fifty! Pah!" He turned from his wife and smiled at me, warmly. "Two windows. But three people commemorated. Again you see—the Trinity! The Trinity!"

The dog peed against the wall. Meanwhile, Mrs. Raynes and Frances, with Kate in her stroller, moved to get a better view of the iridescent windows. I could see them talking and pointing. So could Mister Raynes.

"What was that, what was that?"

We both walked over, the dog straining at the leash, just as eager to get to Mrs. Raynes, who looked fearful but said nothing.

"We're down for the day. Royal Tunbridge Wells." Mister Raynes puffed on his pipe.

"That's one of the places I want to visit." Frances smiled at Mrs. Raynes, who smiled back.

"Splendid. Splendid. You must stay with us!" Mister Raynes crooked another look at me. "Benson, by the way, was the mayor here, for three years. Three again, you see! The Trinity! Furthermore—"

"If I were you," Mrs. Raynes said, turning to Frances, "I'd try and take a look inside—"

"I was talking—*was* being the operative word!" growled Mister Raynes quite loudly. "Not that it matters. When one is talking, one is invariably ignored. Ignored. No matter!" Mister Raynes was almost shouting, squelching his wife's last sentence, her word, her thought. We all stared at him. "That's the way of it in this cunting place."

We couldn't quite believe what we had heard. Frances looked at me with ill-concealed dread and began to slowly move back with the stroller. Thankfully, Kate hadn't woken.

"Ignored. Get to a certain age, and that's what happens. One is ignored. And when I think what I've done for this cunting country. Makes one wonder, makes one fucking think."

Time to go. Quickly waving goodnight to Rosie or Sophie, Frances swung the stroller about and headed for the churchyard gate. Mr. Raynes did not seem to notice. Face blotched like a radicchio leaf, he was a mass of anger, swaying back and forth on his heels, mouthing more foul and obscure words about England. He sounded worse than me! Then the anger, along with the coarseness of his language, evaporated in a puff from his pipe. He asked me where we lived.

"Near Washington," I blurted out, starting to move away.

"Can we stay with you if we visit?" asked Mister Raynes quite charmingly.

"No!"

When I caught up to Frances and Kate, I looked back. Mr. Raynes was scurrying off in the opposite direction, muttering to himself, his wife, or his dog. Hard to tell.

"So, what were you two talking about?"

"I asked again why it's called the Benson window, and she said he paid for it. Then she said that Benson had himself and his black dog put in the stained-glass window. Only in England!"

Before we left the following day, we made it back to the church for a closer look at the West Window, with E. F. Benson in crimson mayoral robes and his little Scottie dog, black as coal! As we walked back to our car, the early morning sun was glistening over the hilly rooftops of Rye like an enchanted fairy tale coming to life. *Molto bello* indeed!

~

We journeyed back across the marsh. Leafless trees rose out of the ground like fingers of an old giant's hand, beckoning us toward the sea. We ignored the summons and drove inland, towards the county of Kent.

Our cottage was located beyond Kent's ancient Saxon shore, on the Island of Thanet, once known as the Island of the Dead, where Saxon nobles were buried. Although no longer an island, Thanet still represented a large chunk of coastal Kent and a very pretty part of the country. We crossed over the ancient Saxon boundary and drove on for several miles. I was looking for a village called Cleve, but no such place seemed to exist. What did exist was a village once called Aycole, whose name had over time been functionally snipped to Acol.

"Sounds like something you put down the loo," I said, somewhat uncharitably.

"We've passed it. The house, I think we've passed it!" said Frances, ignoring me.

Turning around, we drove back through the village. The tiny hamlet looked as abbreviated as its name. Reconnecting with our detailed map, we turned a corner and there it was. Not a village called Cleve, but a residence called Cleve Court. The entire property was surrounded by a brick wall, fattened by ivy, moss, and wisteria. We drove quickly through the large, open gates onto a pebble driveway and saw a magnificent Queen Anne mansion, softened with age and looking more like a giant gingerbread house than anything else.

According to our directions, the carriage house was to the side of the mansion. I could see a gatehouse, the size of a small cottage. Next to that was a small, arched stone gateway, through which was our holiday home. I drove closer, then stopped. The car was too wide to go through the arch. It could not be done.

I reversed and tried to align the car with the narrow gateway. I would have to angle into the opening, then straighten up very quickly. Frances got out and, like someone doing semaphore without the flags, began to guide me through the tiny archway. As the car inched forward, I breathed in, as though that might save the chromium on the door handles. I got through and parked on a small cobbled driveway. Relieved, I got out, stretched my legs.

Set under a large wooden awning, we saw a dormouse-like entrance, obviously scaled down from its once larger size. Through the slightly opened door, we heard the gentle hum of a vacuum cleaner and followed the sound. The expansive foyer was covered in dark wood, like a stage set for a murder mystery. To the right was a large open-plan kitchen and, beyond that, a sweeping dining area and lounge. Much larger than we first thought, yet narrow enough to be quite cozy, the cottage was bright and cheerful with tall ceilings.

The man vacuuming the lounge stopped when he saw us. Small, swarthy, and suntanned, he offered half a smile in greeting.

"You're early. Or I'm running a bit late!" he said, coiling the cord on the cleaner. I wondered if he would have carried on cleaning if we had not have shown up when we did.

At the end of the lounge was a glass wall with sliding glass doors. We stepped out into a lush, green garden with furniture, a children's playset, even a barbecue grill. Either the owner was American, a dedicated griller, or both! The slight breeze was pleasant and inviting. Frances and I looked at each other and smiled.

The caretaker gave us the keys, then answered our questions. Was there a phone? Only for incoming calls. Was there a crib? A what? Oh, a cot? Yes. A separate dryer? Yes. And yes, everything was working.

"What if we need anything, or if anything—"

"No problem. My name is Roy. I live in the gatehouse, just through there." He pointed.

"Oh, Roy, what about the ghost? It's in the brochure."

"Is he friendly?" Frances added.

"Friendly alright. Kicks up a racket though. But you'll discover that yourselves!" Then he darted through the stone arch and was gone.

"You remembered the ghost," said Frances, pleasantly surprised.

"The ghost of the baroness!"

The baroness was Baroness Orczy, who lived in the mansion at the turn of the twentieth century. She wrote *The Scarlet Pimpernel* elsewhere, but she did complete other books at Cleve Court, including *Nest of the Sparrowhawk* and a Christmas murder mystery, both set in the house. Through her writing, or her inheritance, she could afford to live in comfort and style. She even had a stableful of Lipizzaner horses sent over from Hungary. The old baroness must have cut quite a dash trotting about with three white horses abreast. Her carriages were kept in what was now our lodgings, on the ground floor. The liveried groomsmen and stable staff must have slept upstairs.

"How she ever got a carriage through that archway is beyond me," I said.

～

While Kate napped, we explored the rest of our new home. We weren't exactly looking for a ghost, but one could easily have taken residence without disturbing us in one of the house's many bedrooms and irregularly shaped spaces.

Beyond the kitchen and the vicarage-like hallway, a wide staircase led to the upper level. Under the staircase was a carved-out niche with a pointed door. We opened it and found a tiny lavatory. To one side, at the bottom of the stairs, was an old-fashioned library with large, comfy chairs and an alcove like a gentlemen's club in Pall Mall. On the first landing we found a bedroom, a full bath, and a laundry room. Continuing up to the top landing, we entered a long passageway leading to more bedrooms, then another bathroom. But still no ghost.

The evening turned chilly. We cranked up the heat and decided on an early night. Tomorrow, my family would come for lunch and stay for "tea." My birthday. I was not looking forward to it.

Moonlight seeped into the bedroom through small lattice windows. Shadows came and conjured shapes on the wall, but I was asleep before I could play silhouettes.

Clonk. Clonk. Clonk.

I was wide awake. Bolt upright. I held my breath.

Clonk. Clonk. Clonk. Click-click-click.

"Hear that? Frances! Are you awake?" I whispered loudly.

Then it started again. Clonk. Clonk. Clonk. Click-click-click.

"It's the ghost." Frances sounded infuriatingly indifferent. "Go back to sleep."

"Yes, but, didn't you—"

"It's just the plumbing. It's old. Go to sleep!"

CHAPTER 17

In the home of Baroness Orczy

WE WOKE TO THE SOUND of rain pelting the windows in well-regulated bursts. The last day in May and we seemed to be back in the dead of winter. It was freezing.

"It'll brighten up. Just think positive thoughts! And happy birthday!"

Frances was determined to be cheerful. She must have willed the weather to change for, just after breakfast, the rain ceased and the sun tried to muscle out the clouds.

The first car arrived with Pam, Aunt Flo, and Jessie and Lew. I went outside to greet them while Frances frantically finished cleaning up. Kate spied on the new arrivals from inside the doorway, suddenly shy.

"Hello, Pam! Any problem getting through the gate?" I asked, a bit grudgingly.

"Oh, Denis, you're funny, you are! There's lots of room."

I smiled, then gave her a big hug and thanked her for bringing my folks.

Lew was next out of the car. He gave me a hug, and I put my arms gently around his shrinking frame. Then he steadied himself, stood tall, chest out, rifle-straight.

"Good to see you, son," Lew said, looking at me as if I had just passed a test.

"You too, Dad, and you, Mum. Hello, Mum! Hello, darling!"

I was now waving as frantically as Jessie was. She was still in the back seat, waiting not so patiently for someone to open the door for her. Lew wobbled around to the other side of the car without any help, then attempted to haul Mum out.

"Get off me! Get off me!" she yelled, fighting off Lew with flaying arms.

Ghrrr.

"Just look at my big son!" she said, as if addressing an audience. She stood beside the car, straightening her summer coat and waving Lew aside. She tweaked my cheek and asked me, as always, how I had managed to get so big.

"Come on, Mum! Kate and Frances want to see you."

I shepherded everyone inside. Lew sat down in the first armchair he could find. Leaning forward, thin legs tightly crossed, he looked like a pensive question mark. He seemed preoccupied.

"You alright, Dad?" I asked breezily.

He said nothing but waved a gnarled paw, as if to say, don't ask! I decided to leave well enough alone. Like us, Pam and Flo were impressed by the gothic charms of the cottage and surprised by how big it was. They muttered and nodded to each other approvingly. Although walking with a cane, Flo was still getting around, with a little help from Pam.

"Right, then, let me show you where you're staying," I said, taking Flo's bag up to the landing bedroom. "Pam, you and your mum are in here—"

I turned to help Pam with her bag. She grabbed my arm.

"Denis, it's your dad. He's just come out of hospital." Pam spoke with some urgency.

"What do you mean? What's the matter with him?"

"Not now, I'll tell you later." She looked around furtively. "He doesn't want you to know."

"Know what?"

Kate was dragging on Jessie's hand and trying to pull her along. Mum seemed vaguely amused, then she looked up at me and asked where Lew was as if she had misplaced him.

"I'm right here," said Lew gruffly, now right behind her, holding a suitcase.

"I'll take this up, Dad."

"No, you bloody well won't," he said, holding on tightly. He used the suitcase to balance himself, then straightened up and tried to smile. "Lead the way, my son, lead the way."

"I think I'd better have a tiddle first," said Jessie.

Frances guided Mum, who was a little unsteady on her pins, towards our below-stairs confessional.

"What's this, then?"

"It's a loo, Mum," I shouted down from the stairwell.

"I thought I was going to be doing me prayers!" said Mum, disappearing from view.

Halfway up, Lew let me take the suitcase and grasped the thick wooden banister. We reached the second floor and entered the first bedroom. I put the suitcase on the bed. Lew looked around, saw a chair, and sat down.

"Get me breath back."

"Take your time, Dad, take your time. After Pam and Flo leave, we'll move you down to the landing. So, doing alright?" I tried to sound casual, remembering Pam's request.

"Your mother's been driving me up the wall."

"She always has. Tell me something I don't know."

"You're a hard man, my son." He smiled grimly. "You're a hard man. Come on, give me a hand up."

Frail he might be, but his grip was as strong as ever. We made it downstairs just as Jessie was emerging from the confessional loo. Slowly, we moved to the lounge. Lew lowered himself into a sofa. Mum hovered.

"Sit here," said Lew, gruff as ever, smacking the sofa cushion next to him.

Mum ignored him and sat down next to Flo, opposite Lew.

Ghrrr.

"Well, happy birthday, Denis," said Pam.

"Yes, happy birthday, my son. Shame about the weather. Been like this for weeks, it has."

"Birthday? Is it your birthday? Today?"

"You got the present for him, Jessie! In your bag!" Lew was pointing.

Jessie handed me a set of cufflinks wrapped in tissue, and Lew said he intended to treat us during the week. Kate got presents too, a teeny tiny china tea service from her grandparents and a plush toy from Pam and Flo.

"He always loved his presents, Denis did," Jessie said.

"One year, Denny saw Lancelot on the telly or somewhere. And he wanted a suit of armor, nothing else!" said Lew.

"Armor?" asked Jessie.

"For Denis. For his birthday."

"What's he want a suit of armor for, you silly old sod!"

"Not now, woman! Then! Way back when! So, anyhow—"

This time Lew was interrupted by a rat-a-tat on the door, and a slightly tenuous, peering form shuffled into the kitchen. My older brother Tony. Sopping wet, he craned his neck over the counter.

"Oh-oh! Is this who I think it is? Ah, yes! Got the right place, have we? Oh, yes, here you all are! Here you all are! I can see you, I can see you!" Tony cackled and pointed a finger as if he'd caught us all in an elaborate game of hide-and-seek. He was looking a bit more pear shaped, shoulders more rounded, but his eyes were still sharp and inquisitive, his smile still slightly mocking. I got up and walked over to him. Tony held out a hand to wag, which I did.

"Well, hello, Denis, long time no see—as they say, so they say! Ha, ha!"

"Got down here alright, then?" I asked. "Any problem parking?"

"No probs, no probs! Not at all! Now, come on, come on, Wonder Woman, come on then, that's it, that's it." He moved back to the foyer, ushered his statuesque wife inside. Tricia blinked beneath thick pebble glasses, trying to make out the throng of people. She squeaked a hello to everyone, then moved tentatively forward.

"Yes, yes, that's it, that's it, in you get, in you get. Let's close that bloody door, keep the warmth in. Come on, come on, quick, quick! Gotta close that bleeding door! Come on, come on!" Tony flapped his arms about, encouraging her to move faster.

"Do you mind! I'm trying to get me coat off!" Tricia had a small, quiet voice, but she spoke with some authority and moved at her own pace toward the family in the lounge. As I hung up coats, Tony leaned over to me and pulled his face down into an expression of comic dread.

"Wouldn't believe it? This rain, this wind. Freeze the balls off a fucking brass monkey—bastard weather for your birthday! Still, never mind, ay! Ay!"

"Language, Toe, you know, Kate." I indicated his niece, playing nearby.

"Ah, my Gawd, yes, yes—don't worry, don't worry. Say no more, say no more! Not a word. Shame about the weather, but c'est la vie, as the effing French say, c'est la vie!"

"They say it'll brighten up," I said as we moved towards the lounge.

"What do they know? Oh, Denis." Tony stopped in front of the kitchen. "While I remember—happy birthday! Brought your card down. Save posting it." He slipped out an envelope and handed it to me.

"So, I hear you've retired," I said.

"Well, that's what they call it." His face molded into a quivering snarl. "Early retirement. Not voluntary, mind you! Bunch of pratts." He smiled suddenly. "But! But! As it transpired, could have been a lot bloody worse—I could still have been there, ay, ay? Know what I mean!"

"Dad said you're studying again! Good for you."

"Yeah. Chemistry. Thought, fuck it, why not! Sorry, sorry. Go for the old doctorate. What have I got to lose? Fuck all, really, that's what I've—oh, oh, sorry, did it again! Such an effing pratt! Bloody thoughtless, but what can you do, what can you do?"

Tony moved slowly, almost cautiously, into the lounge, pantomiming his discovery of every relative, evoking the odd titter and smile. After the customary hugs and greetings were made, Frances went off to make the customary drinks.

"Ah, yes, I recognize this lot, oh yes! Cold enough for you is it, cold enough, ay? May-the-bloody-thirty-first! Someone must have got a bloody leg over!" He cackled gleefully.

"Oooh-oooh," cooed Mum, waving energetically.

"There she is! There she is! Oooh-oooh! 'Allo, Mother Angel!" He leaned towards her, arms outstretched. They started blowing noisy kisses to each other. Laughter erupted. Kate smiled at Tony and Tricia, not really remembering them.

"Come on, give your Uncle Tony a hug then." He picked her up and bounced her a bit on his arm, "There! That's better, isn't it, isn't it! Eh? Eh!" Tony put his niece down, then let out a long sigh as he saw Lew trying to get up.

"Hello, son. Traffic bad, was it?" Lew straightened up and gripped Tony's hand in both of his, but not in a handshake. He then turned slightly and greeted Tricia with a gentle pat on the back. She was still standing behind the settee. Greetings done, Lew sank back into his seat.

"So, er, you doing alright? Alright, aren't you? Yes? Yes!" Tony inquired.

"We're not doing too bad for a couple of oldies," said Lew.

"Oldies! You speak for yourself, you can! Oldies! 'Ark at him!" protested Jessie.

"Still getting about. Still using our bus passes." Unsmiling, Lew spoke with somber pride.

"Getting about? With bus passes! Well, I ask you—what more do you bloody well want? What more, ay, ay?" Tony looked around, grin in place, playing to the crowd.

"Usual aches and pains, ay, Jess? That's what you get at our age, isn't it?" piped in Aunt Flo.

"Don't you get old. Don't you get old." Jessie started shaking Tony's arm.

"Oh, my giddy aunt, listen to this one! Don't get old? We're all getting old, Mum, and you know what you can do about it? Bugger all. So don't bloody worry about it, eh? Eh?"

"Now I better see a man about a dog," Lew announced, not all that discreetly.

"Anyone else? We've got three bathrooms!" I said with an equal lack of discretion.

"I only need one—" Lew padded off to the confessional loo.

"He only needs one! Hear that? Ha! Ha!" My brother's laughter was a little brittle.

∼

The rain was sleeting down as we trudged into the pub by Manston Airport. The hostelry had a low, cowered roof, as if it had been ducking planes for years. Inside, the saloon bar was as snug as an old slipper. A big log fire crackled in a white stone hearth. Around the walls, tacked on oak beams, were framed photos of RAF bomber and fighter pilots from the Second World War. Well dressed, smartly attired young men, some sporting mustaches above wide grins. They all looked so mature, standing together in the shadow of adulthood, unaware of their destiny and how they would be remembered. The few. The ones who saved a nation.

We ordered roasts for everyone, lamb, beef, or pork, with the usual brown gravy. But I was making the most of my birthday with the wine Lew kept buying.

"Happy birthday to the Great Me!" I said, raising my glass, toasting myself with the name I immodestly gave myself as a child.

"Happy birthday to the Great Me!" Mum laughed.

"That's it, that's it, the Great Me. That was always you, wasn't it, Denis? Yes—'the Great Me'! Gawd 'elp us all! Ha!" Tony's half-laugh faded into a long sigh.

"I was telling Frances about when Denis wanted that suit of armor for his birthday—just before you arrived. Remember that, Jessie?"

Mum shrugged. Lew went on, unconcerned by her lack of memory, determined to finally tell the story. "So we go up to Gamages. No luck. Then, 'Arrods. Oh, my Gawd, Harrods! Flunkies everywhere. And the prices! I'm sweating buckets. Then we see it. A suit of armor. And Denis, he's all happy. But I'm not! Tries it on—but it wouldn't fit him. He was too big. I was that relieved." Lew was now all smiles.

"Too many Mars bars!" said Jessie, pointing to Dad. "Lew fed him Mars bars until he got as fat as butter! He couldn't walk without panting. Panting, he was, panting! I put a stop to that! 'No more Mars bars,' I said."

"Alright, Mum, alright. I was a bit miffed about the armor though."

"It wouldn't have made any difference, he was big. Solid," said Lew.

"How is it, I don't remember Mars bars?" Tony raised a quizzical eyebrow, then he grinned.

"That's cos you didn't get Mars bars, you didn't!"

"Gawd give my strength—that's what I'm getting at, Mother Pet. I never saw any Mars bars, did I? Cos I didn't bloody well get any!" Tony jokingly waggled an accusatory finger at Jessie.

"Well, the war was on," said Mum, shrugging, as if that explained everything. In a way, it did.

"Couldn't get anything then, could you, Jess?" said Flo.

"Some people got things." Jessie was remembering. "Vi got stockings! And chocolate. Perfumes. All sorts of things!"

"I'm certain she did, Aunt Jess," said Pam gently. "But you had Uncle Lew."

"He was away, wasn't he! And when he was home, I never got stockings. Or chocolate. I got pregnant, that's what I got."

"Well, there you are, Aunt Jess!" said Pam, trying to remain serene.

"I was pregnant throughout the whole war!"

"The war lasted five years, Jessie," Frances reminded her, smiling broadly.

"No time for chocolates, eh Jess?" Flo laughed her haughty laugh.

~

A little later, back at the house, I tried to sequester Pam to find out more about Lew's condition, but it proved impossible. She was surrounded by relatives, happily gabbing away. On the pretext of showing Tony the house, I decided to wheedle what information I could out of him.

"Oh, Gawd, fuck me—what's going on now then?"

"Look, don't get upset. Dad doesn't want me to know that he's sick, but I thought you might know what's the matter with him, that's all. I'd like to know."

"The old man doesn't want *you* to know! Well, I don't want to bloody know either!"

"Why're you getting all funny?"

"Look, you don't know, you're not 'ere. I am. He tells me what's bloody wrong only, *only* when it suits him. Gets a problem, then waits for muggins me to sort it! He gets a letter saying he has to go to court. So I get it cleared up. Got no bloody thanks, but that's not the point—the point is, I told him, 'You can't expect me to drop everything and come round at your beck and bloody call to fix things.' And you know what he says? 'Don't trouble your arse,' he says. Then he gets this big grin on his face, full of swank, and he says, 'I'll call Denis; he'll get it sorted.' Can you believe it? Can you fucking believe it—excuse my bloody French—the bloody nerve! So I told him—"

Tony's face contorted with rage, the vein beneath his eye throbbed. He glared at me with the vividness of a memory I did not possess. In his mind's eye, I had become Lew.

"Denis is not here, is he, is he? He's over there. In America! I'm here. And that's the way it is. Whether you like it or not. Or whether I like it or not. So, if anyone's going to sort out your problems, it's me. Not him. Get it! And if it wasn't for Mum—"

"Well, yes—" I said lamely.

"That shut him up." Tony now appeared more relaxed. "So what's the matter with the old man now, then? Having trouble with his waterworks?"

"I don't know, I don't think it's anything, really. Pam, you know, she's concerned."

"Yeah, well, all I can say is—you're fucking well out of it," he said, bitterly.

Not today, I thought, not today.

We moved back downstairs and joined the others. I mumbled something innocuous about the house. Tony was suddenly talking effusively about Baroness Orczy and *The Scarlet Pimpernel*.

"'Is he in heaven, is he in hell, that dark elusive Pimpernel!' Supposed to be a bit of a twat—but it was all a ruse, wasn't it? All a ruse! Ah, yes!" Tony had recovered, moved on, and was cheerfully playing to the gallery once more. I was still floundering in the last scene. Fool to his Lear, reeling from the soliloquy.

"Had a good look around, then? Found the ghost yet, have you?" Lew asked Tony.

"Found the ghost? You hear that, Mother Pet? Now he wants me to find a ghost!" Tony laughed without humor, then gently tapped Lew on the shoulder.

"He'll frighten the ghost off, he will!" Jessie laughed.

Ghrrr.

Lew got up and moved into the kitchen like an arthritic tortoise. Despite his painful awkwardness, he had a smile on his sunken chops. There was no dishwasher, so we were hand washing again. Tricia joined us and kindly pitched in to dry cups.

"Good to get back on me feet," Tricia said.

"Trouble with your plates of meat, gel?" asked Lew.

"An inflammation of the foot."

"Bunion, is it?" Lew was intrigued.

"No, no, this was a boil. Had it lanced." Tricia was focused.

"We saw a boy with a carbuncle last year. In Windsor." Now Frances got involved.

"And my nephews? How they doing?" I said, changing the subject.

"Thought they might come today," said Lew. "Denis and Frances came all this way. I don't see why—"

"Drop it, Dad," I said, cutting Lew short.

"Yeah, right—got some tea going yet, my son?"

I told him tea was brewing. He grunted, moved back into the living room, sat down next to Kate, and started reading to her. Again, I asked how my nephews were doing, trying to patter my way onto safer ground.

"Too many people going after too few jobs. Hopeless, really is, hardly worth trying."

"It can't be hopeless. Someone has to get the jobs there are," said Frances, logically.

"She doesn't know what it's like here, does she, Denis?"

I smiled and looked outside. Rain pellets performed muffled drum rolls on the window pane, and Tricia switched to the weather with the same optimistic resignation. What could you do? Something to put up with. Never knew what it would be like from one day to another. You know what it's like here, Denis. I nodded. I knew what it was like. Frances insisted it would get better, and I knew she was usually right. I also knew she was not talking about the weather.

CHAPTER 18

Whitstable and Minster

I CAME DOWN to a clear blue sky, and it was considerably warmer. The residue of the previous day's rain was rising in ghostly wisps of steam. Kate and Frances were already outside, drying off the playset and chairs and sorting out toys. Lew was happily making tea for everyone.

Tony and Tricia had left after high tea the previous evening. Pam and Flo were packed but intended to spend part of the day with us before driving home. We suggested visiting the ancient port town of Whitstable, which was virtually on their way home. I was anxious to get going.

"I'll go and see what your mother's up to," said Lew. "Bit bleeding cold, innit?"

"Not so bad. Bit of fresh air. Do you good."

"I'm too bleeding old for anything to do me good!"

He gave a wheezy chuckle and went off to find Mum. I ambled outside. After settling Flo in the lounge with more tea, Pam followed me into the garden. Now, with the coast clear, she finally launched into her story about Lew.

"He can't go. He hasn't gone for over three weeks. He almost died."

"He hasn't...for three weeks?" I knew what she meant.

"What caused it?" Frances had joined us.

"Mum's just as bad." Pam could be both tantalizingly forthcoming and reticent. "They're not eating right. No vegetables. No salad. Got very serious."

"I thought they ate salad. You mean he could have died, just because of that?" I said.

"Oh, yes. He was completely blocked. Clogged up. Really worried me when I saw him last week. Looked deathly. That's why I

186

took him to the hospital. And then, two days ago, he said he wanted to come home. He didn't want to miss this trip."

"Silly old bugger. All for a bit of salad!"

"Fruit would do it, too. Anyway, the head nurse said they had induced some movement but not enough. They weren't very happy about him going away, but they gave him something for his— you know—so there we are. But he doesn't want you to know. Bit awkward for me, as you can imagine." Pam noticed Lew walking towards us and deftly changed track. She smiled at him. "Just saying how much you're set in your ways, Uncle Lew."

Ghrrr.

He waved a playful fist at his favorite niece. Then Kate rushed forward and he gave her a toothless grin. I decided not to hound him about his dentures.

"Your mother'll be down. She's tooting herself up."

"I think the weather will hold." Frances was eternally optimistic.

"That'll be grand—but first I got see a man about a dog. Then I'll be ready."

Lew took himself off to the loo, and Pam gave us details we could have done without. No doubt, she needed to tell someone. As we moved back into the house I asked my aunt if she was up for another cuppa.

"Quite alright, thank you, Denis. If I have anymore, I'll have to go myself!"

"Good morning all!" Jessie appeared in the lounge and sat down next to her sister. She blew raspberries at her appreciative granddaughter.

Within a couple of minutes the conversation had turned from the good old days to the dark new ones. "You have to lock your doors now, don't you, Denis. It's got so bad—" Flo was saying.

"Where's Lew?" interrupted Mum suddenly. "Where is he?"

She looked a little scared. I tried to reassure her, but we shared her concern. He had been gone for over twenty minutes.

"Do you think someone should check on him?" asked Frances.

Just before search parties were mustered, Lew reemerged and joined us. There was perspiration on his brow but he was smiling. A glimmer of triumph stretched across his bony face.

"Where've you been?" asked Jessie, a bit relieved, a bit angry.

"You alright, Dad? Want to sit down?" I tried to sound casual.

"No, no, no, I've sat enough!"

⁓

Whitstable sat on the outer edge of the large jagged mouth forming the southern end of the Thames estuary. Not knowing the town at all, we headed for the seafront. I stopped the car just below the sea-wall. Pam pulled up behind us. We dropped everyone by a seafront pub and drove off in search of parking. We found a municipal car park a ten-minute walk away. Unfortunately, the weather had taken a turn for the worse. Gray clouds were mustering above us.

"June the first. Looks a bit bleak." Although it was not raining, the air was damp and chilly.

"Well, it's not the Med, is it? This is England. Denis, you are so funny."

Somerset Maugham renamed Whitstable "Blackstable" in one of his first novels. He had grown up here and hated the place. I understood. Visiting the seaside in the summer is nothing like living there year-round. I remembered the sea around the British coastline as mostly mackerel gray, offset by startling blue skies in the summer. But when it rained, or threatened to rain, the grayness was omnipresent, inescapable. As we approached the harbor area, however, the bleakness softened a bit, with hints of sunlight again piercing the dulled silver sky.

When Pam and I got back to the pub, everyone except Kate was drinking coffee. Surprisingly, the owners had been quite happy to serve hot beverages, even breakfast. My folks and aunt remained in the warmth of the saloon bar while the rest of us explored the seafront.

We saw a couple of fishing boats, squat and sturdy, like tugs, ringed with old rubber tires. The morning catch had long since been dispersed to area shops and restaurants, and what fishy detritus remained was being hosed off the decks. In the sky above, enormous seagulls hovered, occasionally swooping down to the water for the odd carcass, while others screamed at the capricious breeze that carried them far aloft, far from the rotting feast below.

Although small, the quay and immediate vicinity had charm and color, with tiny winding streets and alleys with old fishermen's huts and soft-edged clapboard cottages. Fanning out from the harbor area were art and craft shops, boatyards, tackle stores, and a couple of ritzy seafood restaurants overwhelmed with uniformed staff but not with customers. Stands sold cockles and whelks from tiny plates laid out on metal counters with chained pepper tins, bottles of malt vinegar, and free bits of bread for dunking.

A small stall was shucking oysters to order. The town was still famous for its oysters, and I was determined to sample some. I asked for a plate of Whitstables.

"Not this time of year, sir. You'll have to come back in November for the locals."

"Where are these from, then?" I pointed to a pile of gnarly crustaceans.

"New Zealand. Very nice, those—"

We looked around and imagined the place during the windswept month of November. We would never come back then, so we settled for the bivalves from Down Under. They were quite delicious. I also had a small plate of cockles with lots of vinegar and pepper. Kate teethed on chunks of French bread, and Frances had some prawns, which she insisted on calling shrimp.

Kate and I ran ahead, kicking up pebbles on the beach. Only they weren't pebbles at all, but oyster shells, necklaced in tiny gray-black barnacles or bleached almost white by the surf and wind. A beach of shells, discarded over the centuries and perhaps beyond. Two thousand years had passed since the original oyster beds in Whitstable were laid down by the Romans. We played for a few minutes, collecting shells, then a sudden cold gust drove us back onto the seawall and towards the pub, where Pam and Frances were already waiting.

After lunch, we all toddled to the parking lot and said our good-byes. As Pam was helping her mum into the car, she again reminded me not to say anything about Lew's condition. We waved them off, then Lew asked where we were heading.

"Home? Good-oh! Cos I'm bleeding getting cold, I am!"

~

Clonk. Clonk. Clonk. The Carriage House ghost awoke once more when Lew turned on the heat. As the boiler lurched into life, the pipes shuddered and banged with eerie irregularity. It was quite clever of the owner to pass off the noisy plumbing as a ghost. How could we complain about that? At least the system worked quickly.

"Don't have the heat too high, Dad, okay? It's already pretty warm in here."

"We've got old bones! We feel the cold, not like you young 'uns," he countered.

"Fair enough. Look, we're going to have a nap, okay? Kate's sleeping already."

"Get off out of it, enjoy your nap, we'll be alright!"

"Back down in an hour or so!"

Upstairs, we sweltered in the heat for a few minutes. Beneath us, I could hear Lew's sonorous raspy voice, presumably complaining about the cold. We smiled and decided to postpone our nap for another occasion. We got Kate up and, while my folks watched the racing, we headed out for the nearest town with a large supermarket, to do a little exploring and a lot of shopping.

~

"I approve of that," exclaimed Jessie. "Good to try things, isn't it?"

"Glad you liked it," I said as we cleared plates.

I had made duck breasts for dinner, as I had the year before. Again, Mum insisted she had never eaten duck before. Lew rolled his eyes but said nothing.

Then came the test. Salad. Frances had cleverly arranged the greens on individual plates so they didn't look too overwhelming. But there was no fooling Lew. Food for rabbits, he announced. Fair enough, I said, but be a shame if it went to waste.

"Dad, come on, finish your salad," I nagged.

Ghrrr.

With the ladies retired to bed, Lew and I settled in for our customary nightcap. He sat and contemplated his Jack Daniels for a moment, then straightened his blue pullover. It looked as thin as he did. He squirmed in his seat, sipped his drink.

"I got me works all gummed up," he said suddenly. "I thought I was going to wrap up."

"How did that happen?" I tried to act surprised.

"I dunno. They said it's what we eat. Gave us a diet, they did. Salad. And fruit! All that we had tonight!" Lew said, bitterly. "But I can't see your mother sitting still for that!"

"Well, don't you think it's a bit daft to die for the sake of few lettuce leaves?"

I poured more drinks. Lew looked out of the window, his mood as dark as his reflection. He had often told me he was old enough and ugly enough to take care of himself. And yet, at that moment, he looked vulnerable and worried. I did not know what to do. I was concerned, I wanted to tell him that much at least. Then I remembered the effort he had made to get out of hospital, just to see me and my family. And I realized that a grown son and his father should never fight over lettuce. So that was that. I patted him on the shoulder. He looked at me and nodded his thanks for saying nothing more on the subject. For no particular reason, he said Pam would be visiting the following week. Cheered by the thought, he downed his drink, said goodnight, and went slowly up to bed.

⁓

Flaming June finally arrived. The next morning was bright and sunny and windy enough to smell the sea. Frances, Kate, and I left Lew and Jessie at the house and headed for Minster to see sights. Saint Augustine had made landfall at Minster and, from there, spread Christianity throughout pagan Britain. On the site he had chosen for his mud-and-wattle church stood Saint Mary the Virgin, a classic Norman church, built just after 1066. We went up to the front door. It was locked.

"Maybe there's another entrance?" said Frances, not one to give up.

We looked but found no other way in. Just as we were leaving, a diminutive vicar with irregular tombstone teeth set in a wide smile came up to us.

"Want to look inside?" he asked eagerly.

"Thank you, vicar, we'd love to. But the door is—"

"Locked! Yes, yes, yes, but I do have a key, yes, yes. Do bear with me a moment—"

"I thought churches were always supposed to be open," I said.

"Oh, yes, yes, indeed, but we have to keep it locked now. Robberies. Sadly, yes." He looked a bit forlorn, then tried to put a brave face on it. As he unlocked the large oak door of the church, his mood brightened. "I'll come back in half hour or so. But do, do take your time. Enjoy the church."

"Thank you very much. Can we make a contribution?" I asked.

"Oh, yes, yes, you may, you may indeed. There's…you'll find a box near the door. I'll leave you to it then. Cheerio." And he was gone.

We walked down the nave, pushing Kate's stroller before us. The church possessed a real presence, our footfalls echoed against a thousand years of history. There was no mistaking its Norman shape and size. The tower bells were over four hundred years old, many of the wooden choir stalls and pews dated back to the Renaissance, and some of the brickwork in the towers went back to Roman times, a millennium before that. Everything around us spoke to an age of faith. And now the church had to be kept locked, like a private museum. On our way out, we stopped by the collection box, secured by a large padlock.

A couple of blocks away was Minster Abbey. We'd heard a small community of nuns lived there, making it the oldest inhabited abbey in England. Founded by the granddaughter of the first Christian king of Kent, around 670 AD, the original structure was burned to the ground by the ever-raiding Vikings, then rebuilt some forty years before the Normans invaded. The Saxon foundations and cornerstones still stood, scrubbed clean like a glorious folly sprouting from manicured lawns. We found only one sister, tending the ubiquitous gift shop. I don't think Minster Abbey saw many visitors.

Across from Saint Mary's we found an old inn, now converted into a restaurant and bed and breakfast. Inside, different sitting areas were sectioned off, creating an intimate ambiance for dining. Kate happily ate a plate of smoked salmon. Frances had a seafood platter, succulent and briny, and I ordered crab salad. Of course, we shared. We raved about the restaurant when we returned to the house, suggesting we might all return together.

"We'll see about that. Now, then!" said Lew, as if getting down to serious business. "You three going to have a kip?"

Frances looked confused.

"Forty winks," I explained, then to Lew, "Yes."

And the three of us went up for a kip. We closed the curtains in our bedroom and drifted off for a well-deserved break from the rigors of sightseeing.

"I'm boiling." We were woken, not by the clanking and the clonking of our ghost, but by the heat it created. I was awash in perspiration. I got up and staggered towards the thermostat. I checked the temperature, then ambled back to Frances.

"I don't believe it. He's turned up the temperature again. Jesus wept! Hang on."

I shuffled downstairs, not exactly in the best of moods.

"Dad, why did you turn up the thermostat?" I asked.

"We're cold."

"It's not cold, it's warm in here. I mean, it's really hot. Heat rises, Dad. We're sweating! We can't sleep."

"Well, I'm bloody cold, I am! We're old, and we're cold!"

"We've been cold since we got here," said Mum. She was holding the ends of her thin white summer cardigan, twisting it like a handkerchief.

"Why didn't you bring any pullovers? Why?"

"It's summer; you don't wear pullovers in the summer." Mum was laughing nervously.

"You do in stupid England! You know what the weather is like here, Mum. It's cold, it's hot, it's bloody cold again! You gotta dress for the stupid weather! Jumpers, cardigans, pullovers! Don't you know that by now? Don't you!" I was yelling, making much more of it than necessary.

"I'm sorry, son, but we feel it. The cold," Lew said quietly.

"Christ, Dad! How many years have you lived in this bloody country?" I couldn't stop.

Then Lew started to cry. His face wrinkled up like an old leather sponge and tears poured out. I stood there, shocked. Floundering, I sank into an awkward silence. My anger had shriveled into a lump of raw emotion that almost choked me, but I tendered no words of apology. I did nothing. I felt like a shit. And by doing nothing to rectify the situation, I continued to act like one.

"That's done it now, that has," said Mum without much feeling.

Lew waved away her words as he fought his tears. She, too, remained in place, but seemingly unmoved, unperturbed by the wave of sorrow engulfing her husband.

"Look, Dad, it's alright. I'm sorry, I'm sorry—"

Lew could not speak. He withdrew into himself, pounding his knee with a tightened fist as though hating himself for what he felt. And still he cried. I left the room, walked slowly back upstairs, and explained in short bursts what had happened.

"I've never seen—he never cries," said Frances, shocked.

"He's crying now, and I made him. Christ! They're cold. They're just bloody cold."

I was angry again, but not with them. With myself, the situation, the weather, their age, the house, the country. All of it.

"Come on, let's go down," Frances said the right thing.

We both went down. Mum was still sitting across the room from Lew, unmoved and unmoving. Lew tried to apologize. Words sputtered but made little sense. He could not do much more than shake his head, still a tight wad of helplessness and despair.

"It's alright, Dad, it's alright. Doesn't matter. It doesn't." I didn't know what to say.

"We're going to go buy sweaters," said Frances, with calm good sense.

"Great idea, yeah, let's… That's a good idea, we'll do that. I'll get Kate," I babbled. "We'll be back soon. Pick up dinner, too."

"Take your time," said Jessie, as if nothing had happened.

Lew waved us on, one clawed hand cupped his eyes. It had not registered with my parents, and hardly with me, what Frances planned to do, but it was a very practical idea. And it removed us from a painful situation that only time could rectify.

Kate was happily unaware of the rawness in the air. I caught my breath as I put her in the car seat. It was good to be outside. Frances drove, and I sat and stewed in the passenger seat. We arrived in

Birchington around five. Most shops had already closed. I asked at a newsagent's for a place that sold woollies. Marks and Sparks. Of course! I should have known. The nearest branch was in Margate, he said, just along the coast on the other side of Thanet's North Foreland.

Beyond the deserted seafront, treeless and strung with unlit lights, Margate had a modern, accessible shopping center. We parked easily. People were leaving the area as fast as shops were closing, leaning into the evening breeze, raincoats filled with blustering gusts. Paper bags smacked and twisted against legs as purchases were held close against the biting wind.

We found Marks and Spencer a little after five-thirty, just as the last customer was leaving. A manager was locking the glass door. I slipped past him. I explained the situation. He sniffed and told me to get a move on and be quick about it. I felt like a shoplifter as I grabbed a large man's sweater. Frances pulled out a red ladies' cardigan with gold buttons. We did not waste time looking at price tags. We hoped we had the right sizes. Viewed with suspicion by the remaining staff, they nevertheless marveled at our speed. We made it to the nearest register just as it was closing out. I tried to explain why we were buying sweaters, but the check-out girl was now on her time and did not care a knitted stitch. She would not take our money. Her face set hard in a stare of sheer bloody-mindedness. Finally, the manager came to our aid, and we were allowed to make our purchase. As we were hurried out, the glacial swish of the door closed on our heels. Clink-clank of keys turned in a lock. No matter—we had our woollies!

Frances drove again. I knew she must be really concerned about me to actually drive in England. I was still in a pensive mood, not helped by the now leaking sky, streaked and shiny as a black plastic trash bag. Flaming June looked as if it was about to be extinguished forever.

"Never seen him in such a state," I said. "Mind you, he was in a bad way when Rex died—"

Then I remembered, as a youngster, sitting in our Dagenham kitchen, listening to Richard Dimbleby orate Winston Churchill's funeral broadcast on the radio. Lew had sat in stilled silence. A single tear had welled up in one eye, but he had tilted his head back and held it in check. And that was that. Nothing more. Except for Rex. And now this.

"Pam said he's been a little depressed. Maybe we should be easier on him," said Frances.

"Instead of scolding him to eat the right thing? I've given up on that. Don't worry."

By the time we returned to the Carriage House, the rain had stopped, and the sky was awash in pink and blue pajama stripes.

Lew and Jessie were completely surprised by the sweaters. They put them on, showed them off to us and to each other. They were all smiles. It was like Christmas morning without the nuts and oranges. Apart from having to turn up Mum's cuffs, both sweaters fitted like a treat. Lew gave Frances a big hug and took one of my hands within his gnarled old paws. He shook it hard.

"This is grand, son, this is grand," he said, genuinely moved.

"Are they warm? The woollies? They look warm," I said, craving approval.

"Warm! I should say it feels warm! Lovely and warm, it is. What about yours, gel?"

"Red! It's my color!" Jessie beamed with approval.

"Well, as long as you both wear them," said Frances, but gently.

"Wear them! I'm not taking mine off, darling!"

My folks settled down in front on the TV with Kate. We slipped out to pick up the food we had ordered at the Indian restaurant in Minster. When we returned, the happy smiles were still in place. And so were the woollies.

CHAPTER 19

Sarre and Broadstairs

THE FOLLOWING MORNING produced puffy white clouds anchored in the bluest of blue skies. It was a glorious day, and the sun felt like warm velvet. Much better. Lew inquired about the agenda for the day. I told him about a windmill we had seen coming back from Whitstable.

"I found a flyer about it. Apparently it's the last working commercial windmill in the area. No clear directions, but it is close," said Frances, the ever intrepid tourist.

"They want to see a windmill, Jessie." Lew made his smile just wide enough to see. "But they don't know where it is."

"That's what the car's for, innit," said Mum with dead-on logic. Ghrrr.

Feeling rather quixotic, we chased down Sarre Windmill. As we turned toward the coast, we saw the solitary giant looming across the skyline and threaded our way towards it. A tiny signpost for the village of Sarre appeared, so we knew we were close. We found the windmill on a flattened hill, with delightful views of the rolling coastal hills of Kent.

There had been a windmill on this hilly top for centuries, but the one we saw was built in 1820. Inside, thick and blackened oak beams crisscrossed the millhouse like the interior of an ancient man of war. Shuttered light swirled down and glinted like gold dust, a mere memory of the flour the mill once ground. Sarre Mill Flour might have been ground for the gift shop, but not by the windmill. The wind sails of the mill were tethered and immobile, at least on that day.

Just across from the mill were some old sheds containing a sizable display of historic farm carts and steam-driven tractors. Lew and I smiled as Kate climbed over bits of dormant farm machinery.

Then he recognized a huge cart with thick axles and metal strips girding the wheels.

"That's a brewer's dray, that is, and it's pulled by four of the biggest bloody horses you've ever seen in your life. They got hooves as wide as dinner plates! And strong—Gawd, they had to be. Your grandfather drove a team of them horses. Worked for Manner Crossman. Got the job just after the Great War."

Lew always slurred the name, out of familiarity. Mann and Crossman was a brewer in London's East End, and my grandfather drove a team of their horses. Lew said the dray horses pulled a reinforced cart laden with enormous wooden barrels of beer. Delivered to the pubs the brewer owned, the barrels were rolled down into cellars below, like sacks of coal. My grandfather worked at the brewery for about ten years, until he got sick.

"I knew it was bad," Lew picked up the story. "Came out the gents once, he'd splashed a boot with pee and, by the time we got home, that splash had turned to white powder. Sugar, he told me. He couldn't work after that, went almost blind with it. I was at school when he died. Mum told me. He was having a shave and haircut when it happened. Died in the barber's chair, and the barber was going on about not getting paid. Word got back. Everyone knew everything that went on where we lived. 'Blood money!' I can hear my old gran saying it now, 'He wants his blood money.' So I found out what me Dad owed and collected up return bottles—you got money back in those days—and I took the whole lot of 'em round to the barber and said, 'This is what Dad owes you for his haircut.' Then I smashed the bleeding lot of them right there where he stood and walked out. Couldn't have been much more than eleven years old at the time."

"Good for you." I could think of nothing else to say. Then we saw Kate and Frances by a tractor. Let's find Nanny, I suggested to Kate. Fancy a cuppa tea? Lew said he could go for that. So we did.

⁓

I discovered Broadstairs by myself, not on a family holiday. I had made a literary pilgrimage to pay homage to Charles Dickens, to see the places where he vacationed and wrote. To my delight, I had found a quaint coastal town, somewhat cut off from the ubiquitous seaside swag. I loved it. And I desperately wanted Frances and Kate to like it, too.

"Anything to see, other than Dickens stuff? Ruins? Castles?" asked Frances.

"There's a wonderful harbor and an Edwardian seafront, and a lovely beach," I said, lamely.

"A beach? Well, Kate would like that."

Frances did not care very much for beach trips or literary pilgrimages without at least some historical or geographic interest. Even so, she was happy to humor me and spend a day at the seaside, especially if antique stores and bookshops were nearby.

Broadstairs was situated on a headland unapproachable from any coast road. We had to weave our way inland, through a funnel-like conduit, bouncing around various roundabouts before swooping under the railway bridge and into the town's High Street.

"Look, that's where Dickens stayed. And that's where he wrote *The Pickwick Papers*. The house isn't there now, of course! There! D'you see? There's a blue plaque."

No one cared. I drove exceedingly slowly to avoid the pedestrians who darted across our path in every which way, like schools of fish in a giant tank that was being drained. Most disconcerting.

"Is it market day or something? Or is it always like this?" asked Frances.

"How the hell do I know?" The crowds were making me anxious.

"Don't panic!" said Lew, calmly.

"I'm not panicking," I said, sounding rather shrill.

At the end of the high street, the sea suddenly appeared, then disappeared from view. We turned onto Albion Street. Gaily painted double yellow lines, as well as the usual no-parking and no-entry signs, greeted our arrival. We sped past the sights I wanted to show Frances. I was far too busy quaking with dread at the street's loopy quaintness to point anything out. Just past the harbor pub, the Tartar Frigate, I was relieved to find a waterfront car park tucked into the lea of a cliff. I stopped the car, got out, stretched my legs.

Originally built by Henry the Eighth, the harbor jutted out like a giant, slightly curved anvil, protecting its brightly colored fishing fleet. And there, closer inland, a crescent of custard-colored sand: the pristine footprint of Viking Bay. I smiled.

We had a glorious view of the cliffs, the old Victorian bathing huts, the cliffs walkway leading up to the bandstand, and Broadstairs' boxy skyline. Everyone murmured approval. I pointed out places of interest, ancient streets, flint-covered fisherman cottages, antique stores and bookshops and tearooms and flower gardens, all close by. Ever practical, Frances searched the lot for a parking ticket machine while Jessie and Lew and Kate enjoyed the view. I assembled the stroller.

"We can't park here," said Frances as she walked back to the car. "Permit only."

Everyone waved me on as I carefully drove back up the hill. I found a car park a few blocks away, then made my way back down to the beach. I stood in the curve of the harbor, saw my family organizing deckchairs close to the seawall. I smiled. I watched the donkeys marking time by the water's edge, waiting for rides. Kids were making sandcastles. Above them seagulls gusted against the breeze like kites without strings. Kicking off my shoes, I slid into the warm, gritty sand.

"Did you bring Kate's bathing costume?"

Frances looked at me as if I were an exhibit in a museum. "What century are you living in?"

"What?"

"A bathing costume, who says that?" Frances shook her head.

"Alright, alright, but did you?"

"No," said Frances firmly. Then she smiled. "But I did bring her swimsuit."

"Oh, very funny. I think I might just tear these down and paddle a bit." I indicated my jeans.

Frances was already in tee-shirt and shorts; the rest of us were not far behind in our preparation for English-style sun and fun. Mum had taken off her hat and shoes and cardigan and started to nap. Lew had unbuttoned his shirt, taken off his shoes and socks, and rolled up his suit trousers to his knees. I ripped up my jeans trying to create shorts as Kate squirmed into her swimsuit.

Moments later, Kate and I were jumping in icy, gray waves that formed perfect semicircles on the smooth, flat sand. Plucking up courage, we raced into the water. I gasped. My legs turned deathly white as blood fled my frozen pins. Kate just laughed. After some extensive water play, we clomped back to the shore and tried to persuade Frances to join us for a paddle, but she saw through our bold fibs regarding the tropical nature of the ocean blue and declined.

Lew suggested tea. Inured by now to the fact that my family and I drank hot tea year-round, Frances was nevertheless amazed to find this strange predilection actively encouraged at the seaside. Hot tea was available right on the beach.

"The beach tray," I said, with joking effusiveness. "Well, it's part of the English seaside tradition. Like donkey rides, Punch and Judy, and saucy postcards."

"You're so weird," said Frances evenly, shaking her head, trying not to give my blathering any encouragement. Undaunted, I set off with Lew to buy a pot of tea with extra hot water, a jug of milk, sugar dishes, and proper cups and saucers and spoons, all of which we majestically carted back to our little bit of beach and half-constructed castle.

~

The tea was finished, the castle was built. Time to move on. We took the steps that zigzagged the cliffs up to the promenade, to the outdoor terrace bar of the Royal Albion Hotel. My parents would go no farther, and why should they? The day was lovely, the view perfect, and they were soon happily embedded on a sofa. We ordered drinks and food for them and set off to explore the town.

We turned onto Harbor Street. Just past the York Gate, about halfway down, was the Old Curiosity Shop, an old chandler's shop that now sold the usual nautical swag and seaside souvenirs. We walked up a tiny footpath beside the shop, towards Bleak House atop the hill. We stopped and stood in front of the outer wall of Dickens' home. It was surrounded by a battlement of sorts, greenish-brown and pockmarked with pebbles.

"Converted into a house. Used to be a fort. Wish we had more time." I sighed wistfully.

"Think we better head back." Frances sounded concerned. "Your parents will be worried."

The afternoon sun had cast a net of amber light across the bay, softening the skyline. We took one last look, then slowly made our way back to the Albion Hotel. My folks appeared to have taken up residence in the delightful refuge. On the way out, the owner walked with us, pointing out where Dickens had stayed when he wrote *Nicholas Nickleby*. He was obviously proud of the hotel's connection with the author. He urged us to return for Dickens Week. Next year, we told him. Perchance! Indeed, sir!

By the time we got back to the Carriage House, the perverse weather had turned cold again. We cranked up the heat and, right on cue, our resident ghost started thumping on the ancient walls.

∿

The following morning, Jessie and Lew decided to stay in the house, sit in the garden, and watch the racing on TV. Frances wanted to visit Quex House, that extremely local country house we had been driving by throughout the week.

Quex House was the home of Major Powell Cotton, a great white hunter of the Victorian era who traipsed about the "dark" continent looking for sport within the crosshairs of a telescopic sight. It was all on display in the Powell Cotton Museum within. On first glance the large, hall-like rooms looked like the inside of a frozen zoo, with herds of exceptionally tolerant animals of vastly different species. Big, small, they had all been shipped back from Africa and displayed together. The major's trophies looked like pieces in a wax museum but, unlike waxworks, these creatures had once lived and roamed free. It was a singular experience. Other collections were on display—we saw acres of oriental carpets and endless mantles filled with Chinese porcelain. But it was the musty-smelling, glassy-eyed stares of the animals that held our attention and evoked our sympathy.

"Come on, let's go see the roses! Remember, old roses! They have scent," Frances said.

The grounds consisted of almost two hundred and fifty acres of parkland dotted with paths leading to unexpected color splashes and heady aromas. In stark contrast to the museum, the gardens were being brought back to life. Unlike cottage gardens, where plantings are haphazard, these were designed to create spectacular vistas. The beds were wide and deep. In front of the roses were great clusters of lupines and delphiniums and gladioli in a variety of colors. Staggered in size, the plants appeared to form a delicate, frothy wave that cascaded down against our feet in a flurry and became pink-and-white groundcover.

That evening, after another great big fry-up of leftovers, we told my folks about the gardens, the museum, and the herds of stuffed animals we had seen. Lew shared his experience as a great white hunter in India—shades of Major Benjy!

"I went on a tiger shoot. So, we're sitting up in this platform in a tree, and we're told to wait. So we wait. They told us the platform was near the tiger's favorite watering hole. So there we were. And there we stayed. We stayed up there for two bleeding days. And then—"

"And then?" I prompted.

"Nothing. Bloody tiger never showed up."

The following morning, Roy, our neighbor and keyholder, inspected the house and duly returned our fifty-pound deposit, most of which went to gasoline for our big car. We took a last look. It had been Frances' favorite house so far, a place to return to when the weather was warmer and a ghost would not go bump in the night.

We made it back to Dagenham in under two hours. What traffic we saw appeared to be heading in the opposite direction. The first thing Lew did was turn on the front room gas heater full blast. Then he came out to help me with the luggage. Jessie shuffled towards the garden, blinking and smiling at the familiar surroundings.

They were sad to see us leave but relieved to be home, treading well-worn steps, settling back into the familiar curves that marked the boundaries of their lives. Lew was even planning a trip to the library that afternoon, and, despite copious amounts of tea, Jessie's tummy remained happily dormant and untroubled. It was a good time to be on our way.

CHAPTER 20

Woodstock, then back to London

BY THE TIME WE ARRIVED in Woodstock, the sun was drying up frigid puddles, and unsightly water marks on rain-drenched buildings were fading fast. Even so, the downpour had brought some unexpected benefits in its wake. The mugginess in the air had been washed away. And the rain had spruced up the square and pulled the grayish blue stone and honey-hued buildings into sharp focus.

Frances had picked the little town as a stop-over because of its proximity to Oxford and Blenheim Palace, Winston Churchill's ancestral home. Yet, with or without a stately home close by, we found it all so charming we decided to stay, leaving Oxford for another time.

Woodstock stood on the edge of Cotswold country, with a long history dating back to Henry the Second, who kept a mistress here. It was the birthplace of The Black Prince. Over the centuries, various royal princes and other noble sons and daughters came to hunt and kill the deer and boar that lived, somewhat precariously, in the sprawling forests surrounding the town. According to Frances, little was left of ancient royal comings and goings, except at Blenheim Palace, England's answer to Versailles. Tourists flocked there in droves, happily bypassing the elegant little town.

The Information Office found us a small bed and breakfast above a teashop, near a side entrance to Blenheim Park. While the room was being prepared, we set off for a quick tour. We ignored the modern bits stuck onto Woodstock's edges and stayed on the older thoroughfares with cobblestone walkways, teashops, antiques stores, and ancient inns replete with bone-colored flagstones, musty-colored oil paintings, and big fireplaces. Most of the simple, elegant houses in the main market square were in the Georgian style, with mullions filled with swirling glass panes tinged with a pearl sheen.

Window boxes were ablaze with color. Large framed doors gleamed in black or red lacquer. Even the cobbles on the street appeared to shine. Amazing, I thought, what a cleansing squall of summer rain could do.

Our tearoom accommodation turned out to be an old converted shop with large windows and lace curtains. Tiny tables draped with white cotton tablecloths were topped with tiny bouquets of real flowers. Our "family room" upstairs was quiet, clean, and comfortable. Peering out the window to the left, we could see the edge of the Town Gate, a giant wrought iron gateway to the ducal estate. The gates, we found, were opened early in the morning for locals to stroll or jog or walk dogs, free of charge. Then, at nine, they were manned and admission was charged.

The following morning, leaving Frances to enjoy a leisurely sleep-in, Kate and I begged a bagful of stale bread from the kitchen and headed out in search of ducks and sundry waterfowl. Before nine, just like the locals.

We left the tarmac behind. The roadway beyond the Town Gate turned into a broad, swirling pathway covered with tiny yellow pebbles. We followed the path to a large ornamental lake edged by chunks of oblong cut stone. I had read that Blenheim's park-like setting was completed with great panache by the master landscape artist of the eighteenth century, Capability Brown. Blenheim must have presented quite a challenge. The surrounding land had been as flat as a pancake. Not anymore. Presumably using a host of burly yokels, Brown dug out an enormous, saucer-like lake, creating the earthwork foundation for the delicate hillocks he envisioned on either side. A local river was then diverted and dammed, the lake bed flooded. Kate and I were now admiring the result. Well, I was doing the admiring. Kate was doing the stone throwing.

Beyond the curve of the lake edged by feathery willows, the land rose in a gentle slope where sheep happily munched, conveniently trimming the grass. Squat green oaks on the ridge gave way to tall and slender beech trees standing like sentinels on either side, framing the palace in the distance. Picture perfect, as planned. This was Brown's vision of the English countryside, an ideal touchstone for the Age of Romance about to blossom in the late eighteenth century, and a stark contrast to the rigid structure and perfect symmetry of formal French gardens. Blenheim presented a vision of pastoral England as unreal as its French counterpart. And yet, this was the landscape that contoured my imagination, what I liked most about England.

The lake appeared to be a haven for all manner of waterfowl. We learned much later that birdwatchers regularly descend on the place to spot rare ducks, coots, kestrels, finches, grebes, and other feathered creatures. Kate and I could only pick out the ducks, the extra large geese, and the aloof-looking swans. They were out in force, cruising the lake for suckers like us.

The birds must have sensed the bread in Kate's bag, for they all glided purposefully towards us, as though they were being positioned by plotters on a war map. And war it was. Kate threw some bread into the water, but these fowl were undeterred by such maneuvers. They knew where the food was coming from, and they headed right for it. They stormed the beach, waddling towards us in a pincer movement. The birds encircled us. Kate threw the bread high in the air and very sensibly legged it, with me close behind. Her diversionary tactic caused the more aggressive fowl to break ranks. Black-hooded geese honked at swans, who hissed back, snapping and snarling while smaller water birds gobbled up the bread chunks. Laughing, we hurried back for our own breakfast.

An hour later, our entrance fees paid, we were back inside the park and heading for the palace. As we walked around the lake, carefully avoiding huge mounds of black goose poop, we were trailed by another gang of mooching waterfowl that wisely kept their feet in the water but their eyes on us. The lake began to narrow slightly. Spanning it was a folly—a large stone bridge placed there to provide a focal point for another view. As we crossed the bridge, our vigilant gang of ducks swam beneath us and into the main body of water.

Beyond the lake, we could see what was left of the old royal hunting forest. At the end of the park was the village of Bladen. In its churchyard was the unadorned, modest grave of Sir Winston Churchill, buried beside his parents. We headed instead to the place where he was born.

Pushing the stroller over a dirt track was not that easy, but Blenheim Palace was now in sight. Only it was much bigger than we imagined and still quite a march away. We pressed on. Close to the palace entrance were sporadic bits of topiary and a large reflecting pool with a stone pillar in the center, commemorating something or other. We took Kate out of her stroller to better tackle two stories of stone steps, and climbed to a very large courtyard that looked like a parade ground.

Walking on, we came to the main entrance. Here, massive ochre-colored plinths held up stone sculptures with wings. Rising above this was an enormous clock tower surrounded by stone vases and topped with a large golden ball. With its pillars and porticos, windows and arches, chimneys and turrets, and columns and capstones of honey-colored stone, Blenheim looked like a colossal Baked Alaska left in the oven just a bit too long.

Having enjoyed the estate's gardens and grounds so much, we seriously considered staying outside, especially since the sun was shining. But we had bought our tickets, so we went in. The staterooms were big, impressive, and rather gaudy. Except for the room in which Churchill was born. Apparently, his mama was "taken short," as Jessie might have said, and gave birth to the pug-faced Winnie in a glorified butler's pantry, below stairs! I thought it was the most personal and endearing part of the entire palace.

Outside again, we visited a stunning butterfly house, skirted a maze, rode the miniature train, and clambered through an adventure playground, ending up on a wide stretch of lawn beside the tearoom. Happily exhausted, Frances and I slurped tea while Kate joined another family for a game of cricket. Then, suitably revived, we headed out through the main gates and returned to the quiet charms of Woodstock.

~

Our hotel in London was on the Brompton Road, within a few blocks of the imposing museums of South Kensington. In the opposite direction were the glittery shops of Knightsbridge, dominated by Harrods, that vast emporium of expensive edibles, collectibles, and wearables. Beyond that was Green Park and the West End.

The squally cold weather we'd experienced was now behind us. London was unusually hot, so I decided to wear my cut-down jeans, vowing to buy a pair of shorts the first chance I got. Strapping on my sandals, I rolled up my sleeves and started to relax. We had every intention of doing a little shopping in Knightsbridge. But first, afternoon tea at Harrods.

The side entrance had steps and, as I struggled with Kate's stroller, a young man in morning coat and gray-striped trousers rushed out to me.

"Oh, thanks so much, I was having a bit of a—"

"I'm sorry, sir, I can't let you in."

"Excuse me?"

"I can't let you into 'Arrods," he said, blocking my path politely but firmly. "I'm sorry, sir, but cut down jeans are not allowed in 'Arrods, sir."

"You must be joking."

"Jeans are allowed, sir, but not cut downs. It's the 'Arrods dress code. Sir."

"A dress code? In a store?"

"This is priceless." Frances was amazed but, unlike me, she was smiling.

"This is bloody ridiculous! Bleeding stupid place. Bloody rules. What a joke!"

For Frances, this was just quirky old England with its rules and rites, its pomp and pomposity, where everything seemed to be at odds but somehow evened out eventually. But for me, at that moment, it was all about being found out. Caught with my hands in the till. By now, I had attracted a small group of smiling onlookers. A man nearby leaned forward. He said he knew what it was like.

"My wife bought a dress here, one of them expensive ones with holes in it," he explained, trying to make me feel better. "When she wore it the following week, they wouldn't let her back in! 'No clothes with holes,' they said! 'But I bought it here,' she told 'em. Still wouldn't let her in, though. Coming to something, innit?"

Frances loved that story, but I didn't. I rolled the stroller back down the steps and turned away, full of sulk and bitterness. I refused to look up, steeped in self-pity and bile.

"Come on, let's go to Fortnum's!" Frances suggested, brilliantly.

As I turned the stroller towards the underground, Frances caught my arm and waved down a cab. It was a nice touch. By the time we arrived at Fortnum and Mason's, London's oldest department store, I had calmed down. We were shown to a corner table in the lovely Fountain Room. We ordered the afternoon tea—watercress sandwiches, cucumber sandwiches, freshly baked scones, clotted Devonshire cream, and a choice of jams. Kate had a large piece of chocolate cake.

After our feast we ambled about the food hall and stocked up on those distinctive green tins of tea. I counted seven kinds of Stilton! Before leaving, we visited the toy department, where we found a magnificent hand-carved rocking horse. The creature sported a mane and tail of real horse hair, and real leather tackle! I suddenly remembered Lew and my suit of armor. Fortunately, Kate remained in her stroller, the horse a little out of her range. It was certainly out of our range. Attached to the beautiful horse's hand-tooled leather bridle was a three-thousand pound price tag.

A block from the store, in the forecourt of the Church of St. James, we came across an antique market. We bought a couple of watercolors of the Thames riverbank, obviously painted at an idyllic stretch of water I had yet to find. I wondered if I ever would. You'll just have to go back, Frances said. Maybe she was right.

Inside the church, rich wood carvings adorned the paneled walls. It felt more like a pagan temple than the castle-like places of worship we had seen on our travels. A tall vaulted ceiling added to the openness without detracting from the simplicity of the design. Built by Christopher Wren to hold almost two thousand people, on that afternoon the church held just the three of us and remained largely ignored by the thick stream of tourists and Londoners alike. And yet, its quiet elegance provided a true refuge on this, one of London's busiest streets. And I had finally noticed it.

～

"Oh, Denis, it's absolutely marvelous! I don't know anyone who's been banned from Harrods. How fantastically clever of you!" said Isabel with great enthusiasm.

We had arrived for dinner at my friends' elegant town home near Kensington High Street.

"It didn't seem clever at the time," I said, defensively.

Frances rolled her eyes before darting after Kate, who was throwing cushions around the living room. Colin was getting glasses.

"We should drink to that—" he suggested.

"And celebrate the banishment of Denis from Harrods!" said Isabel, finishing Colin's sentence. Then she added, "You should have wrapped your jacket around yourself and worn it as a kilt!" Her eyes glinted with intense merriment.

Colin's grin stifled a nasally chuckle, then he shook his head with mock disbelief and said, "Of course, the whole place is turning into a vast tourist trap. Wise to move on."

"So then, you went to Fortnum's? Much better. And the tea's so good, isn't it? And Kate had a good tea? Too many cakes, all sticky fingers and smiles?"

"Drinks!" Colin called out, pulling up bottles from a cabinet. He found one that brought a smile to his face. "Now! Denis. Sherry? No? No. Oh—" Colin sounded a little crestfallen. "Yes, wine. Of course. Nobody drinks sherry anymore, do they?"

He put the bottle down and deftly picked up another. Happy with his choice, he began to pour. Colin was still in his pinstripe suit, trying to unwind from a day in the City. Isabel, on the other hand, had been painting all day and was far from winding down. Stylish, yet casual as ever, in skin-tight jeans and a floppy silk shirt, she moved around the room, going from person to person, spilling over with infectious fun and loads of energy.

"I've so much to tell you—we'll be up half the night at this rate. More than happy for all of you to stay over, if you'd rather. Up to you. Say the word. Not a problem," said Isabel quickly.

"No, the hotel's okay. A bit dowdy, but—"

"But alright? It'll do? In a pinch? And just down the street from ghastly Harrods."

Then Isabel was gone. I was not keeping up. I had barely said a word. I followed her downstairs to the small but well-equipped kitchen. Expertly Isabel shuffled pans and trays around, stirred pots, basted a roast, dealt plates, rolled napkins, and happily kept up a stream of bubbly chatter. Moments later, everyone was in the kitchen, trying not to get in the way but not wanting to miss any of Isabel's culinary magic. Soon we were clanking more glasses and toasting each other and our enduring friendship. It was fun to be back with old friends, gulping down wine between bursts of lively conversation and much laughter.

"And Mister Noisy—how's he doing?" I asked.

Mister Noisy was their son, Mark. Very bright and just a bit cheeky, as a lad he was always rather loud and loquacious. The nickname stuck.

"Doing splendidly." Colin was effusive. "The world's his oyster. Really!"

"He's now 'our man in Singapore'!" Isabel crowed with feigned grandeur.

"Spends a lot of time there. Not yet thirty—quite marvelous."

"Imagine Mister Noisy managing lots of lovely lucre!" Isabel guffawed at the thought.

"Actually, Denis, I haven't told him, but I'm really very proud of him, the way he's carrying off the whole thing, you know—" said Colin with quiet admiration.

"Why not tell him?" I said.

"Tell him?" Colin pulled a face, then his jowls sank, and he slowly shook his head. "Not something one does over here, you know. Ah, Denis, you've really become rather American."

"Have I? Guess I have, a bit." I shrugged.

Colin smiled at me, but not unkindly, then added, "Not such a bad thing, all said and done."

~

If nightingales ever sang in Berkeley Square, they certainly did not sing there now. The square—it's pronounced bar-clee, I kept telling Frances—was noisy and dirty. Even as a teen I remembered taxi drivers and other knowing motorists using the square as a cut-through to avoid Oxford Circus. The few trees in the square's center looked forlorn and grimy, and the grass covered the earth like a bad comb-over.

I had an appointment to meet a literary agent, and his office was in a large, old fashioned office block probably built in the nineteen twenties. The cage elevator rattled as it slowly ascended and finally came to rest on the top floor. We checked the doorways. No luck. Then we spied a set of twisty stairs and an arrow pointing up.

Above us, on a small landing, stood a man with a cigarette. He held it at the tips of his fingers, rather like a Gestapo agent from a bad World War Two movie. The man blew smoke towards the ceiling.

"I'm looking for Jim Bell?" I inquired, smiling, trying to be charming.

"There's no Jim Bell here," the man said with frosty coyness. Then, quickly, "But there is a James Bell. And you must be Denis Lipman. Do come in, make yourself—comfy?" He sounded vague. He proffered Frances a chair.

"Beryl, my agent, told me to stop by. So! You're in charge?"

"It would seem so." He waved a dismissive paw at the tiny office, as if he had better things to do. "I'm doing this—helping out, as it were—holding down the fort."

I was getting a bad feeling about this. He was being arrogant; I was trying to be polite and just sounding meek. We were both play acting.

"I really wish Beryl would stop sending over plays. Frankly—" He shook his head despairingly and waved toward piles and piles of scripts leaning against the wall.

"Oh, I see—"

"As it happens, I glanced over your script. Interesting story—but why is it you 'mericans think you can write Cockney?"

Frances shot me a glance. It was a lost cause. We left soon after. A strange reversal of what had happened to me when I was an impoverished playwright, chasing a very junior position in advertising. I got interviews but usually ended up getting harangued. "Who do you fink you are then, ay? Some bleedin' playwright at the RSC, fink you can stroll over to advertising then, do ya?" Everyone seemed to bristle at my rather modest credits. I couldn't get a job. A fresh start was in order. I wound up in the States, where my short resumé raised interest, not hackles.

In Britain, I had been out of step. Now, years later, according to Jimmy Bell, I was out of words. Oh, well. We quickly fled windswept Berkeley Square and ended up on Old Bond Street.

Jumping the stream of people like spawning salmon, we made landfall in the gas lit precincts of Burlington Arcade. We caught our breath and slowed our pace, more in step with this unruffled Regency oasis. Below the arcade's glass-paned roof, flower baskets hung and giant brass gas lamps shone. Beadles in top hats and liveried tailcoats discreetly patrolled the polished floors, protecting this pedestrian-only thoroughfare as they had done for almost two hundred years. An ornate jewel box of a shopping mall, Burlington Arcade was filled with very tiny, very expensive shops that sold select items ranging from leather goods, jewelry, medals, and swords, to cashmeres, bespoke suits, hunting jackets, and handmade boots. Frances bought me some hand-rolled handkerchiefs and my favorite aftershave as late birthday presents. By the time we sauntered out of this unhurried haven, I felt rather relaxed, indulged, and slightly pampered.

Then Kate wanted a bus ride. Why not! We caught a number fourteen bus back to Knightsbridge. Kate loved the big, red, double-decker London buses and took great delight in sitting upstairs. In fact, she enjoyed London as much as Frances did. And sitting up front, on the top deck of a number fourteen bus, I could see why. While Kate "drove," Frances and I enjoyed some of London's best views.

The bus sped down Piccadilly, then slowed at St James' Street. Kate glimpsed the chocolate box sentries on duty outside the Palace of St. James. We picked up speed, swept past Green Park, glimpsing the subdued grandeur of Mayfair and the big hotels. We swerved around Hyde Park Corner and the back garden of Buckingham Palace, then into Knightsbridge. Slow again, our bus rumbled along as thick streams of people crested on either side, surging in waves from one elegant store to another, oblivious of traffic or each other. Much to Frances' relief, I actually smiled as we passed by Harrods and its impeccably dressed patrons. Bad memories, like bad moments,

were casting smaller shadows across my path. I think I was beginning to enjoy London as much as my family did.

~

The following morning, I called my folks from the airport.

As I spoke to Jessie, I could hear bellows-like breathing in the
background. Lew was obviously listening. I heard the usual snatches
of rattled conversation. Don't tell me what to do! What you saying
that for? Aw, shut up! Hell, next! Lew asked Jessie to say good-bye
on more than one occasion. It was like a music hall routine that just
wouldn't end.

"Now listen, son, I'm sorry I got in such a blinkin' state. Hope it
didn't spoil your holiday."

"Oh, don't be daft, Dad, of course it didn't! You alright now,
aren't you?"

"Not doing too bad—soldiering on. Pam came 'round this morning. She's a godsend to us, you know, Pam, she is, really—"

"I'm glad she comes to see you, Dad. I wish I could come over
more often."

"You and me both, son, you and me both."

"So, next year, Dad. We'll go somewhere else. You up for that?"

"If we're still here—we'll be there."

Fair enough, I thought, and smiled. Fair enough.

A Coastguard's House on a Pebble Beach

CHAPTER 21

In Royal Tunbridge Wells

THE PLAN WAS to cut across to Royal Tunbridge Wells for an overnight stay before heading to our rental house in the Cinque Port of Deal. This was, of course, the home of Mister Raynes, the nutter we had met in Rye. At least he had not put us off visiting the historic spa town. Tunbridge was "discovered" by the eighteenth century dandy and socialite "Beau" Nash who, along with a gaggle of aristocrats, wasted oodles of time in the place, pontificating about fashion and gossiping a lot. The royal family followed the leaders of fashion and soon made Tunbridge Wells a much-favored watering hole. Queen Victoria eventually bequeathed regal status on the town.

The directions to the hotel were very clear: across the green on the hill above the town, then left just past a gas station. I made an immediate and very sharp left turn and, to my amazement, there, before us, was the hotel. Originally built as a private mansion and converted into a hotel in the late Victorian era, the Royal Spa Hotel reminded me of a rambling country house. With some time to kill and a throbbing head to clear, I suggested taking a turn around the grounds, but Frances and Kate had another idea. Breakfast!

"I'll just have some coffee and toast. That will do me," I murmured pitifully, still feeling the effects from that last little bottle of wine on the plane.

"Fine, have toast, then. Look, Kate, look! Ponies!" said Frances.

Sure enough, bobbing just outside the breakfast room windows was a posse of young girls on ponies. They all looked quite earnest, led at a walking pace to the stables on the hotel grounds. Then breakfast appeared.

A polished canopy was whisked away with a flourish, revealing two large, juicy Cumberland sausages. Kate's eyes and smile widened accordingly. A vast platter showed up for Frances, with eggs, sausages, bacon, fried bread, baked beans, mushrooms, tomatoes, and hash browns. Then, imprisoned within a wire frame, toast triangles were placed before me.

"Oh, splendid." I tried to sound enthused as I freed toast from its silvery cage.

Kate was madly happy with her sausages. Her English side was obviously asserting itself. I was now feeling much better and bitterly regretting my cheap moment. Frances felt the same, as Kate and I picked continuously at her plate, dipping buttered toast into the baked beans and stealing the odd mushroom.

By the time we finished, our room was ready, and we felt replete and revived enough for a long nap.

~

"Ah, The Pantiles. Oh, yes, you'll want to see them! Everyone does!" The desk clerk said with relish, as if I had asked about "panties" instead of "Pantiles." Or perhaps he was trying to forget he'd been asked the same question a thousand times. "It's just through the park, down the hill."

With just a few clouds framing the edge of a picture blue sky, we set off for a leisurely walk. The town center had elegant Regency vistas filled with wide spaces and long rectangles. The famed Pantiles turned out to be two rows of expensive shops with covered colonnades. The wide pedestrian flagstone roadway was once paved with ceramic tiles. Hence the name. It was all rather reminiscent of an upscale strip mall, relocated from the eighteenth century. We found fine antique shops with museum-like auras, elegant art galleries, the odd tourist-parlor, even an ironmonger's. And of course a sweet shop where Kate insisted on buying herself a Cadbury's Flake, which had replaced Smarties as her number one Brit treat.

At the end of The Pantiles was the original Chalybeate mineral spring. Discovered in the sixteenth century, the spring water apparently contained properties to revive flaccid bits of external anatomy, soothe enflamed livers, and cure dropsy—whatever that was.

Just above the spring, looking like a small Roman temple, was the Georgian bathhouse. Even though it was closed for renovation, water still flowed from a bath tap connected to an exposed outcrop, all rocky and mossy and glistening with purifying dampness. Sitting on a chair beside the spring was a middle-aged woman in period garb. She wore a long, white cotton dress and drawstring blue vest, a frilly linen bonnet, and a light blue shawl. She smiled and nodded and looked quite deranged.

"Good morning," I said. "I see you're dressed the part."

"Oh, yes, yes. Well, it's what they used to wear, isn't it? Yes, yes." She sounded as batty as she looked. She waved a metal cup on a chain that clanked like Jacob Marley's ankle bracelets.

"Can you tell us about the place?" asked Frances.

"Oh, no. No. I just dip. Want me to dip some water for you, dear?"

The woman dipped for some water and handed me the cup. It looked like a toilet bowl in need of a flush. Manfully, I drank a mouthful. The smell of rotten eggs hit the back of my throat and escaped through my nostrils, as if someone had thrown a stink bomb in my mouth. The costumed dipper smiled and nodded knowingly as my face wrinkled into something resembling a topographical map. Frances rolled her eyes and thought I was, as ever, exaggerating. Then the cup was re-dipped and Frances tasted the water. Now it was my turn to smile and nod knowingly.

"Revolting, isn't it? Mind you, you know what they say, the worse it tastes, the better it does you! Oh, yes, yes." The dipper sounded almost sympathetic. "Have some more if you like. It's free!"

"Is it good for hangovers?" asked Frances pointedly.

"So they say. Mind you, I prefer something fizzy, myself. Yes, yes!"

At a nearby teashop, we ate a very light lunch, just a few finger sandwiches and a big pot of tea. We were saving ourselves for dinner with an old friend.

~

Donned in a white linen suit and candy-striped shirt, Adelard stood before me, occasionally plucking at a hand-rolled hanky flopping from his top pocket. He leaned into his huge, rolled-up brolly and twirled on it slightly. I looked at my old friend. He had not changed a jot. His thick black hair and beard still glistened with pomade, and his eyes with mischief. A bon vivant by nature and a chef by profession, Adelard had long ago shed his Canadian accent, made his way to London, and found success as a private caterer to various stars and jet-setting types. Always wonderful company, a globe-trotting boulevardier who would go to the ends of the earth for a theatrical first night or a great party. He even made it over to the States for our wedding.

"Take this, go on, go on!" The ever-ebullient Adelard, who had come from London to have dinner with us, pushed a rosy-red cocktail in my hand. "I'll get one for myself. Think I could manage a splash." Then, dropping his voice an octave, "Or two!"

"Thanks!" I said, wondering how this drink had appeared so quickly.

"Enjoy!" said Adelard expansively, before flitting off to retrieve a drink for himself.

Despite his colossal bulk, Adelard moved adroitly and, before I had finished my first sip, he had returned, errant drink in paw.

A few minutes later, Frances and Kate showed up. Adelard bestowed warmest greetings, then insisted on getting Frances a glass of the gratis cheer.

"What is it?" she asked, intrigued by the orange and cucumber strips, lemon quarters, and mint leaves. No wonder a straw was needed to locate the translucent crimson liquid.

"They're Pimm's, quite luscious on a warm eve. And they were just sitting there, going to waste. Still quite chilled. So, I thought—" He took a long sip, his chops imploding as he inhaled his drink through the straw deftly held in a curled pinkie. "Waste not, want not!"

"I've never had this before," I said as I sucked up my drink. "It's good! I believe the Queen likes them, too. Or so I've heard."

"Well, I wouldn't know about *that* queen. Hmmm. Dee-lish! Left over from a reception, I shouldn't wonder. You're supposed to make it with fresh lemonade but I use Seven Up, myself, and no one knows the difference. Chin, chin! And look at Katie. So pretty!" He peered at Kate over his stomach. "God I'm sweaty!"

He whipped out his top pocket handkerchief, the size of a baby blanket. He flapped the hanky around his face, and Kate waved at him. Adelard smiled his big smile. Not really a smile at all, he simply opened his mouth very wide, and looked very, very surprised. That was his smile.

"Oooh, I'm enjoying this Pimm's something rotten. Aaah, my hero!" he said, as I discreetly replenished our drinks. "So! Kent! Never been to Royal Tunbridge Wells before. What made you pick *this* place?"

"We wanted a day on our own before we head down to the cottage," said Frances. "And Denis' family."

"Ah, yes, of course! That's right! You're entertaining them, aren't you! Sweet of you, that. Hmmm. And how are they? Lew and Jess? Must be getting on, poor loves."

"Still quite spry, actually, pretty active, when all is said and done," I said.

"Spry? Spry, I like that! Spry! Can't ask for more than that now, can you. Now, back to me. So, what'd you think?" Adelard took a step back and waved his arms around himself as though he were an illusionist who had somehow magically produced himself.

"Well, can't you tell? I've lost thirty pounds!" he trilled.

"Marvelous!" I said, a little too quickly.

"Good for you!" Frances spoke with an equal lack of conviction.

"Feel so much better, trimmer," said Adelard. "Right, then. Dinner!"

Before I could stop him, Adelard had purloined three more Pimm's from the abandoned tray. We did not say no. He led the way into the dining room, looking like a bearded pirate under full sail in his large white suit. Upon dropping anchor, Adelard performed a quick pirouette for Kate's amusement, then graciously deferred to me as the hostess approached and showed us to our table.

"Oh, I can't sit on that!" Adelard waved a dismissive flipper at the elegant dining chair. "Have you got something without arms? Thanks. Awfully!"

A big, high-backed, armless chair was brought and positioned by two waiters. The hostess fussed attentively. Adelard wiggled slightly as he sat down. The chair held, and he visibly relaxed.

"Hmmm. I think I'll have the lamb. The saddle!" Adelard suddenly leaned around his menu. "You are both having starters, I trust? You are? Good! Hate eating alone. But I will if I must!"

After a sumptuous dinner Frances and I ordered an ice cream concoction for Kate, coffee for us. Adelard chose the soufflé with caramel sauce, which he consumed with ease. Then he proceeded to finish Kate's leftover ice cream.

"I don't think I can manage anymore." Adelard flopped back in his chair, sweating like a tenor after a particularly emotive aria. He looked as exhausted as we felt. Jet lag. After many hugs, Frances took Kate to bed, leaving me to catch up with my old friend.

We strolled towards the terrace. The grounds looked particularly beautiful. The cusp of darkness at the edge of this vast canvas hinted at a pastoral setting just beyond the frame.

"What are we doing out here?" snapped Adelard rather harshly.

"Well, look!" I said, somewhat defensively. "The sun's only just fading. And the view—"

"Oh. I don't much do views. But very nice, all the same. Now! Let's go to the bar and let me ply you with a little cognac? Hmmm?"

"No, I don't think so. Been a long day. Tired. Now it's getting to me."

"Well! I might as well be off, then. Oh, Denis! Darling!"

Adelard gave me a big hug, the bristles of his beard sank into my face and suddenly my cheek had become the wrong half of a brush and pan set. He released me from his grasp, checked his watch, and smiled. "Oh, this is perfect. There's a train in twenty. I'll be back in the Smoke before you know it! Well, this has all been very nice, Denis, my love. You and Frances and Kate. Been too kind. Now, you go off, have a lovely holiday. Give my best to your folks! Tah-rah!" He spun around and, without another word, swung his umbrella in a forward motion and followed it down the hill to the station.

～

Deal was quite large, larger than we'd expected. We pulled up on the seafront promenade, across from a row of stately Regency townhouses and a large whitewashed Victorian hotel. Sprawling along the coast road was a hodgepodge of small hotels, shops, pubs, restaurants. We glimpsed small weathered cottages painted in soft yellows and greens, some with Dutch gabled roofs, some pointed or turreted or conical. Houses were pleasantly huddled together close to the pier, as if vying for the best sea view. Down the straight coast road, rows of tall Victorian and Edwardian terrace houses made up the skyline of this unspoiled seaside town.

Beyond the pier were a couple of fishing boats lying askew on the pebble beach like a pair of exhausted sea lions. In the opposite direction, nothing except dunes of pebbles. We wondered where the harbor was. We later found out Deal had always been a port without a harbor. The safe haven the town provided ships in the age of sail was created by the Goodwin Sands, a natural sandbank a mile or so off shore that could, on occasion, be seen at low tide above the waterline. Between the Sands and the coast was a stretch of placid water called the Downs, where the sailing ships had once harbored.

Looking beyond Deal towards Walmer, we saw grand and imposing houses. In the other direction the homes looked a lot less regal, tapering off into a line of modest dwellings. And that's where we were heading, down the front on a small street that ran parallel to the sea. The brochure had promised a coastguard's cottage. Perhaps, at the end of this drab little road, we would find a wonderful, weather-beaten, clapboard cottage with a rusty old anchor in the garden.

We found our house near the end of the terrace, beside a big thick concrete seawall and the beginnings of a windswept municipal golf course. A coastguard might have lived here once, but there were no nautical knickknacks or seafaring foolery at this end of town.

We had been told to enter at the back. In the tiny garden, a lone rosebush stuck out like a piece of Meccano, flanked by a couple of planters and a large trash can. The entrance looked like a lean-to covered in tarmac paper, its windows rippled with thick impenetrable glass.

We rang the little plastic door bell and a small gray-haired man with a gray sweater answered the door. I introduced myself.

"You can't leave the car there. Take it round the front. But get your luggage in first, yeah?"

He made no attempt to help us. As Frances and I shuffled the bags inside, Gray Man made it clear this was not his house, it belonged to his sister in-law. She was away, working overseas.

The first room we walked into was the kitchen. It looked dingy. Just beyond was a tall hallway with stairs leading to a bedroom landing. The sound of vacuuming ceased, and a heavy-set woman came into view.

"Just tidying up. Down in a minute." She smiled without humor.

I moved the car to the front. Technically, our house did face the sea, but thanks to the thick, concrete seawall we could not see it. I walked down the large front garden and entered the house through a glass-paneled mud room. Beyond this was the main lounge, which had narrow windows covered with parchment-colored lace curtains. The furniture was old. Not antique, just old. Frances and Kate were now in the dining room.

"It's not just musty. It smells—damp." Frances looked right at me.

"Very. Damp. Don't you think?" I glared at Gray Man.

"Difficult airing it out. Can't open the window when no one's around. But I'm glad you're here, to live in the place, like."

"And why's that?"

"Well, the house was burgled. So it's good to have people around. As you can imagine."

Frances' eyes widened. She was about to say something, but Gray Man put up a hand, as if to ward off any further comments, then stumbled back towards the stairs and called for his wife. He obviously couldn't wait to leave.

I noticed an old rotary phone perched on a little table. The dial had been padlocked, rendering the phone as immobile as a booted car.

"How can we make calls?" I asked.

"No. It's er, er, just for incoming calls. The phone is—"

"I see."

"I don't," said Frances. "We were promised a phone. That means a phone we can use."

I lifted the receiver. The phone was as dead as a doornail.

"And when were you going to tell us the phone's not working?" I fumed.

"I've been onto to BT about that. Twice, I have." He stammered out the words. "Thought it'd be back on by now. I'll call them again." Gray Man tried to laugh.

"Good," said Frances. "We want this phone reconnected. And unlocked. It's on our list of amenities."

"Give me your number. I'm sure we'll be in touch." I was firm.

"I'll try and get someone in—about the phone." Gray Man's voice quavered, his words hung in the air without conviction. Then he and his wife were gone.

We followed Kate as she scampered upstairs to a bathroom with a toilet bowl as big as a witch's cauldron. Along the landing were two smallish bedrooms and one larger one with a bay window facing the front. Below us, other people's barren gardens and sheds, but when we looked up and out, there was the sea, with a clear view to the far blue coast of France.

So there it was. We had rented a house at the wrong end of town. Even so, we wouldn't have to drive everywhere. We could get newspapers and Flakes from a newsagent two blocks away. There was easy access to the promenade, shops, nearby attractions, and the prettier part of Deal. So we decided to put a brave face on things and make the most of our week.

We unpacked, then took off along the promenade toward the pier. The sluggish sea shimmered like newly poured concrete. The first order of business was to find a suitable place for Sunday lunch, then stock up on sandwich stuff, salads, and cakes.

We peered into the whitewashed Edwardian Royal Hotel—a little too formal for my boisterous clan. Then we found the perfect place, a storefront, bistro-type restaurant with big windows. It looked bright and cheerful, with checkered tablecloths and, most importantly, a varied menu including the traditional Sunday lunch I knew my family would expect.

As we ambled back across the wide promenade towards Walmer, Kate ran ahead to look at the sea. Frances found the spot where Julius Caesar first came ashore fifty odd years before the birth of Christ. She was pleased as punch. Caesar and Rome had supplanted Merlin and Camelot in her literary interests, a case of might over magic.

"Caesar landed in a better part of town than we did." I sounded sour, unconcerned with historical significance.

"Oh, do cheer up. I know, let's go out tonight."

And so we decided to forego cooking and treat ourselves to a nice dinner. Somewhere close, somewhere nice. We found just the spot along the prom on the way back to the house, a delightful little seafood restaurant with just half a dozen tables or so. Kate had a fancy version of fish and chips. As we were just a few miles from Dover I just had to order the sole. My favorite. For once Frances followed my lead, and she was glad she did. The large fillets were perfectly grilled, the firm flesh sweet and flavorful and served with tiny buttered potatoes flecked with parsley.

After dinner, we walked back across the prom. Kate found stones and plunked them into the fast approaching water. It took only minutes for the tide to cross the pebbly beach and come gurgling around the bottom steps of the seawall. Waves crashed then shimmied back down the beach, pulling at the stones as if trying to gobble them up. The sun had gone down. A few lights glinted on the distant French coast, like fallen stars held fast on a dark blue horizon.

CHAPTER 22

On the front at Deal

WE OPENED what windows we could. Warm, fresh air breezed in. After a late start, we finished unpacking and sat down with our morning cup of coffee. Suddenly, around eleven, "Colonel Bogey" blared throughout the kitchen. Normally whistled, the World War Two ditty seemed to be playing on a carillon of bells built into the walls or ceiling of the house. At first, we thought it was an alarm. We checked the radio, the TV, the kettle, the phone—still dead— then we looked at each other.

"Can't be the doorbell," I said, firmly. "It's too much."

The ghastly tune rang out again. I saw a shape in the fuzzy glass door at the back of the house.

"Oh, God! It is the doorbell! It's them!" I was near to panic.

"It can't be," said Frances, with some certainty. "They won't be here before noon. Relax."

"The telephone repairman? They said they were getting someone in." I smiled.

"Wouldn't that be something!" Frances sounded impressed. "And on a Sunday!"

I opened the door to a large man, about forty, graying temples, somewhat overweight, with a friendly face. Definitely, I thought: an off-duty repairman.

"Denis?" he asked.

"Yes! Good. Well. Come in, come in," I said, eagerly.

"Wanted to make sure I got the right house."

"You got the right house." I led him to the padlocked phone. "There it is."

"Don't see many like this anymore—" He picked up the phone and examined it as if it were an antique. "We don't come across this model much."

The guy seemed to know what he was doing, so I left him alone and moved back to the kitchen. Frances was still standing in the back doorway, looking down the street.

"Denis, look at that car," said Frances, calling me over. "That car there. The older woman. She looks just like your Aunt Flo."

I went outside for a better look. I saw a youngish woman and a stately, older woman. I walked slowly towards them. The older woman started laughing and waving at me. She did look vaguely familiar.

"Oh, my God. Aunt Mary!" Grinning, I waved back, then quickly legged it back into the house. The large guy with the friendly face was still holding the phone.

"Sorry, mate, but this phone is buggered!"

"Are you my cousin Kevin?

"I thought you'd twig it eventually!" He started laughing in that unmistakable Evans cackle. This laugh sounded as if the world had just fallen arse over tip. My mother's entire family owned that laugh. I looked again at this cousin I had not seen in years. I remembered him looking like his thin-faced dad, but time had filled him out, which fit his friendly, exuberant personality.

"I had no idea you lot were showing up."

"Lew called us. So I brought Mum down. And Maxine—you haven't met the wife."

"No, no, well, it has been a while! Fifteen years? At least!"

"Must be! And you must be Frances." Kevin gave Frances a hug. "Lew sent us pictures! And this is Katie! Hallo, Katie! Bet you don't know who I am!"

Kate ran around the room, confused but fascinated by the flurry of activity. Maxine helped Mary into the house. Mary was still chuckling away.

"Hello, Denis, lovely to see you, it is, weally. Been so long!"

"Come in, come in!" I was grinning.

"This wally thought I was the repairman!" yelled Kevin, pointing at me.

"Looks like one, doesn't he?" Maxine smiled. "And just as useless."

Although Maxine was dressed in a two-piece suit, as if she had just come from church, she was as comfortable with her newfound relatives as if she'd known us all her life.

"Lew never said you were coming down," I said, in my defense.

"Well, we weren't too sure. Mum's been a bit under the weather, but she's alright now, so thought we'd have a run down," said Kevin.

"Well, of course I'm alwight. Funny, you are, cor!" Mary laughed, then smiled at me, before catching her breath and going on, "So, how are you Denis? Been a long time, hasn't it. Goes so quick, though. Time." She tut-tutted, "Makes you wonder, where it's gone!"

Gently guided by Maxine, my aunt moved slowly into the living room, quietly huffing and puffing with the effort.

"Not too bad, is it, Denis. Homey, yes, homey." Mary tried to be diplomatic.

"At least it's close to the sea." I shrugged.

"Any closer you'd be in a boat!" Mary giggled happily. "Love a cup of tea, Denis!"

"Coming up, Mum. Frances has got it on the go," said Kevin.

With a contented sigh, Mary sank into the sofa and pointed at her son. "Look at the size of him now, Denis! He's got a corporation on him, hasn't he!"

"Leave it over, Mum. I've got a lot of shares in this corporation!" Kevin tapped his ample stomach then started laughing, not caring a damn about how he looked.

"When I think of his dad! Always wiry, he was." Again she tsk-tsked.

My Uncle Bert had been like Lew, as thin as uncoiled rope. Although unrelated, as they got older, they began to share the same emaciated appearance. The same scowl.

"So when's the ring leader showing up?" asked Kevin.

"I suppose you mean Jessie? About half an hour or so." I checked my watch.

Kevin laughed, then legged it back to the kitchen. I sat down next to Mary. She leaned across and tapped my hand, wanting me to pay attention. I did.

"You know, Denis, I still go and see Bert, at the cemetery. I talk to him. I know he's there, listening. Comforting, it is, weally—" Mary's "r" sounds always came out as "w," a very upper class speech impediment, and quite strange for an old East Ender. "Kevin thinks I'm off my wocker."

I held her hand for a brief moment, then Kate barreled in, chased by Maxine. Mary laughed and clapped her hands for Kate's amusement. Then Frances and Kevin came in with tea, just as "Colonel Bogey" reverberated throughout the house again.

"What the bloody hell—" Kevin looked up at the ceiling.

"They're here," said Frances, bracing herself.

Mary insisted on getting up to greet everyone. I opened the front door and there was Pam, quite unchanged, smiling her smile of quiet bemusement. "We made it," she whispered. "Had our moments— but everyone's alright now. We're alright, aren't we, Aunt Jess?"

"I'm alright, I am! Is this Denis? It is! Come here, then! Come here!"

I gave Mum a hug. She seemed a little distracted, there was a certain vagueness, but her smile remained as infectious as ever. She shuffled along at an imperceptible pace; her lower legs and ankles were swollen, and her feet appeared to be bursting from her soft slippers. Even so, she looked healthy and tanned, convinced she would improve as the weather did. She poo-pooed my suggestion about getting a walker.

"I'm not having that—look like an old lady." Mum was adamant.

"What about a cane, then? Give you a bit of support," I suggested.

"I don't need a stick; I've got 'im!" Mum pointed to Lew.

Ghrrr.

Mum laughed, and Mary giggled. Lew rolled his eyes in the time-honored way. I gave Lew a hug and said it was good to see him. He nodded. He could not speak; neither could he hide his emotion. I offered to take their suitcase, but he waved me away, and I let him be. With stick in one hand, he hauled out the luggage with a still-strong right arm.

Despite his apparent reticence and softer demeanor, he seemed a little healthier, a little sturdier than the previous year. But there was something else. His hair was no longer slicked back, but closely cropped, spiky. And gray. I pointed this out. He jabbed a finger towards Jessie, then gave the thumbs up sign to show she approved his new look.

Aunt Florrie was last getting out of the car. Cane in hand, she prodded the path before her as though testing for quicksand. She pulled a face while Pam opened up a wheelchair. Embarrassed by her lack of self-reliance, Flo bravely laughed at the fuss Pam was making. Everyone exchanged a cackle of greetings and kisses.

~

As soon as everyone settled inside with tea, the usual chin-wag began in earnest. Scolding, cajoling, and laughing, the three sisters gossiped about other family members and the eight decades they had shared yet remembered so differently.

"That was one of Tom's stories—can't believe everything he tells you." Flo was firm. She put no store in the veracity of my funny uncle, her diminutive and recalcitrant husband.

"I wemember what Tom told me. And what Mum said!" Mary went on, the loudest of the three. Her voice, like her memory, was a little less wobbly. "Mum had melted down a bowl of suet fat. And she forgot all about it—larking awound with Tom, wasn't she? Such a funny little bugger. He was, funny!"

"Still is." Flo's voice was tinged with bitterness and mild contempt. "A funny little man."

"So anyway…" Mary was keen to get on to tell her tale. "Tom pwobably went upstairs to see Wose. And Mum more than likely went off for a nap, didn't she. Ha! Ha! Just like Mum, ay, Jess—just like her, wasn't it. So anyway, the fat on the stove must've caught fire. Flaming up, it was, or so she said. To this day I don't know how she did it, but she wakes up, takes the pot outside and pours it down the outside lav. Then Tom comes back, goes off outside and sits down to do his business. Then he's back, ain't he! Quick as a flash. Sqweaming blue murder, he was!"

"Well, he would do! Got his tackle splashed with hot fat," Lew said with a grunt.

The three sisters cackled with fiendish delight. The rest of us grinned, shaking our heads. When the laughter subsided, Flo asked Frances if she had ever met Tom. Frances said she had not; Aunt Flo smiled a withering smile and said Frances had not missed much.

~

We arrived at the restaurant at the allotted time. I went in ahead to explain there would be three extra people in our party. No problem. More chairs and another table were hastily aligned. Wine was served, and everyone settled in.

Our roast lamb lunches arrived and were soon drowned in mint sauce, and Kate's burger was soon smothered in ketchup. I made a toast. Glasses were clanked, good wishes muttered between bites of lamb.

Then I heard it. A scudding sound. It was loud. A chair scraping back on the wooden floor. Somebody screamed. Cutlery rattled. Everyone was talking at once. More chairs were moved. Plates were being cleared. Everything turned loud in my ears. I looked up just as Frances did. We froze. It was Flo. She appeared rigid, stricken to her chair, vomiting with considerable force across the breadth of the table.

"Gawd 'elp us! It's a fit! She's 'aving a fit!" exclaimed Lew, with tabloid subtlety.

Flo suddenly slumped back against her chair, and the rigidity ceased. Dark green, porridge-like bile dribbled down and around her chin. Pam put a supportive arm around her mother, and Kevin swathed her in napkins and tried to keep her steady and upright. She seemed unconscious. The manager was hovering. He was looking around furtively. He probably wanted us gone. I couldn't blame him. I just stood there. Frances walked Kate to the bathroom. She resisted, wanting to witness the unfolding drama. Mum noticed the commotion and turned to Lew.

"What's a matter with Flo?"

"She's having a fit, woman! She's having a fit!" Lew scolded impatiently.

I heard several there-theres and other kindly inanities laced with panic. An ambulance. Should we call an ambulance? Pam firmly shook her head. Lew now stood, looking this way and that, arms bent back, not knowing what to do. None of us did. Jessie, confused and flushed, tried to get up. Lew told her to stay put. Frances and

Kate, now back, sat down next to Mary and Jessie, who pulled a face of pantomime dread that masked her true feelings of concern and fear.

"Let's get her outside. Get some air," said Kevin, taking charge.

"Oh, my Gawd, oh, dear, I feel all faint meself." Mary laughed nervously.

I helped Kevin take Flo outside. Her feet dragged a bit, but we managed. Pam assembled the wheelchair, and we wheeled her across to the promenade. Flo sank down one side of her chair, leaning into a pillow of cool breeze that blew across from the sea.

"Better," she said softly. "Better—"

Pam stayed with Florrie, Kevin and I went back inside the restaurant. People were still gawking but trying not to. Some attempted to express concern. Others just wanted to get on with their lunch. Lew was at the register, having had the presence of mind to settle the bill. When he returned, I said we should all go.

"Aren't we going to have a bit of sweet?" asked Mum, innocently.

"Come on, Jessie, we're going now," said Lew as he helped her up.

"Why you grabbing me? Get off out of it!"

Ghrrr.

～

Back at the house, we somehow got Flo up to one of the small bedrooms. Pam produced various phials and pill bottles, stacked them in neat piles, and told us to wait downstairs.

"I'm glad you two blokes were here." Lew pointed to me and Kevin. "I would never be able to lift her. Barely lift meself."

"What was it, Denis?" asked Maxine.

"Pam will be down. She'll tell us; she knows what's going on—"

"Turn up for the books, innit?" said Mary. "You alwight, Jess? Alwight, aren't you?"

Mum burped, then nodded and smiled. She was alright. The living room became a doctor's waiting room. Time trickled by as slowly as wet sand in an egg timer. Conversation was strained. Snippets. Muttered phrases. Then periods of silence punctuated only by Mum's burps and Kate's giggles as she played with Maxine and Frances. Mum twisted a handkerchief absently. Lew poured out small measures of Jack Daniel's and passed them around like drinks at a wake.

Pam reappeared. Much to everyone's relief, she said Flo would be alright. In time.

"It's petit mal. Mum's had it before."

"She epileptic, then? Bad, that. Nasty. Very nasty." Lew growled.

"That's grand mal, Uncle Lew, this is a very mild case. So there's no need for concern. But I'll monitor her condition." Pam spoke quietly and professionally.

"How did it happen?" asked Frances.

"The excitement. The heat. Seeing everyone. Anything can bring it on, really. It's happened before, like I said. I'll call the doctor in the morning. But it'll take a couple of days for her to get—you know—to recuperate. Get back on her feet."

"Hooray! I get to sleep down here all week!" said Kate.

With only three bedrooms in the house, we had planned for Kate to sleep overnight in the lounge. Now she would have stay there longer. Kate could not have been happier.

"Shall we get on with tea?" I asked nervously.

"Oh, I'd love some tea, Denis. What a good idea!" Pam smiled.

Frances and I got up and went to the kitchen. No one was leaving. And that meant the able-bodied members of my family were expecting to be fed. Nothing changes. Have to keep our strength up, Denis, won't help if we starve ourselves! I could hear them saying it. So Frances and I boiled eggs, buttered bread, washed salad, cut cake, and dealt out salami and ham and cheese slices onto flowered plates. Something to do. Pam went back upstairs to check on the patient. She was now in total nurse mode. A few minutes later Pam returned, assured us Flo was resting comfortably, then started looking around the kitchen.

"Have you got a bowl, Denis?" Pam asked.

"A what?"

"A bowl. You know, for Mum."

"A bowl? For Mum?" Instinctively, I pushed the salad washer out of sight. I looked around, trepidation glazing my face.

"You know, a commode. Do you have one here?"

"A commode. Ah, yes. No! No!"

I shot Frances a glance of sheer panic. Oh, God! My aunt had a seizure. She can't be moved for days. And now Pam's searching for a commode! It was something out of P. G. Wodehouse. But there it was. And there we were.

"A bed pan, then? That'll do. I looked in the toilet; doesn't seem to be one there," said Pam.

"We did not request one. Well, I mean, it was not on the list of amenities. Nor was a commode, actually. Have you tried the lav? The other lav—down here, you know—"

"Yes, I looked in that one."

"Oh, dear. Well. Well," I said, floundering.

"I'll look around, if I may. I'll find something, for, you know—"

"Go right ahead," Frances finished my thought. "Let us know if you—"

"I will, Frances, don't worry." Pam took off, scouring the house for a bedpan.

"I wonder what she's going to use?" asked Frances, forever curious.

"I don't want to know!" I babbled on, "Oh, my God, what if Flo goes in the bed? Kate is supposed to sleep there. Oh, Christ. We're not equipped—I'm not good at this! And if there's an emergency, the bloody phone doesn't work! And there's my parents in there, and the other lot. Oh, God!" I started laughing.

Frances told me to get a grip, but I continued laughing. With thoughtful eagerness, she offered to smack me. I declined her kindly offer and took deep breaths instead.

"Better?" asked Frances, sounding a little disappointed, then asked me to help put out the tea things. Good idea. So that's what I did, and my hysteria gradually subsided.

Soon, everyone was eating, drinking, and nattering as though nothing unusual had happened. Kevin and Maxine regaled us with stories of trips and family get-togethers until, eventually, the conversation wore down. Flo's condition, the events of the day were starting to take their toll. Even my ever-ebullient Aunt Mary was beginning to fade. Mary, Kevin, and Maxine said their heartfelt good-byes and expressed well wishes for Flo. It had been a bittersweet family reunion, but we all muttered optimistically about getting together when everyone was better. Just as they were leaving, Pam reappeared and announced Flo was now sleeping normally.

"Come here, Mary, Mary quite contrary!" Mum shuffled into the kitchen for another hug good-bye with Mary.

"You are silly, Jess, you weally are!" Mary laughed. "You should be sitting down."

"I do enough sitting down," Mum shot back at her sister with a wide nervous smile.

And then they were gone. While Frances and I cleaned up, my folks and Kate explored the garden. We told Pam to relax a bit. She sat down, exhausted, grateful for a break. As she talked, I interjected with oh, really, did she, oh, yes, poor thing, with a few oh, dears and there-theres thrown in for good measure.

"Her urine is very strong," Pam suddenly announced.

Oh, God, I thought. Had Flo made it to the toilet? The sheets! Oh, no. Wait. Maybe Pam had conjured up a commode? Had she improvised with a bowl? Which one? Oh, God. Oh, God.

"I'm a little concerned. I may have to take a sample. For the doctor. I just need to put it in something. Something I can close."

"Of course!" said Frances. "Oh, look, it's Kate's bedtime!"

"Well, we'd better find her then! Oh, yes, she's in the garden!" I said.

We fled, leaving Pam to look for something to put something into. Something with a lid. Something we could replace. We never asked.

CHAPTER 23

From Henry's castle to Sandwich

MONDAY MORNING cracked open with all the dull, warm grimness of a half-formed egg. At least it was not raining. Breakfast went off without a hitch. Toast, cereal, tea for my folks, gold-top milk for Kate, coffee for us.

Pale and drawn, her long gold hair combed but untended, Pam finally joined us. She looked like a distraught character from a Victorian novel. In a way, she was. She smiled wanly and drank her coffee strong, with just a shot of milk. We waffled on about the weather before finally broaching the subject of her mum's condition.

"She's nodding off, then coming to, you know. But getting better." Pam sighed heavily.

"What about you?" Beyond my own panic and selfishness, I did feel concerned.

"Thank you for asking, Denis. I do what I can. I don't get a lot of help from the family. They have their lives."

Assuring us we could do nothing more for Flo at the present, Pam insisted we go out and try and enjoy the day. Even so, we did not feel comfortable venturing too far afield. Deal would fill the bill perfectly. Apart from the old town, Deal boasted two castles, some royal apartments, and a museum. As Mum's legs were playing her up, my parents decided to stay close to home. Frances and Kate and I would go alone.

In the annals of literature, Deal has not been viewed too kindly. A Regency travel book described the town as "a villainous place filled with filthy looking people." A century or so before, the diarist Samuel Pepys called Deal "pitiful." Well. We enjoyed our walk in a delightful part of the old town Pepys must have missed. Especially when the sun quite unexpectedly took a shine to us.

Some of the smaller streets and alleys were cobbled, and the houses at least two hundred years old. With Kate in her stroller, we spent a pleasant hour zigzagging from the high street hubbub down to those quieter, more picturesque alleys and turnings, before finding ourselves back on the front looking out at the emerald-gray sea.

During the Napoleonic era, with its strategic nearness to France, Deal became one of the busiest ports in Britain, the only one without a harbor. Of course, with all those sailors on shore leave, this ancient Cinque Port boasted more pubs and prostitutes than any other town in England. In the early part of the nineteenth century, any hovel big enough to hold a keg of beer could describe itself as a hostelry. As the demand for the demon drink rose, so did the number of pubs, hundreds of them. It must have been like spring break all year long.

Of course, the hole-in-the-wall pubs and prossies, like the capstans and slipways, were long gone. The old Naval Yard was sold off in the mid-nineteenth century, and the town became a sleepy, rather quaint shell of a place. Even so, Deal was well-populated, and locals still took to the promenade while anglers happily dropped lines on either side of the pier, jutting out into the sea like an immobilized Gulliver stranded in the waves.

On the pebble beach we saw fishing boats, reminiscent of Aldeburgh, selling their catch. Farther along, set back from the promenade and surrounded by grass, we came upon a vestige of military might, a strange edifice built by Henry the Eighth to ward off the French. It looked quite unlike anything we had ever seen before.

Deal Castle was primarily an enormous turret tower sunk into a dry moat, a huge gun emplacement that could fire upon incoming ships yet remain virtually hidden and secure. On the flat top of the castle, massive guns had once been wheeled and turned to fire from any conceivable angle. I was quite impressed. The stronghold was fashioned in the shape of a Tudor rose. We wandered around the wall "petals," one within the other, many feet thick, protecting the stone heart. The strange circular layout started to make sense. Deal Castle was austere and functional, built only for defense, without any thought to regal splendor. Ironically, this stronghold never saw any action. This particular invasion from France, expected in Henry's time, like the one threatened by Napoleon several centuries later, never materialized, and the big guns remained silent.

~

Lew was standing in the foyer at the back of the house. He had been waiting for us. I moved ahead and saw an anxious Pam scurrying down the stairs.

"Oh, I am glad you're back, Denis. Mum's had another episode, on the way to the lavatory."

"Dead weight. I couldn't lift her. I knew I couldn't—" Lew's face was set grim.

"It's alright, Dad. Frances, best to keep Kate down here—"

Kate had scampered up the stairs, a child's morbid fascination with sickness. As Frances retrieved her, I bounded up the stairs, Pam just behind me.

"Be careful, Denis, there's vomit!" she called out.

"Right. Fine. Got that. Okay."

Flo was prostrate on the landing. As I was trying to get a grip around her back, Lew almost stumbled. I knew he desperately wanted to help, but he could not. I asked him to wait downstairs, keep Mum company. He nodded, relieved to be on his way. As Pam and I began lifting, Flo started to come to. She bore the pains and the indignity of her plight with quiet fortitude. Eventually we got her back to bed.

"What's that smell?" I heard Kate ask.

"Look, Pam, your mum should be in a hospital," I said, almost pleading.

"She'd hate that, Denis. I've spoken to her doctor; he's not too concerned."

"Well, he's not here, is he!" I said testily.

Kate broke free and bolted up the stairs.

"Kate!" Frances called out.

"Everything alright up there?" Now Lew was yelling up the stairs.

Before going back downstairs, Pam and I mopped up the landing and stair carpet. Eventually the vomit stain merged with the existing carpet stains. But the smells remained. Toilet pong mingled with industrial strength cleaner and clung to the upstairs like wallpaper. Oh, God. I sighed. I looked in on the patient. Flo was awake. She tried to smile. In a rather gravelly voice, she apologized for being a bother. I suddenly stopped feeling sorry for myself and told her she was no bother at all.

~

"Your mother's gone upstairs, to the room."

Lew spoke without looking up from the racing section of his newspaper. I assumed Mum had gone off for a nap. Not a bad idea, I thought, sitting down. Frances was in the garden with Kate. Apart from a ticking clock and the occasional flutter of paper as Lew turned a page, all was quiet. I dozed off.

When I woke up it was five o'clock. Lew was in the kitchen, putting out cups, brewing more tea, shooing Pam and Kate from under his feet. It would soon be dinnertime, and our cupboard was bare. What to do? We didn't feel like cooking. Then I remembered that boon of English cuisine: take-out Indian food.

It was Mum. I saw her first. She was smiling and waving as she slowly made her way down the stairs. A vision in pink, pearls around her neck, hands flashing with gold jewelry. I just stared. And stared. Mum gave me her wide winning smile, a fixed star in a crimson universe.

"Well!" she said. "I'm ready!"

"Ready?" I asked.

"For dinner. We're going out, aren't we? Going out for dinner?"

"Where did you get it in your 'ead that we're going out!" Lew was somewhat flummoxed.

"What about Aunt Flo, Mum? She won't be able to make it," I tried to explain, tried to sound conciliatory. "And Pam can't leave Flo now, can she?"

"What about me?" Mum protested. "What about me!"

"We'll get something in. Something Indian. Curry, you like curry. Okay? Yes?"

"But I'm not sick. Don't see why *we* can't go out!" She sounded belligerent.

The seriousness of Flo's condition had somehow been dislodged in Mum's memory. We explained that it wouldn't be very nice or appropriate to abandon Pam and Flo. We were staying in. Mum pulled a face and fell into a crested silence.

An hour or so later, we sat down to king prawn madras, lamb curry, and jasmine rice. I cooked up an egg for Kate. I told Mum we would go out another night. She shrugged her sloping shoulders and said she was not bothered. I could tell she was a little downcast, but she cheered up with a glass of wine and some chicken tikka.

$\sim$

The sun shone long into the evening. It seemed the day would never end—in more ways than one. We milled around the living room, causing happy distractions for Kate, who wanted to stay up. Eventually, Mum toddled off to bed, followed by Pam and Frances. Lew and I walked across the roadway to the seawall. We stood for a few moments watching the waves as they crashed across the stony, deserted beach.

"I'm going to be ninety this year. The time goes by. Goes quick, it does. And I'm having a bugger of a job keeping up with it."

Hackle. Hackle. Hackle.

Then I noticed something. Glasses! The flinty gray eyes were now buried deeper than normal, almost hidden behind the glint of thick goggles. Lew noticed I had noticed his new look.

"Yeah, I know, me old lamps are fading. Mind you, it took a while."

We watched two naval ships, slow and silent, pass each other on the horizon.

"I always wanted to be a sailor, as a kid. Join the navy. Always liked ships," I said.

"I hated them. I was only ever on troop ships going to India! Time it took. Boring!"

"Yeah, I remember you telling me you were fed up most of the time. In India."

"Fed up. Gutsed up. Read a lot, though. And those religions over there, read up on them, too. You know, the Muslims just have to say 'I divorce you' three times and that's it, you're divorced. Thought about that for a while."

"About getting a divorce?"

"Being a Muslim. Thought about it."

"You did?" I was surprised.

"There was this nurse who saw me through my malaria. She was Muslim. Indian. But Muslim. They all thought I was going to die. Got a brass plaque made for me. They had the gun carriage waiting, telegram for Jessie was all but sent. But I pulled through. Thanks to that nurse. She prayed to Allah for me, she did. Nice of her, that was. When I got better, I got to know her and her people. I used to eat with them. Sat 'round this big bowl. Everyone dug in, rice, curry, meat. No plates, just used your fingers and the chapati to mop up the sauce. Bloody lovely."

"Ever read the Koran?" I inquired.

"Parts of it. But I never—never went beyond that."

"Didn't think you were much for religion," I said.

"Nah, wasn't. But I read up on it. Did a lot of reading out there. Like I said, nothing much else to do. Shakespeare, a lot of Milton, Lord Tennyson. And Elroy Flecker, you know, *The Golden Road to Samarkand.* 'To the oceans now I fly, and those happy climes that lie where day never shuts his eye, up in the broad fields of the sky…' That's all I can remember."

The verse had cloaked him in a kind of confidence I had rarely seen. He seemed more comfortable with himself, his age, with me. Somehow the poem had unlocked the portals to Lew's inner memory, and a long buried sense of self had finally started to emerge. It surprised him as much as it startled me.

～

Tuesday morning rolled around, and Flo was definitely on the mend, much to everyone's relief. We decided to visit the nearby town of Sandwich, which was a little bigger than Deal. Mum's legs were still playing her up, so she decided to stay home with Pam and Flo. Surprisingly, Lew said he would come along, even though we'd probably be walking around quite a bit. No problem, he said. He brandished his cane like a rifle, said he was fine to walk. Pam shooed us out of the house with a list of pharmacy supplies she needed.

Sandwich was once a busy medieval seaport—until the sea tightened its tides and pulled back several miles leaving Sandwich, like Rye, clinging to marshy inlets and the banks of a sluggish river. The town was not on the tourist trail. Beyond a few shops and perhaps a few old buildings, our expectations were not exactly high.

The car park was surrounded by glass and blast structures. Not a promising start. Then, within a few yards, our footfalls landed on soft, rounded cobblestones laid down in the Middle Ages.

We made our way through a beautifully shaped archway and onto a plaza. To one side was the rusty red Guildhall built in the sixteenth century. The Guildhall's forest of intricately carved wooden beams, faded red and gold-painted panels, and stone masonry melded together into a vast reminder of the town's prosperous past. This was a find. Tucked inside this building was an Information Office and a very helpful and obliging staff member happy to tell us more about her virtually unheralded town.

Apparently, Sandwich's wealth was created, in part, by the influx of immigrants from the Netherlands. Some years prior to their arrival, the elders of Sandwich saw their town's fortunes, like Rye's, drying up along with the harbor. They feted Queen Elizabeth the First, treating her to as much pageantry and flattery as the town could afford, all in the hopes she would come up with the coffers needed to dredge the harbor and make it viable again. The Queen did not oblige, and the town fell into a slump until the Dutch arrived, fleeing religious persecution. They established a cloth trade and contributed their skills as dike builders, enabling the locals to reclaim much of the marsh and turn it into profitable farm land.

We decided shopping could wait. Frances was in her element, I was relaxed, and Kate was happy in her stroller. Even Lew was game to explore. Carry on, he said, I'll keep up. And he did.

We walked to St. Peter's Church, a town hub since the Dark Ages. The church's curfew bell was still rung at eight each evening. Once called the "pig bell," it tolled the time when animals could be let out onto the streets. A "goose bell" was rung at five in the morning, presumably to wake the geese. Why anyone would want to wake geese at five in the morning was beyond us.

The vicinity around the church was festooned with narrow alleys and winding streets with names like The Butchery and Holy Ghost Street and No-Name Street! Kate loved that. Guildcount Street boasted a lovely row of cottages and Potter Street had lopsided-looking houses. This area was crammed with all kinds of shops, thronged with people. Locals. Other than ours, not a telltale guidebook or camera anywhere in sight.

With bags of groceries dangling from Kate's stroller, we came upon the longest intact medieval thoroughfare in the country. Strand Street was dotted with ancient stone and terracotta brick buildings, including the Sandwich Mint and the King's Lodgings, built in the fourteen hundreds as a guest house for pilgrims visiting Canterbury. We found black-timbered and wattle-walled houses, and walked on sidewalks trodden almost flat to the road after hundreds of years of use. Nearby was a wonderfully old-fashioned teashop, with a window displaying homemade cakes and oversized scones, beckoning us to come inside. It was teeny tiny, with thick oak beams and white plaster walls, shiny horse brasses, and sconces with different-shaped teapots, stuffed with lavender and blossoming thyme. Lace tablecloths and flowers adorned the tiny tables.

A friendly gray-haired lady presided over the tearoom. She had a genuine smile and obviously took a great delight in children. Kate soon had the run of the place. Although she wore the traditional black dress and white pinafore of a waitress, the woman was, in fact, the owner. More importantly, she told Kate, she was also the baker and scone maker. And a good one, too! Her scones were light and fluffy, and the glistening chocolate cake was moist and dense. Even Lew indulged his sweet tooth. We made a note of the shop's address and promised to return. We reluctantly made our way back through the Guildhall archway, back to the long gray metal fences and low biscuit-colored buildings of the twentieth century.

In the car, on the ride back to Deal, Lew read from the pamphlet Frances had picked up. The town of Sandwich was first recorded in the seventh century and had Saxon origins, though many believe it was settled much earlier. The name was derived from the Place of Sand, but it was the origin of the edible sandwich that intrigued us most. In the mid-eighteenth century, the illustrious Earl of Sandwich called for beef to be placed between two slices of bread so he could eat without getting gravy on his playing cards or ruffled shirt sleeves. Ironically, the first Earl of Sandwich, Edward Montagu, only took the title because his fleet docked at Sandwich prior to sailing for France to pick up King Charles the Second and return him to the throne of England. Montagu could just as easily taken his title from another town along the coast.

"Anyone for a roast beef portsmouth?" I asked.

We thought about it for a moment; it did not sound as strange as I expected.

"Could work," said Frances. "Although roast beef 'rye' would be better."

"Rye! Yes. Clever. Very." I smiled.

~

Nothing untoward had happened at the house. We found Mum napping in the garden; Flo was still in bed, as expected. As we unpacked our groceries, Pam gave us the latest on Flo's condition.

"I've checked her urine. Not as strong as it was," said Pam casually.

"Oh. Good. Yes. Is she…better?" I floundered.

"She's sitting up now. I think she could make it to the toilet. With some help, of course."

Of course! I stood in silent dread of being asked to help. Frances nudged me, and I asked if we could be of assistance. Luckily, Pam managed quite well without me, and I was most grateful.

When Pam suggested we go out for dinner, Jessie's mood darkened. Perversely, she did not want to go out. Something told me Mum was still harboring some resentment for the night before. She was also a bit miffed at the constant attention being paid to her sister.

"I'm not feeling too good meself," Mum announced with great vigor.

"Well, don't fret, Aunt Jess, you can stay here with me and Mum. I'll get us in some Chinese food. Mum likes that, and I think she'll be up for it a bit later. Do you like Chinese food, Aunt Jess?"

"Chinese food! Hell next! I'm not eating that sort of thing." Mum was firm.

"Come out with us, then," said Lew, trying to be encouraging.

"Where you think you're going!" Mum was harsh, uncompromising.

"Well, I'm going. You can please yourself!" said Lew, defiantly.

Jessie looked astonished, but Lew, for once, held his ground.

"Oh, come on, Mum. I want Dad and you to come with us. You wanted a night out."

"No! A bit of bread will do me. No butter!" Mum spoke with a martyr's firmness of purpose. And then spoke no more. She intended to suffer in silence. So that was that.

Frances, Kate, Lew, and I walked down to the large whitewashed Edwardian hotel on the promenade. We had a pleasant dinner, but not a very quiet one. Next to us were twenty or so middle-manager types on a golfing trip from Canada. Loud and raucous, they were very friendly and, as soon as she'd finished eating, Kate ran off to be part of this merrier group.

When we returned to the house, Flo was downstairs at the kitchen table. She looked a little gaunt, but smiling, a cup of tea by her side. Mum was finishing her Chinese dinner!

"So Mum did okay with the Chinese food?" I whispered to Pam.

"Did very well." She spoke a little louder. "You enjoyed it, didn't you, Aunt Jess?"

"Never thought I'd ever eat Chinese food. Quite tasty really. I surprised meself," Mum announced reluctantly. "I just hope I can keep it down—"

Then Lew gave Mum a drop of cherry brandy. She certainly kept that down. Her mood improved all the more when he switched on one of her favorite TV shows. Everyone was happy to relax and watch the box, except Kate, who wanted to go throw stones in the sea.

∼

"Granddad! It's your turn!" said Kate, smiling broadly.

Lew and I had volunteered to take her out. I was happy to go, the house had gotten a little stuffy, and it felt good to be in the sea air. We took turns with Kate throwing rocks from the railing. It was high tide and the waves were sloshing against the wall like water in a fire bucket.

"Your mother's still gutsed up about not going out last night," said Lew, growling quietly. "And if I say anything, she turns on me!"

"Same as usual then! You're used to that," I said, trying to jolly him up.

"Made a rod for me own back with her, I did. Gave her everything I could. But it was never enough. I wasn't what she wanted."

"What did she want?"

"Buggered if I know. I still don't know. Mind you, I'm bloody pleased about how things turned out for you. The things you've done. You've always done what you wanted to do, you have. I never stopped you."

"No, Dad, you didn't."

"I only ever wanted you to do one thing. And that was get in the print. And you did that. You got in. A union shop. And you didn't even have a relative to get you in. You had to take an exam, remember? And you passed! You was in. I was as proud of you as a dog with two cocks."

That was a new one, even for me. Luckily Kate was out of earshot, blissfully throwing stones in the sea. Lew went on about the importance of getting a job with security, a pension. I felt he was speaking as much for himself as he was for me. Despite the decades that separated us, we felt the knowledge of things we reluctantly shared, a knowledge of the England we both grew up in.

"You didn't last a week in the print. Not a week! What a turn up that was!" He chuckled.

After just two days on the job I was already bored. At five minutes to five my boss told me to stop the press. I told him I could complete the job in less than a minute. Again, he told me to stop the machine. To re-ink and reset for a few sheets in the morning seemed a waste of time. I had only six sheets left to print. I carried on. My boss was furious. He shut down the press. And it was not even five o'clock! Clean up time, he said. Five to five was clean up time.

Then there was the tea. According to shop rules, I could only make tea for the members of my own union. So I had to take tea to three printers from my union four flights up, and the boy on their floor brought tea down for the three members of his union on my floor. Barmy! Unfortunately, I made the mistake of saying so. Considered unruly, I was told to shut it or I would be shunned, and if I wasn't careful I'd get my testicles painted with black ink. I had just turned fifteen years old.

The following morning I called the magic shop, got my old job back, and handed in my notice. Word got out. "Don't teach him anymore," the foreman told my boss. The father of the chapel told me I was a bloody fool. On my last day, the works manager showed up and lectured me about being the first apprentice he had ever known to quit. All I could think about was getting out of the place with my balls un-inked. I left at five to five. I didn't bother cleaning up.

"At least you tried," said Lew now. "Still—"

Still. I tried to make light of it, but Lew was back there, thinking how things might have been. How I might have stayed in England, if only I had stuck it out. I reminded him, "things" had been better for me because I *hadn't* stuck it out.

Kate ran ahead of us. Colored shards, unseen images flickered on the living room window as we made our way down the garden path, toward the house. Lew stopped suddenly.

"You're happy, aren't you, son?"

"Yes, Dad, I am."

"That's all that matters." He smiled. "Come on, let's have a drink, me and thee—"

CHAPTER 24

Back to Broadstairs, on to Walmer Castle and Richborough

WEDNESDAY MORNING brought lots of hot sun. The rise in the temperature also rose our spirits. Flo was all for getting up and about. For the first time in days the house felt like a holiday home and not a hospice. The place was filled with happy chatter. I was anxious to go out and enjoy the day, but the older members of my family, except Lew, were more than content to stay put and catch up on missed gossip. Again Pam shooed us on our way. Lew jumped at the chance to come with us.

Kate and I had a yen to go for a swim. Forty five minutes later, we were back at Viking Bay in Broadstairs. We took off shoes and socks, grabbed deck chairs, and headed out across the beach. The sand massaged our feet and seeped between our toes like warm, rough silk.

While Kate and I jumped the warm bathwater waves, Frances read a book, and Lew sat nearby, a tight grip on the cane thrust into the sand. He stared out to sea, as rigid as the old Scottish sentinel ironclad to the coastguard's office on the harbor wall. I lay for a moment like a starfish on the water's surface, bobbing with the gentle ebb of the harbor waves. The sun smoothed the waves into a lake-like sheen. As I gradually turned in the water, I could see the tiny fishing fleet anchored nearby, the gold white curve of the sandy beach, the ivory cliffs like crumbly shards of Wensleydale cheese, the hat box shapes on the Victorian skyline above. Then Kate splashed me. The reverie was over. I roared with laughter and dove after her as she splashed her way back to the beach.

"Ice cream!" yelled Kate.

"I guess you're not cold!" Frances sounded amazed.

"I'm bleeding cold, I am! Cold as charity." Lew growled as he forced a smile.

The weather had changed inexplicably. A wind was now gusting. The sand underfoot felt like frozen bread crumbs. We hurried for shelter. Then the capricious wind blew away the iron-clad clouds, and the warm blue was back for the rest of the day.

"This is it! This was the fish shop I wanted to take us to last year!" I was smiling at the small, oak-paneled restaurant on the curving incline of Harbor Street. I had forgotten it was there.

"Fish local caught?" asked Lew.

"Right off the harbor wall," said the owner as he took our order.

The fish was hot, fresh, delicious. The chips crispy and golden.

"Good this is—lovely haddock," said Lew, between mouthfuls.

"Remember Mum making haddock?" I asked.

"Well, it was different from this!" He leaned slightly towards Frances to explain. "Jessie bought it already smoked, then she'd poach eggs with it. Lovely, it was."

Our memories differed somewhat. I recalled a slab of fish that looked jaundiced. Mum would submerge the haddock in a large pan of boiling water and cook it for at least an hour, until the tail curled up in a quivering gesture of surrender. The fish made my teeth shudder when I bit into it, for it possessed the texture of sliced candle wax. At least it did not taste fishy.

"It was hot," I said truthfully.

"Jessie always put out a hot dinner in the evening. Always."

And that, for Lew, was the most important thing: a hot dinner, lots of it, and bugger the taste. After lunch we walked back to the harbor, enjoying a view of the town that, for me, had mellowed in the cask of time, becoming richer, deeper with each visit.

～

Back at the house we found Jessie and Flo happily chatting about their bouts of illness as though talking about a favorite hobby. Then the conversation changed. The two sisters were now happily complaining about being cooped up. They announced they felt well enough to take a quick turn along the promenade. So be it!

Our merry band was soon back on the Deal seafront. Pam wheeled Florrie into a pleasantly bracing breeze while the rest of us watched a fishing boat being winched ashore then unload its catch. We caught up with Flo and Pam at an outdoor shellfish stand. Pam was delicately eating cockles while Flo happily forked up bits of eel with jelly clinging to the moist flesh like clusters of turquoise diamonds.

Frances found the sight of jellied eels a bit disturbing, but it started my parents and Flo reminiscing about Kelly's Pie and Eel Shop and going "down the Roman" years ago. The Roman Road had hosted their local market street, where the sisters and my Nanny loved to go. I was always bored with these shopping expeditions, and couldn't wait to pull away to Kelly's for pie and mash. I would always linger at the eel stall just outside, for some grisly entertainment.

"Just one'll do," a customer would say. Glistening and slithering with a fishy kind of mucus, an eel was extracted from an open metal box. I stood and watched, fascinated, as the fishmonger beheaded the creature, which then curled up into a shuddering horseshoe. Whacked flat, the eel's underside was sliced open, bloodied innards swiped into a bucket. The gutted eel was chopped and wrapped in blood-splattered newspaper, then handed to the customer.

After seeing eels slaughtered I never fancied eating them, jellied or not. Pie and mash was another matter. A classic East End dish. They were individual-sized pies, the pastry filled with gravy and ground beef, baked until brown and crisp on top yet with a wonderfully soft, chewy underside. When cooked, the pie was tipped out of its metal container onto a plate. A large spoon of thick mashed potato was smeared clean against the plate's rim, the mash covered in a thick, emerald green parsley sauce. The only condiments were salt and malt vinegar in big pewter containers chained to long marble-topped tables. Wooden benches worn smooth were the only seats. It was all a bit rough and ready, but the food was served quickly and tasted delicious.

"You always ended up there, you did, at Kelly's," said Lew.

"Mary, where's she gone? Mary!" Mum looked worried.

"Went 'ome. Days ago," said Lew, brusque as ever.

At least Mum knew Mary had visited.

After Pam and Flo had finished their seafood, we all tottered back to the cars and were back at the house within minutes. Suddenly Mum said her tummy was playing her up and she had to have a lie down. She did look a little flushed. I helped her upstairs. Lew hovered solicitously.

"I'll be alright, I'll be alright," Mum kept saying. She even smiled.

"Well, you better be!" said Lew as he propped up her pillows.

I went back downstairs. Ten minutes later Lew came down, looking troubled.

"She feels queer. Worse than normal. She says she hasn't settled." Lew was distraught. He looked at Pam. "Do you think you could give us a ride home, girl?"

"I could, but won't she be alright in the morning?"

Lew shook his head. Pam, Lew, and I all trooped upstairs. Mum was propped up in bed in pink satin sleepwear, smiling bravely as her audience clustered around her bedside.

"It's no good," she whispered loudly. "I want to go home. Feel lousy. Rotten!"

"You need a rest, Aunt Jess. Let me open the window." Pam was back in nurse mode. She poured water. Fluffed pillows. She took Mum's temperature. Mum tapped Pam's hand.

"Thank you, Pam. I thank you—" Mum sounded sad, a faraway look on her face. "I need to rest, to sleep—"

Pam and I shuffled out of what was now Mum's sickroom. Lew stayed with her. A few minutes later, he came back down, shaking his head. "It's no good. She won't budge. I tried. Gawd help me, I tried! You talk to her."

"I thought she was nodding off. Going to have a nap." I was a little confused.

"Wide awake, she is! Wide awake as a bleeding alarm clock! Nothing wrong with her!"

I went up to see for myself. When I saw her, she did not look ill, just morose. I thought, perhaps she was feeling short-changed. We'd all been lavishing care and concern on Florrie. Her night out had been thwarted. Worse yet, we had gone out and left her to spear balls of pork in a livid red sauce. Even so, this was all a bit much.

"Might as well go home. Pam's going." Mum sounded forlorn but adamant.

"We came over to see you and Dad, Mum, and for you to see your granddaughter."

"Well, I've seen you now, haven't I."

I was momentarily taken aback by her casual indifference, her selfishness. I wanted to say I knew she was shamming, knew she was jealous of someone who was genuinely sick. But I remembered how distraught Lew was and how much he wanted to stay. I looked at her and suddenly realized I wanted her to stay, too.

"It's alright for Florrie; she's got Pam. What have I got? I haven't got a Pam, have I!"

"You've got Dad. He looks after you," I said forcefully.

"Not the same, is it? Not the same—"

Mum wanted a Pam, a caring daughter who lived in. But all she had was me and Tony. Sons. Far away. Far apart. I sat and listened to her complaints. Then she went on about her ailments. Bilious, she said, then added she was "gastric," as if that explained everything.

"I'm sorry you feel so bad, Mum. Really. But I'm hoping you'll feel better in the morning. It would be such a shame if you went home now. I'd miss you. I really, really would. And we've got to have at least one or two evenings out, don't you think? By ourselves. Just the five of us. Yes?"

"I wish I had me Epsom salts. That always works me right through. Clears me out, it does."

"Try some of this—" I waggled a bottle of pink stuff. I could tell her resolve was weakening.

"You take that?"

I told her I took a lot of it. Especially on that trip, though I didn't say that. She picked up the pink bottle and took a big swig. She smiled and said she really was tired, and I finally believed her. She said a good night's sleep would do her good. She would see how she felt in the morning, and decide then.

~

Later that evening, Lew and I walked along the seafront, looking at the lights in the distance. I tried to reassure him the danger was past, Mum would stay. I told him I had made a bit of a fuss over her. I had listened to her, if only for a few minutes. It was probably all she wanted.

"I nearly strangled her once."

"Who?" I asked, thick as a brick.

"Your mother," said Lew, quietly.

"Oh, really?"

Oh, really. I couldn't believe that's what I'd said. It was not what I was thinking. I was not thinking at all. Perhaps he wanted me to ask him why or how or when, but I simply muttered oh, really…oh, dear…oh…well, then words failed. Lew filled in the blanks. Only his blanks were loaded.

"I was just standing there one evening. She was rapping on about something, and suddenly, suddenly, I just couldn't hear her anymore. Bearing down on her, I was, with me hands around her throat. She didn't try to do anything—didn't try to stop me, like. As if she accepted it."

"And?"

"Then I saw what I was doing and I stopped. I sat there with her on the floor for a moment, then I helped her up. Begged her forgiveness. She said nothing. Not a word. So I made her a cup of tea. Then went to work."

"You went to work?"

"I was working nights then. And you know what's bloody funny? When I got home next morning, it was like nothing had happened. She never mentioned it again, not once. Not ever."

He smiled slightly, shook his head as though disbelieving his memory. I thought his desire to strangle his wife, however fleeting, stranger than her ensuing reticence, but I said nothing.

"Did you ever again, with Mum—" I inquired casually about subsequent homicidal urges.

"Oh, no, no, it was just the once!" He sounded almost cheerful, very matter-of-fact.

Our evening walks had become confessionals. Cast in the unwanted role of frockless or feckless priest, I never knew what to say. So I just listened. His marriage, his hankering for exotic religions, the poetry, and now, the attempted murder of my old mum—why was he telling me all this? Perhaps Lew's revelations, like Mum's illness, were his way to articulate the loneliness he felt. I asked him if he fancied a drop of Jack before going to bed. Before he could reply, I assured him that I most certainly did.

~

Eeee. Eeee. EEEEEEEEEEEEEEEEEEEE.

The alarm at Walmer Castle sounded like a high-pitched monkey screeching at high speed. Kate was standing beyond a thick red plaited cord she should not have crossed, staring at a door she should not have tried to open. As I retrieved my daughter, the alarm seemed to whoop and screech all the more. A young security guard came sprinting down the long corridor towards us. She was a very young woman, tall and thin with a pleasantly angular face and long, straight dark hair. She looked like a student in a guard's uniform. She quickly took in the scene, eyed the young culprit, and smiled. Then we heard jangled voices on her walkie-talkie.

"All clear. Standing down. Standing down." She switched off the com-device that continued to cackle and splutter in her hand. "She whisked back a curtain revealing a gray alarm box, inserted a key, and the electronic monkey ceased to chatter.

"You can't go in there, I'm afraid. That's the Queen Mum's private apartment. She'll be here tomorrow. She's the Warden of the Cinque Ports."

Kate was far more interested in the attendant than the imminent arrival of aging royalty. She asked the guard her name.

"My name's Kate. What's yours?"

Kate beamed. They had the same name! Moments later, little Kate's new friend was taking us on a guided tour of the almost deserted castle. A nice way to keep our daughter on the right side of the red ropes. Frances asked lots of questions, and we happily lingered without seeing another soul.

Although Walmer Castle shared Deal Castle's austere design, it had adapted to a time when invasion threats were taken a little less seriously. Beyond the round bailey, living quarters had been added. For hundreds of years Walmer had been the official home of the Warden of the Cinque Ports, then the Queen Mother. In the middle of the nineteenth century, the honorary title was bestowed upon the Duke of Wellington. We visited his apartments, meticulously preserved. And something else. Within an hour or two of Wellington's demise at Walmer Castle, the local undertaker had applied some kind of plaster goo to the poor old sod's face to obtain a likeness. So the thin lips, toothless mouth, incredibly long nose, and sunken cheeks of one of England's greatest military heroes were preserved for all time. And it was still there. Wellington's death mask, propped up on a bedside table, beside a candlestick, like a Halloween novelty.

"You made it back in time, then," said Jessie, smiling merrily.

We had left my folks, Pam, and Florrie in the castle's teashop. Earlier that morning, the all-clear had been sounded. Mum had made an amazing recovery and decided to stay. The storm cloud had passed. Lew was happy. Pam was taking Flo home, but they had joined us at Walmer Castle for one last natter. My elderly relatives weren't charged admission by the considerate museum keepers, after we explained they would not be taking the tour with us. They had been quite content to sit while we gadded about the place, soaking up history and innocently tripping alarms.

"Seen all you want to see then?" asked Lew, predictably.

We recounted the highlights of the castle but they were only interested in Kate's adventure. Kate the guard gave Kate the intruder a good-bye hug, and our multi-generational caravan slowly made its way back to the cars.

"Well, Aunt Jess, we'd better make a move," said Pam. "See what Tom's up to."

"Tom? Is Tom like him?" Mum pointed to Lew.

"I wish he was like Lew, I really do."

"You can have him, if you want him! Take him! I can't get a good night's sleep with him, all bones, he is. Bones sticking in me. Like sleeping in a graveyard, sleeping with him."

Ghrrr.

Flo apologized again about her "turn for the worse," regretting any inconvenience she had caused. I told her we were glad she had stayed and had recovered so nicely. I liked her. I was sad to see how the years had weighed her down. One day, she insisted, she would be herself again. One day.

"So long, Katie! Look after your mum and dad," said Flo, in a hoarse but friendly whisper.

"Flo! Flo! You're my sister," Mum gripped Flo's hand tightly, as though clinging to a memory. Flo tapped Jessie's arm and said she and Pam would visit when things were back to normal. We waved good-bye and headed back to the house.

Later that afternoon, we decided to go back into Sandwich. We walked near the banks of the Stour that gently meandered around the ancient port town before flowing into a maze of marshland, as if to delay its final rendezvous with the sea at Pegwell Bay, a few miles away. Here we found a quieter, more residential part of the old town. Down both sides of one street, the houses were fat with age, lolling over the narrow sidewalks like nosy neighbors checking who was coming and going. Outside one house, bunches of flowers were piled on a bench. A sign informed us that the flowers were two pounds per bunch, and money should be put in the plate. We put down our money, and Frances selected a bunch of Sweet William from this absent but trusting flower seller.

Walking back to the car we found an Indian restaurant, so for the second time that week we ordered the usual spicy mix of platters, and roast chicken for Kate. When we got back, Kate presented the flowers to a beaming nanny. More smiles appeared when Jessie and Lew found out Indian food was back on the menu.

After dinner and a bit of playdough sculpting, Kate went up without a fuss to what was finally her room. Then Jessie tottered off to bed after a bit of telly.

"Don't stay up late," said Frances as she took to the stairs a little later, waving goodnight.

I padded into the living room and stretched out as Lew set shot glasses before the huge, diminishing bottle of Jack. Using both hands he carefully poured out the soothing amber. I took a breath.

Another nightcap of nightmares! Then again, it was hard to imagine he could have much else to confess. We talked about where I lived, things we did. I talked of our friends, how much I liked America. He stopped me suddenly. He spoke quickly, as if he might forget what he was about to say.

"You know, I've realized why I hated the Americans. It was in the war. I was jealous. Jealous I was, and it stayed with me. For years. You see, son, we were a ragtag lot. Uniforms, equipment... and boots barely fit. Had to scrounge a pair that came close to fitting. But the Americans, they were properly kitted out. And the food they had! Never saw anything like it. My lads were hungry. I got this truck, drove it over to the American sector. I told 'em what was up. They filled up the truck with food. I used to see their quartermaster, regular like. He fixed me up, all the grub I ever wanted. Called me the bee's knees. I called him a mug."

"They were generous, Dad."

"Yeah, I suppose they were. And I suppose they could see what a bleedin' state we were in. Could've rubbed our noses in it. Could've told us to eff off out of it. But they didn't."

"They were being friendly. We were allies, after all."

"Yeah, taken me all this time to see that. Funny, innit? And when I saw how wonderful America's been for you. Well, it changed my opinion of the Yanks, I can tell you."

"Took you long enough."

~

The following morning, Lew said if he and Jessie were feeling adventurous they might totter across the road and stare at the sea. We should go off and do whatever it was that made us happy. He spoke of our touring and sightseeing as he always did, as if it were some strange, incomprehensible rite of passage. Frances, her enthusiasm for ancient history undaunted, had found yet another Roman fort to assail. Fine. It was not far away, just beyond Sandwich, quite close to home base.

"Rutupiae? Sounds like an expensive vegetable," I grinned at my cleverness.

"Very funny."

We drove through Sandwich and crossed the river Stour, passing beneath the old Barbican Gate. From the time of King Canute, this gate until recent time had been collecting toll money. Built in the fourteenth century, the gate was enclosed within a large, squat medieval tower with red-hued walls and a conical roof that looked like a misplaced part of Carcassonne. Beyond the gatehouse, the road dipped and soon joined a much larger one connecting the coastal towns of Thanet. We took a much smaller road, signposted for Richborough, and eventually pulled up in a small graveled area by a wooden hut that served as a ticket office, gift shop, and museum for Britain's oldest Roman site.

Despite its size and archaeological importance, Richborough Fort attracted few visitors. We only saw one other car. Caesar may have landed a few miles away at Deal, but it was the Emperor Claudius who actually completed the invasion of Britain ninety years later. His legions made landfall at a place they named Rutupiae, which later became known as Richborough. We stood beside the trenches they had dug, part of a fort that held the inhabitants safe for centuries.

Beyond the earthwork were the remains of a small Christian chapel built towards the end of Roman rule. We also came upon foundations and walls of a fort built some three hundred years after the initial invasion. The structures were encrusted with stony protuberances, like toothless faces imbedded in the concrete stonework. Concrete. Invented by Romans, the stuff still played a vital part in our modern lives; it somehow narrowed the distance and connected their time with ours. The walls were massive, big enough to keep marauding Saxons at bay and protect an army of civil servants and administrators. For it was from here that Rome ruled over most of Britain.

Frances and Kate headed to the museum and gift shop to view cracked bits of pottery and fragile-looking utensils, and to find a Roman toy for Kate. I decided to remain on the battlements to enjoy the brisk salty breeze coming off the sea-drenched marsh. With the river snaking past, I could imagine how the fort looked when the sea lapped closer and Roman triremes harbored nearby.

The views from the other battlement were less evocative. I saw the cooling towers of a disused power station. Closer in, the view became worse. Puffing smoke and covered in plastic tubing and metal ventilation pipes, a large chemical plant stood before me like a disemboweled office block. A tufty-haired, mottle-faced man in a quilted anorak sidled up to me.

"Viagra," he said cryptically.

"What?" I asked, surprised.

"That's where they invented it."

"Really?"

My slightly indecent docent made a couple of lewd gestures, no doubt expecting a nudge in the ribs and a yuk-yuk laugh. I slowly moved away and looked back at the site. If only they could have planted trees to hide the pipes, cover the gaskets, the fencing—

◠

"Been a week," said Lew, raising his Guinness to us. "Ended up alright, though, didn't it?"

We were in the King's Arms, a pub in Sandwich founded around 1580, enjoying a fine traditional meal of meat pies and fresh vegetables. For dessert, a light and fluffy toffee pudding, glistening with copper-colored treacle and a rich, warm, pourable custard was placed before me. The perfect end to dinner. We raised the last of our wine. A toast to Flo. On reflection, the week had, indeed, not turned out too badly. We had gone back to Broadstairs, discovered castles, and enjoyed the quiet charms of Sandwich. Seen more ruins. And I had spent time with my folks.

When we got back to Deal, Kate went up to bed. Downstairs, we talked a little about our visit to Richborough. Then I told Lew we would be turning in early. I said I needed to pack, but I just didn't want to hear any more. Lew nodded silently, raised his hand as if to indicate that whatever I wanted was okay with him. Then I relented. I quickly poured a couple of drinks. We remained standing as though in a pub, having one for the road. In a way, we were.

"Tony," said Lew, gazing at his drink, "Your brother's gawn and taken away our whiskey—"

"What? What whiskey?"

"Me and your mother, when we get a bit down, we have a session with the whiskey, and then we have a laugh, and have a good cry—"

"Christ, Dad, what were you thinking? Mum's not a whiskey drinker. It makes her go mad!"

"That's what Tony said," answered Lew quietly. "Poured it all out, he did. Every last drop. Shouldn't have bothered his arse. We're not getting better, getting worse! And I won't be a burden, I won't be a burden to anyone. Your mother feels the same. That's why we've got a suicide pact."

"A what?" I stared, and words rushed through my head faster than I could speak them.

"A suicide pact. Me and your mother. Oh, it's alright, I've already told our social worker," Lew went on reassuringly. "She was a bit taken aback when I told her, mind."

"I'm not surprised."

"Shame about all that whiskey, though. But don't worry, I'll make sure nothing comes a cropper with this lovely drop of stuff!"

"That's a relief."

Lew savored his drink and breathed its vapors as if he had just stepped into an icy wind. But he was smiling. I had never seen Lew so cheerful. We finished our drinks, and, before we slowly ambled towards the stairs, he gave me a two-hand handshake and wished me goodnight.

CHAPTER 25

In Windsor and Eton

GRAY MAN showed up mid-morning. While he checked over the house, Lew and I walked Kate across the street to throw one last bunch of pebbles into the turning tide.

Plop.

"You've been good, my son. Listening to me going on this week." Lew smiled.

"You are a bit of worry, aren't you," I said, fearfully.

Plop. Plop.

"Don't worry, we'll go on, your mother and me. We'll happily nag each other to death!"

"Well, that's alright, then."

Plop. Plop. Plop.

We used up our stones. Kate waved to the sea. We turned back to the house and regained our deposit money. Gray Man never asked if we enjoyed our visit, although he did check the padlocked phone. Still dead. We didn't bother complaining.

As soon as we got to Dagenham, I went upstairs to my old bedroom for my annual last look. This time I was surprised. Beside the bed were some of Lew's books. Also, his hairbrush and hair cream. I found some of his clothes in my old wardrobe. He had moved in. I asked Lew about it when I got back downstairs. When did you move into my old room? Ages ago, he said. Why? He disturbed Jessie. And she didn't like him reading late. So that's that! I did not push.

After a last cup of tea with my folks, the three of us headed to Windsor to relax and unwind.

~

Something new. The only way to our hotel was through a pedestrian-only roadway. What were we expected to do? We sat there for a minute, then decided to chance it. We'd been promised parking, after all. We drove down the car-free street, feeling like smokers in an organic restaurant. We pulled up in front of the Christopher Wren House Hotel, also situated on a pedestrian-only street. We spotted a teeny tiny arch that led to an inner courtyard car park. I sighed.

The receptionist was most understanding. "No problem, sir, give us the car keys; we'll take it from here. Don't worry."

Our room was delightful, airy and comfortable, decorated in an early Georgian style. On a low table by the large oblong window was a complimentary fruit basket, a bottle of designer water, and a reassuring decanter of dry sherry. Frances was very pleased. We all were.

We were right in the curve of the Thames, at its prettiest and leafiest. We ambled around, enjoying the mellow warmth of the late afternoon sun, following the crowds that flowed towards the park-like settings that led to the banks of the river.

As we crossed the Eton Bridge, the river beneath us flowed with all the languid gentleness of maple syrup. Our pace slowed accordingly. Just beyond the wine bars and restaurants clustered around the Eton bank of the Thames, we lost the crowds and found the quiet and privacy of a pretty English village. Down tiny courts bordered by vast rose bushes and old gas lamps encased in big glass lanterns, we discovered cream-colored Georgian houses with tall windows, framed by wrought-iron fences. Almost hidden were Tudor cottages sandwiched between Victorian storefronts and funny little shops. One tiny store sold nothing but cat-based paraphernalia, with tea cozies, placemats, cups, creamers—naturally—and spoons and bowls and teapots and coasters. Everything was fair game for a cat paw, cat shape, or cat design. Hard to imagine a place could survive just by selling to feline fans, but there it was. We thought of Oscar, our large black cat, and smiled.

Blissfully lazy and not wanting to scour around in search of dinner, we decided to eat in our hotel's restaurant and enjoy its delightful view of the river. Originally the home of Christopher Wren, the architect of the Restoration who built London's Saint Paul's Cathedral, the hotel that now bore his name had preserved all the characteristics of the grand old home he had designed.

The evening sunlight shone with warmth and softness, and the river scene was perfect. Small pleasure boats chugged beneath the soot-black arches of the Eton Bridge. Rowboats were moored on the opposite bank. We had dinner on the terrace. Between courses, we watched people stroll from one riverbank to the other, stopping to see the swans glide through the warm, pink shards of sunlight reflected on the water's surface. The sun seemed reluctant to leave this tranquil scene, and so was everyone else.

Dinner was over all too quickly. The river backdrop, the warmth of the evening, and the delightful ambiance of the terrace had been enough to keep us in smiles through each course. Afterwards, we strolled up the hill into the town. A whiff of anarchy was in the air, tension was cracking the evening's tranquility. The streets below the castle, just beyond the hotel, were teeming with inebriated, half-naked soccer fans displaying huge Union Jacks. As if we had any doubt as to what team they supported. Lines of police stood on sidewalks. Streets were cordoned off. I asked a constable if he expected trouble.

"It'll be alright, I should think. England won!"

England had won. We decided to avoid dropping into any pubs and ended our evening, quite pleasantly, in the hotel's comfy bar. Later, we heard roars and yelling and some occasional shouts of "England," but none of it stopped us from getting a great night's sleep.

~

"Oh, look! Over thaar! Thaar's a doe! Do look, I'm shaah it's a doe! Over thaar!"

A large voice carried with aristocratic authority right across the length and breadth of the breakfast room. We had chosen a table by a window so we could eat and watch the swans take their morning promenade. Frances was already sitting, drinking coffee, when Kate and I joined her, carrying plates of sausage and eggs.

"Oh, Kate, that man said there's a doe out there—she must mean a swan. Want to look?" said Frances, looking out the window. Kate ran to the window while I looked around. The only swan-gazer was a woman of middle years in a silky top and tailored blue pants.

"What man?" I asked.

"Yaah, I'm shaah it's a doe!" the swan-gazer said again.

Frances turned to look, not quite believing her eyes. Or her ears. For although Swan Lady sounded like a pantomime dame with a voice burnished by years of drinking single malt, she really was a woman. A reedy looking thing, with severely straight hair, a long, thin, curved neck, and a pointed chin. She mirrored the creatures she was watching quite perfectly.

From the hotel patio, Kate and I walked down to a small gate that led onto the embankment. Feeding ducks or swans had become one of those things we did together when we were in England. The swans came from all points. They knew something was up. When we opened the bag the restaurant had given us, we discovered not bread crusts but patisserie treats—brioche, apple Danish, cinnamon buns. No wonder the huge white birds were gliding down on us as fast as a fleet of feathered hydrofoils.

"They're owned by the Queen, you know. Every one."

A squat little girl with a suspicious look had sidled up close to us. Her red socks were rumpled, and she wore a PVC rain mac over a print dress.

"Which ones are the Queen's?" I asked, trying to be friendly.

"They are all owned by the Queen. Every one," the girl said, darkly. "If you kill one of them, the penalty is death!" She pronounced "death" as in "deaf."

"Well, we'll be sure not kill any, just feed them, alright?"

"I suppose—" The girl began kicking pebbles into the water.

"Do you want some bread?" asked Kate.

The child shook her head, then turned and walked away. Odd. Kate shrugged and carried on feeding the birds. They slopped up croissants like gannets eating fish.

~

Windsor was putting on a show for its most illustrious resident. Red, white, and blue bunting crisscrossed street after street. Pictures of the Queen were everywhere, as well as homemade signs saying "Happy Birthday, Ma'am!" Union Jacks and other patriotic motifs hung from every other window. A carnival-like atmosphere filled the streets.

We wove our way through the patient throngs. The crowds were growing. Both sides of the High Street were now lined thick and deep. For a better view, we climbed the stairs to the town hall, unusually stilted on brick pillars. The huge reception hall was open and, not being told otherwise, we ambled inside the vestibule that overlooked the street.

I think it was a private gathering, but no one told us to leave. We were surrounded by flower-hatted ladies in tartan pleated skirts squired by chaps in top hats and tailcoats talking in that nasally, almost strangled pitch of the English upper class. Some were characters right out of Dickens, with pudding-round faces and greasy tops, or long ears like pulled pastry. Pinched-faced ferret types listened and nodded to fellows with heart-attack red complexions. A woman with a ski jump chin conversed with a man whose nostrils appeared longer and narrower than slits in a toaster. And dotted within this fruitcake mix were soldiers in crimson and gold dress uniforms with sashes and swords. All jammed together in happy accord. And, of course, a military band was playing nearby, raising, we felt sure, the odd lump in many a throat.

And why not? It was, after all, a day for pomp and patriotism. The Royal Standard flew, the Queen was in residence. Her birthday. The event seemed to bring out all the classes of English life. And whether they were in reception halls or on street corners, they all gravitated to their various stations without rancor. No one felt deprived, no one left out. And, somewhat caught up in it all, my little family was having a lot of fun. And so was I.

We squeezed our way out of the Guild Hall. On Castle Hill, a horde of slightly dumpy ladies of a certain age bustled with gently contained exuberance towards the castle gates. I saw no end to this procession of wavy blue hair. Most of the ladies wore dangerously tight, shiny print dresses, little hats with starched bits of veil, and long cotton gloves. We found out they had been invited to a garden party within the castle grounds. They were very excited and seemed to clack and flap at each other with great enthusiasm. Apart from different dress patterns, the ladies looked remarkably similar, as if they were in a queenie look-alike contest, only they never knew it.

After a relaxing lunch in a small Italian restaurant, we took a boat trip up the Thames. It was a wonderful little voyage. We followed the soft curves and undulations of the grassy embankments that bordered the languid milky green flow of the river quite perfectly. People were out boating, strolling the towpaths, feeding the ducks, fishing, pushing prams. Some stopped and waved as we gently chugged past them. At last, I had discovered the perfect way to see the river.

Too soon for our liking, our little river cruiser turned in a huge arc and swung back. On our return to Windsor, we chugged past small, thickly wooded islands. Every now and then, waterfowl ventured forth paddling in elegantly feathered convoys. I could barely imagine this was the same Thames that flowed past my old home in industrial Dagenham, where only rainbow-colored patches of oil rippled the river's surface.

After docking beneath the dark crescents of the Eton Bridge, we walked back along the river, beside a row of beech trees and a curving willow. The sun was setting, shimmering pink across the surface of the Thames. The last of the light illuminated the leaves of the trees, weaving black threads of shadow between them, like intricately sewn lace.

We walked past our hotel and climbed back up the hill to the castle.

The Queen's birthday celebration was over, but many garden party ladies were still clustered around the cobblestones on Castle Hill. No doubt fortified by cucumber sandwiches and, perhaps, the odd drop of Bombay Blue, these regal look-alikes milled about, trying to prolong the excitement of the day as long as they could. One such lady brandished her printed invitation at us. Neither snobbish or aloof, just eager to share her experience, her excitement, with anyone who would listen. We were happy to lend an ear.

"I couldn't see Her Majesty," she said, quite honestly. "But I did see the top of her hat as she went by. Lovely, isn't she! Lovely day for it though, isn't it?"

Her sensible shoes had yet to touch the ground.

~

The following morning, we made an early start, but not before our last English breakfast. The journey to Heathrow was fast and easy. As always, I called my folks just prior to boarding. I spoke first to Jessie, and asked after Flo.

"It's funny how Flo got sick, and then I got sick as well!" said Mum, merrily.

"I know, Mum, but you're better now, aren't you?" I could feel Lew rolling his eyes.

"I'm always better when I'm home! Now, where you off to then?"

"Home, Mum! We're off home!"

Then I spoke to Lew. I reassured him everything had turned out fine. I wasn't sure how much he heard. Or how much he believed. But it was true. Despite everything, I had enjoyed seeing more of the country in which I once lived. I no longer felt the constant urge to escape. And somehow, in that metamorphosis from native to tourist, something of the country, something of my parents and myself was becoming entwined, binding me anew. Family. People. Places. All of it, closer than I had ever imagined.

"Next year! You talking about next year? Ah, my Gawd! Let's get over this one first!" Lew sounded out of breath. I think he was trying not to laugh.

"Oh, it wasn't so bad! Just don't get sick, and you'll both be alright," I said.

Ghrrr.

YEAR SIX

A Regency Cottage on a Bridle Path

CHAPTER 26

From Cuckfield to the Hundred Acre Wood

THE SKY WAS BRIGHT and, despite Lew's dire warning, the weather looked promising. I looked up and grinned as we left the airport. Not bad, I thought, not bad at all. Nothing above us but a few fluffy clouds. Landing at Gatwick, in the Southern Home Counties, put us within striking distance of our final destination, and close to our first one.

The Hilton House, located just beyond the village of Cuckfield, had nothing to do with the hotel chain. We smiled as we drove up through the tree-lined grounds to the parking lot. Gently converted into a private hotel, the Victorian country mansion remained very much intact. The hallways were comfortably furnished, the lounges had lots of settees and overstuffed armchairs, and there was a music room with a baby grand. An intimate bar was located beside a delightful conservatory filled with pineapple plants, orchids, and a wide array of exotic foliage. Glass doors to tumbling rose shrubs, climbing vines, and a carpet of green. Stone birdbaths were surrounded by islands of geraniums, well-weathered park benches, and a picnic table perfectly placed to enjoy the spectacular views beyond the garden. Unmarred by any building, the Sussex Downs rolled out before us, like waves of green racing to meet the shiny turquoise sea some fifteen miles beyond.

Of course, nothing is perfect. We peeked into some bedrooms on the spacious first floor landing; they had high ceilings and were wonderfully appointed with four-poster beds. Rooms for couples traveling alone. We were given the original servants' quarters at the very top of the house. Even though our "family" room was huge and filled with charming furniture, we were still in the attic, at the top of a long narrow staircase.

"They've put us in with the servants, madam!" I groaned rather dramatically.

"Must have known you were from Dagenham," Frances smiled.

In spite of myself, I grinned back.

Dinner that evening was served in the original dining room. Most appropriate. I had a succulent fillet of lamb, Frances had a tenderloin of pork, and Kate had a hamburger, which made her very happy indeed. Oddly, we had to order our food forty-five minutes before coming into the restaurant. A quaint English ritual, but there it was.

After dinner, we took the remains of our wine to the patio and watched the sun make its slow descent beyond the mottled emerald line of box and oak.

~

After a sumptuous breakfast, the following morning we headed out to Sheffield Park, home of the Bluebell Railway and its working steam trains, with a restored track stretching to Horsted Keynes twenty miles away. Sheffield Park was a beautifully preserved country train station, thronged with more people than it ever saw on its busiest day as a stop on a small branch line. Many unprofitable lines were closed in the late nineteen fifties, and this was one of them, but a preservation society later reopened the rail line, attracting steam train enthusiasts of all ages.

We joined crowds of people and loads of families with young children. Lots of smiles and squeals of anticipation all around. On one platform we found a restored station buffet, tall cast-iron girders, wooden eaves, big glass windows, polished tea urns, and a big marble counter. We peered in, then took off, looking for trains! We climbed aboard a luxurious Pullman, an old Great Western restaurant car, and one or two freight cars. Beyond the sidings were locomotive sheds, a museum, and another station buffet. So much to see. Kate got on the footplate of another train's engine as it stood beneath a water tower getting a drink, then she took off for a ride on a miniature train.

By then we all wanted a trip on a train—a proper train! Two were running that day, one with an engine over a hundred and thirty years old. After buying return tickets, "round trip" Frances called them, we walked the length of the platform, eyeing the waiting train, debating where to sit. As there was no surcharge, we decided to travel first class. Inside our carriage, the framed mirrors were of etched glass, leather straps lifted or lowered wood-framed windows. Walnut-framed maps adorned the compartment. Polished brass fittings sparkled. Lace doilies draped the headrests. Kate particularly liked the footrests. The seats were as large and comfortable as armchairs, upholstered in spiky royal blue velvet. Gold braid tassels held back curtains. A small side table stood beneath the window with a vase holder for flowers. This was the way to travel!

A whistle blew, a flag waved, the train hissed. Engine wheels spun until they caught traction, and our car juddered and shook ever so slightly. We were on our way.

When I was a kid, steam trains were still in service, wheezing, smoking, billowing steam, and sounding like metallic raspberries. Holiday trips with Jessie and Lew always started at one of London's main-line terminus stations, Victoria Station for the South Coast or Paddington for the West Country. Large, glass-covered edifices, filthy from the soot of locomotive smoke built up over the great age of steam, a gummy-brown legacy of times gone by.

As the trains slowly pulled out of the station, the soiled backsides of buildings and bile-colored embankment walls would pass before me. The air was always thick and soot-ridden, but the train cut through it all, moving farther, faster, below iron-girded bridges with hints of street life above. Concrete-and-brick gullies, gorges, and tiny road tunnels gave way to suburban back gardens; red flashes from London Transport trains slithered this way and that and were gone. A signal box. More houses, walls of bricks, wooden posts. Faster and faster. Green embankments on either side of the train were the winged flights of the arrow that sped us forward, straight and true. Clickety-click, clickety-click. Never stopping. Small villages, county towns came and went, hurtling by in a hushed scream.

Heavy grease, coal soot, and tangy smoke. The smells I remembered most were stirred again, years later, in Sheffield Park.

~

Our vintage train chugged out of the platform, billowing thick smoke, puffing and spluttering along, unhurried by timetables. We had to close the window every time we passed under a bridge or went through a small tunnel. But when we could, we leaned out the windows, enjoying miles of magical woodland and embankments tumbled with wildflowers. Tall grasses and hollyhocks seemed to sprout from the sides of soot-red bridges. Regiments of pink and purple foxglove stood to attention as we passed by and aptly, great swaths of bluebells gently swayed in the train's wake.

On the return from Horsted Keynes we stopped off at the recently restored Kingscote Station and ambled around the platform. The trains and stations were maintained and run by members of the preservation society. One old chap in period garb was busily sweeping the platform. He wore a blue-striped shirt, a red polka dot kerchief around his neck, big blue dungarees, and a peaked oil cloth cap. The station porter was quite happy to stop and talk to us. He had a rich, sonorous voice, a voice I had heard before but could not place.

"You don't sound much like a porter." I smiled.

"We're all volunteers, actually. You know, Preservation Society. We just re-opened this station as a matter of fact. Quite derelict. We've been fixing it up. A bit of a job, as you might imagine. Come with me. You won't believe this."

He led us down to a tunnel beneath the rail bed connecting both platforms. An Aladdin's cave of shiny white porcelain bricks plastered and lined with very ancient enameled, baked metal posters for Camp coffee, baking powder, soap, cigarettes, and products long gone from shops. Kate particularly liked the Fry's chocolate poster.

"It was completely filled in," our friendly guide explained. "Didn't even know it was there until someone found the beginning of the steps. Quite a job of excavation, as you can imagine."

"Wonderfully preserved," I said.

"Isn't it just!" he exclaimed. "A perfect record of an another era!"

"Why did they fill it in?" Frances asked reasonably.

"Haven't the foggiest idea!" The volunteer porter chuckled like a big old walrus.

We said our good-byes, the porter went back to sweeping the platform, and we caught the next train back to Sheffield Park. Then I remembered. He was an actor I had seen on the box, years ago, but never in a role he played with such relish.

~

"Kate will love it. I will love it! We can see the actual locations she has read about!"

Truth be told, Winnie the Pooh was an enthusiasm I had come to recently, with my daughter. As a boy, I knew nothing of Christopher Robin or, for that matter, the Railway Children, or Narnia, or Mister Toad and the other river bankers. In fact, I hardly knew any children's books at all.

My parents bought me toys and I had lots of stuffed animals, but books rarely made it onto my list. After baby books, I didn't know interesting kids' books existed, and I don't think my parents did either. Yet all the books I read to Kate were in the library at my old school, and at the children's public library in Dagenham. All I needed was a library card. And to get a library card, all I had to do was recite the alphabet. Easy peasy. Anyone could do that. Anyone, that is, except me. Absurdly, I always fumbled the test. The annoying thing was, by the time I was seven, I could read quite well but still could not memorize the alphabet.

I took the test every other week, and every other week I failed. Finally it happened. Despite a few pauses and the odd stutter or two, I made it through to zed and got my library card. I was ten years old by then, and too old for whimsical tales of river creatures and bears with a fondness for hunny. So, along with Kate, I had recently discovered a wonderful pantheon of children's literature. And now, on a sunny day in June, we had a chance to visit Pooh Corner, find the Enchanted Place. Quite impossible to pass up.

Hartfield was on the bottom edge of Ashdown Forest, a small, pretty village with a teashop, a couple of pubs, and a few stores, one of which had been renamed Pooh Corner. The very same tuck shop where A. A. Milne's son, the real-life Christopher Robin, once got his weekly ration of sweets. Every bit of available space in the tiny shop was devoted to Pooh and his pals. From doorstops to gob stoppers, everything was emblazoned with the bear. Everything. Even so, the shop had retained its charm, and I could easily imagine Milne and his son ambling in from their summer home, just a little way up the hill. We decided to continue onward for the Hundred Acre Wood and Roo's Sandpit—the Enchanted Place!

We parked and set off on foot in search of that fabled glade, in actuality the Five Hundred Acre Wood. The Ashdown Forest was not just a huge clump of trees but, rather, a wild mix of sandstone ridges, gullies, cracked stone openings, and scrubby moorland. The upward path was banked by trees and covered in soft golden fern and leaf mold. After about fifteen minutes, the path opened to a clearing surrounded by huge boulders, like cliffs squeezed together on a coastline. Below we saw the sandy bottom, Roo's sandpit. We walked around the dense woodland and rocky outcrop and found a way down. I looked around and smiled. Silence. It was so still.

Kate, of course, was far too busy playing in the sand to get caught up in my literary imaginings. Frances rolled her eyes. After a bit, we carried on. Somewhere in the Ashdown Forest was a statue of Winnie the Pooh. We never found it, but we did find a plaque dedicated to A. A. Milne, tucked away in a semi-circle of trees, almost hidden, overshadowed by the forest he immortalized, those acres of woods he planted in the imagination of so many.

~

On Saturday morning we made our way toward a real country cottage in a tiny village not too far from the sea. Our rental home was close to Sandwich, the delightful, historic town we had enjoyed so much the previous year. Familiarity, I hoped, could also breed contentment. I would soon find out.

Our keyholder had said to take a turn at a "kind of crossroads," and there would be a signpost for Hammill. Sure enough, we found an old, white wooden sign, pointing down a one-lane road burgeoning with fat clumps of grass on either side. Following the tiny lane, we drove past a magnificent estate with stables. Frances stared wistfully at the house, Kate longingly at the horses.

We passed barns and farm buildings, then the lane turned into an even smaller, graveled track. Moments later, we reached a small row of old, farm worker cottages flanked on either side by a woodland glade, shrubs, and bushes, peppered with bluebells. The one at the end was Madrigal Cottage. Our home for the week. I pulled up on the small driveway. This was it. Storybook England. I had finally turned to the page I always wanted to see. The one I always imagined.

We got out of the car, and I just stood there for a moment. The walls were plastered and whitewashed, secured in part by a cross of black iron staples. On the little garden wall and in front of the house were tubs of geraniums and clusters of irises and daisies. Bordering the cottage, as if to celebrate our arrival, a sprawling hydrangea burst out like rosé champagne in a gush of fizzy pink plumes shooting skyward and spilling onto the small gravel driveway.

A few steps led us to an entry porch, under a gabled roof with rounded terracotta tiles. Our genial keyholder, Joy, was waiting for us, a cheerful, rosy-cheeked woman who lived nearby on a small farm. She bustled about, putting away various mops and brushes, then gave us her undivided attention. The cottage looked spotless, and Joy was more than happy to show it off.

Madrigal Cottage combined two small farm workers' cottages into one rather spacious, comfortable home, but the artful renovation had not gutted the place's aged charm and coziness. The sun streamed into the long, modern kitchen. To the side was an oak-beamed dining room, with French doors onto a patio with garden chairs and a table. Beyond a mossy wall, a few stone steps led up to a small but lovely garden thick with roses, delphinium, and irises, with smaller flowers tucked into a lush bed of soft grass bordered by a variety of culinary herbs. And to the side more daisies, and hollyhocks as tall as me! The flowers continued their raggle-taggle journey to the front of the cottage, merging into a hedgerow and small copse. Beyond the garden was open farmland that swept down and across to the bluest of blue skies.

From the dining room, we backtracked through the kitchen into a generous sitting room with cream-colored walls, candle sconces, and a large, open fireplace. Across an uneven hallway was a twin bedroom with a small bathroom, perfectly situated for my folks. Between this bedroom and the living room was an old staircase leading to a narrow passageway with three more bedrooms and a very large bathroom with an enormous bath under the window. I looked out over the fields, heavy with crops and thick with budding fruit trees, divided by tall hedgerows, dense and dark green with blunted tops burnt gold by the sun. My enthusiasm got the better of me, and I told Joy this was the first house we'd rented that I would love to own.

Frances was just as enamored of the place as I was. We found potpourri clustered about the place. Some of the furniture was antique, some just old and re-upholstered but comfortable. Towels were rolled and stuffed in wicker baskets. Herbal and oatmeal soaps rested in antique bowls. Dried flowers burst forth from tiny vases. It was all wonderfully twee. Apart from the magazines glorifying Australian manhood in the upstairs bathroom, I would not have changed a thing. According to Joy, the owners were two young men who lived most of the time in London. They had bought the place and spruced it up after the couple who united the two original cottages had, conversely, split up.

Downstairs we found an excellent music system and, not surprisingly, a video player with a slew of old musicals. The kitchen was perfectly equipped. Our first dishwasher in England! The knives were all sharp. The owners obviously knew how to cook.

After finishing the tour, Joy said, if we had any problems, or needed any help, just come by the farmhouse. There was no phone in the cottage. I did not even care. I loved the house. We all did. Somehow, Madrigal Cottage already felt familiar to me, but I could not put my finger on why.

Out for a walk, just beyond the cottage, we realized we were snug in the midst of working farm country. Yet we never caught a noseful of those bracing farmyard smells suburban types like me find so vile. The only aromas were pleasant and flowery. Naturally, there were some horsy, leathery smells nearby, but that was fine by us. Kate couldn't wait to find their equine owners.

We took a nap. Afterwards we retraced our way and drove into the village of Woodnesborough, a mile or so away. Not much there, either. Just a church, two pubs, and a small shop with a small post office that sold newspapers, cigarettes, and candy. As we were close to Sandwich, we decided to press on, stock up, and rekindle some pleasant memories.

On the way back through Woodnesborough, we pulled up at the first pub we found and booked Sunday lunch. We had no idea if The Charity Inn was good, bad, or indifferent, but it was close to our cottage, easy to get to, and the lady who ran the place was very friendly and said she could handle our burgeoning tribe. We would be nine for lunch!

Stretching out like pink and amber toffee, the long days of summer were being drawn out into warm light evenings that went on and on. We found our way back to the cottage about seven o'clock and made ourselves a picnic supper on the back garden patio with cold cuts, fresh bread, and salads. Drinking in the coolness of a glass of Vouvray, with its hint of sweetness and floral bouquet, we savored the night. All we could hear was the rustle of leaves and the soft buttery thwack of a pair of doves ascending into the nearby woods. We watched the sun as it reluctantly sank below a leafy horizon, along with our wakefulness.

CHAPTER 27

Hammill to Woodnesborough

THE MORNING SUN shone soft streaks of gold through the kitchen window. Coffee brewed and filled the kitchen with pleasant aromas.

"Is that one of the tapes your dad sent over?"

"No," I said, excited. "It's *The Archers*—on the radio. Live!" I couldn't have been happier.

Right after breakfast I padded upstairs and turned on the taps for a nice long bath. The tub was huge, but it filled quickly, and I was soon splashing around, up to my armpits in warm watery coziness, listening to the faint rustle of leaves, enjoying a morning breeze picking up across the fields beyond the open window. I leaned back and stared out at a cloudless sky. I heard the soft clip-clop of a horse and rider trotting past our cottage. None of it seemed real, but it was. It was!

Just after eleven Pam showed up with my folks. Lew was first out of the car. He gave me a grin and a big gnarly hug. He was even thinner than I remembered. Dangerously thin. His cheeks were like sinkholes, the sides of his forehead looked depressed, outlining the shape of his cranium. Even the flesh beneath his ears had sunk into empty pools. His sleeves were rolled up; the tattoo on his arm had faded into a blue-green haze. Mum's name was barely legible. Although tanned, his skin looked as thin and fragile as French toilet paper.

"My skin is like an old wafer," he said, as though reading my mind. "I can cut meself just by drawing me thumbnail across it. You want to see?"

"No!" I said, with the merest hint of panic. "You don't have to, I believe you."

Hackle. Hackle. Hackle.

"Grand to see you, son, does me heart good, it does. And Katie, she's growing up. Just look at her!" Then he turned to Frances and grinned. "Come here, darling, give me a hug."

With a bit of help, Mum walked across the gravel clearing. She was also thinner, her back now permanently curved like a fading rainbow. When she got her bearings, Jessie cocked up her head and gave me her wonderful sunny smile.

"Come here, my big son."

She flapped her arms towards me, the usual look of disbelief on her face. As I helped her into the house, she asked what kind of a place it was. A two-hundred year old cottage, I said, fixed up as good as new. Older than me? she asked. Yes, I said. She laughed.

"Right in the heart of the country, Mum," I went on.

"Bit isolated here, aren't you. Couldn't live in the country, meself. But you like that, though, don't you," said Mum, not as thrilled with the cottage as I was.

"Yes, Mum, I do. I really like it here."

"Well, at least you brought the sun with you; you were lucky." Lew was grudgingly pleased. "Right up to last week, it was raining cats and dogs, it was."

"Of course!" said Frances, with a smile. "We always bring the sun!"

Pam gave us a slight, almost reticent smile. I gave her a comforting hug. Words, for the moment, were left unsaid. Pam's mum, my Aunt Flo, had sadly passed away earlier in the year. A brief illness. And so another was gone. I always imagined my stalwart aunts would be around forever, but now old age was finally tripping them up, and no amount of medicinal gin could stave off the inevitable.

Looking around, Pam said how much her mum would have liked our cottage this year. We shared some fond memories. I offered everyone tea, tried to get back to the moment.

"Flo was my favorite sister, she was," said Jessie, suddenly.

"Your sister Mary will be here soon. So don't let her hear you say that or there'll be trouble," growled Lew.

"Oooh-wah! Mary's coming all this way here?"

"She only lives at Ashford, Mum, it's not far," I said brightly.

"Everything's far if you don't have a car." She shot a look at Lew.

Ghrrr.

With my parents settled comfortably in the living room, a pot of tea before them, Pam and I strolled into the garden. We looked across to the sheep on the hillside.

"They don't want to stay over," said Pam suddenly.

"What?"

"Lew's blaming Jessie, but it's him. Uncle Lew is feeling very anxious, doesn't like being out of his own world any more. You know what they're like. At their age. But I think if he settles in, he could be persuaded to stay. Just thought I'd warn you. It might come up."

"Should I have word with him?"

"I would leave it for now. I would, really."

So that was that. I was to play dumb and ignore the suitcase on their bed, unopened and unpacked.

Moments later, Cousins Kevin and Maxine showed up with my Aunt Mary. I was delighted to see them. Their smiles and laughter managed to crack even Lew's leathery face into the hint of a grin. Mary settled herself on the settee beside Mum, resting her double chin comfortably on her neck. She then gave her sister a squeeze and looked about the place, smiling broadly.

"Done alwight here, Denis. Lovely, isn't it, Jess, ay, ay? Lovely, isn't it?"

"Not bad for a week away, eh, Mum?" I tried to evoke an optimistic response.

"A week!" Mum sounded shocked.

"Not bad, Denis. Better than last year. Tucked away up here, aren't you. But very nice, though. Very nice." Kevin glanced around and nodded approvingly.

Maxine pulled out snaps of their new trailer and started passing them around like baby pictures.

"Like a home from home, it is. Lovely inside. Wemember those old caravans we used to have, Jessie? You wemember, don't you, ay, ay?" Mary tugged on Jessie's sleeve.

"Can't say I do." Jessie shook her head, sounded disinterested.

"Well, it's nothing like that. Oooh, no! You can weally live in this one. You can, weally."

Everyone seemed enthralled by the photographs. Maxine explained how this and that opened, how table and chairs folded into beds. Like magic, apparently. Frances seemed fascinated.

I was pleased when Kate started whining about hunger pangs. I helped Jessie and Lew to their feet, then Kate started shooing the others to the door. And at last, we were on our way to lunch.

After the brightness of the outside, the pub appeared a bit dark, but we soon grew accustomed to the pale ale-colored light. The Charity Inn had lots of atmosphere, keg smells, with just a hint of smoke lingering from the fire that recently roared in the grate. I looked around, taking in the low ceilings, faded peach-colored walls, old oak beams, and a three-sided bar that served both the public bar and the saloon part of the pub, where we sat, quite alone. The other side of the bar was crowded. No one was eating. As this was Sunday and the whole country was having roast lunch, our solitary dining status was not reassuring.

On the plus side, there were no noisy slot machines, no piped muzak. It was a good old-fashioned village pub with patrons knocking back pints, throwing darts, talking, playing cards, even a pianist who took requests like a human jukebox.

Our group was a bit subdued at first, but we settled in when drinks were served by our friendly hostess. Thankfully, she had no problem with the "under age" member of our party. Pretty soon, everyone was catching up on the past year. I went over and sat next to Pam, who was keeping somehow to herself, looking rather sad and pensive.

"Mum would have loved this, to be here, with everyone."

"I know. With us in spirit, eh?" I said gently.

"Hope so!" Pam looked up and smiled. "I do hope so."

Table service was very attentive. Not surprising, perhaps, as we were the only customers eating. In fact, we were waited on by the landlady's entire family. In short order, more wine was poured, more pints of Guinness pulled, and our classic English Sunday lunches served. The roast beef, lamb, pork, and turkey all looked the same. After a little taste-testing we discovered the meats also tasted identical. Not that anyone cared, except Kate, who only ate a few carrots. Even I was more amused than annoyed. At least the food was plentiful and the Cote du Rhone drinkable. Happily, the desserts proved big winners: apple pie, bread pudding, and spotted dick moated by a thick, vivid yellow custard, steamy hot and sweet. Kiddie food. Lovely. Of course, by this time, we were quite merry and susceptible to just about anything.

The hubbub of the pub was pleasant and, seeping through it, I heard "Roll out the Barrel" from across the bar. Lew was merrily singing along. Jessie was knocking back the red wine, chatting with her sister Mary, as if her memory problems never existed. After finishing his song, Lew tottered around the table and hunkered down with Mary. I didn't quite hear what they said, but Mary laughed and told him what a silly old stick he was. That I heard. I moved a little closer.

"Oh, it's lovely, isn't it, Lew, it weally is. Getting the family together like this—and it's not even a funeral!" Mary burst out laughing. Lew grinned and nodded, unable to speak or even laugh.

"Bloody funny, that is, bloody funny, but you're right!" he finally blurted out.

I caught bits of conversation. Their chatter was like an old song with a familiar refrain I'd heard many times before, but it still made me smile. Kate was playing musical relative, running and sitting from one to another. Following suit, we all began swapping places. Mum was suddenly holding onto Pam's hand as Mary held forth about something or other. Kevin and Maxine grinned and groaned at what she was saying. Frances was now talking to Lew. Trying to keep an eye on Kate. My family. It was shrinking, but holding on. I was happy to be a part of it. Happy to be back.

The other customers were very friendly and took great delight in Kate as she ran around with Frances in pursuit. Eventually, my two ladies ended up by the piano player, who was more than happy to serenade two new fans.

"You've had enough," Lew murmured to Jessie ominously.

"Get me a short, you know what I want. Go on, get on with it!" Jessie gave me a quick furtive grin, as if she was getting away with something naughty. Lew muttered disapprovingly but nevertheless headed towards the bar.

Ghrrr.

Jessie unexpectedly grabbed my arm and held on very tightly.

"Do you believe in heaven?" she asked, a hopeful smile on her face.

Without thinking, I said no, I did not believe in heaven, and went on to say with unctuous sincerity that I was not a religious person. Her smile melted into a puddle of disappointment.

"Being here, enjoying yourself, that's what counts, Mum. Family. Friends," I blustered on, already regretting what I had said.

Mum looked up at me, seemingly unconnected to her surroundings, the noise of the pub, the laughter, the warm chatter, the closeness of those around her. I tried to make amends for my thoughtlessness.

"Look, Mum," I said. "I really believe we carry on, through our children, through our friends, and if you remember someone, they don't really die, do they? I mean, look at your sister, Flo—"

"What about Flo?" asked Mum.

"Well, you know, Flo died, but you're not going to forget her, are you now?"

"Flo dead?"

An actor once told me he wanted a portable stage trap, a device he could carry around and use on certain awkward and difficult occasions. Just like this one. Alas, no trap opened for me.

"Well, at least you're here. And I am, too!" Mum began to cheer up.

"You certainly are, Mum, you certainly are," I said, with heartfelt relief.

Mum was smiling again. She shook my arm in her tight grip, and I gave her a hug and kissed her brow.

"Have a drink with me," she said, as if no-one else was there. "And find out what Lew's doing with my Benny."

Pam sat with Mum as I went to retrieve her drink, and get one for myself. I found Lew at the bar, waiting his turn. I suppose she still wants her drink, he asked. Yes, I said. She's had enough. He shot me a look, I shrugged. Benedictine, he said. I smiled. As if he didn't know. Then a narrow-faced man in his fifties shuffled towards us. He was smiling, friendly.

"Like it, then? This pub?" the man asked. He was balding, a bit overweight, a beer glass swung back and forth from his mouth to his side, like a hand bell. "Bit different from America, ay?"

"We're having a good time," I said.

Narrow Face's friend came over. This new guy had a bright red, round head pulled tight like a half-inflated balloon, tightly cropped hair, and tight clothes. The only loose thing about him was his smile, which drooped a bit, making him appear a little demented. Balloon Head was more than a few sheets to the wind. He steadied himself by placing a hand on Lew's shoulder.

"Your marines. We did a few jobs with them, we did."

"My marines? What do you mean *my* marines?" Lew seemed confused.

"I like the U. S. Marines, we trained with your lot." Balloon Head was not really listening to anyone. "We did, we trained together. Good blokes."

"I'm an Englishman, I am. Cor strewf!" Lew shook his head in disbelief.

"But you look American, you do!" Balloon Head insisted.

"You must be blind drunk, mate! London born and bred, me. In the army! Sixteen years! Royal Artillery!"

"Royal Marines!" Balloon Head pointed to himself with his thumbs, chest extended, obviously very proud, and very vocal. "Royal Marines!"

"Royal Artillery, me! Royal Artillery," Lew yelled back.

So the ex-battery sergeant major competed with the ex-Royal Marine in a strange but friendly shouting match. There was much eye rolling. Narrow Face broke ranks to come over and tell me his friend was basically alright. Quite safe, really, just a little off.

"He's got a silver plate in his head," the friend said, making it sound as if the plate was a medal. In a way, I suppose it was, and I said as much.

~

"He thought I was an American! Never thought anyone would ever take me for a Yank!"

"I know exactly how you feel, Dad," I said, with a rather smug smile.

Drinks in hand, we weaved our way through the throng, back to our table.

"I wondered where you lot had got yourselves to!" Mary was bright red and glazed of eye, but perked up when offered another drink.

"Benny! I love Benny, I do."

Inexplicably, both aged sisters started laughing. Lew looked at me with the usual disbelief on his face. I looked back to the bar, saw Kate happily perched on the piano player's lap while Frances took pictures. I walked over, offered the pianist a tip. He told me he did not need money. He only played for beer. He said there was no better way to spend a Sunday afternoon. He had a point. I bought him a drink.

By three o'clock, the drinks were dead and the coffee long gone. Even with the iffy food, lunch had been a success. We said good-bye to the landlady, her family, the veterans at the bar, and Len, our friendly pianist, then drove in slow, stately, and most careful procession back to the cottage, where Mum and Lew and Mary and Kate napped out. Pam said she was happy to read the paper and hold the fort while the rest of us went for a walk.

Tree-sheltered footpaths, ancient farm tracks, and horse trails beckoned just beyond our front door. We walked around the edge of a large cornfield and soon found ourselves in a strange concrete clearing, thistles and combs of grass bursting through cracks. The encroaching hedgerow had softened and disguised a World War Two aerodrome. The fact that it was completely unmarked made our discovery all the more fascinating. I looked up at the sky, tried to imagine it. Spits, Hurricanes. Mosquitoes? What planes had landed on this strip? Who were the men who had taken off from here, what unmarked space held them still? Framed by weeds and the flaky rust of the decaying missen hut, this forgotten field was as poignant to me as any war memorial built of marble and inscribed with gold. We walked the perimeter of the old airfield and picked up another path between a hedgerow stuffed with prickly shrubs of wild berries and clusters of Lady Orchids and silk thin poppies, blood red and orange, a vivid reminder of a previous war, the one that was supposed to end all wars. We picked our way through a canopy of oaks. Beyond the hedge, a few cows squatted in the shade and, far beyond, unshorn sheep, all fat and rounded, grazed in deep green pasture like forgotten woolly golf balls. The path opened up and curved in an arc, and we found ourselves just below Madrigal Cottage.

~

We came back to find Lew bolt upright in a chair, bristling with indignation. Jessie was on a sofa nearby, smiling and shrugging her shoulders. Pam was in the kitchen making tea. Frances said she wanted to check on Kate and escaped up the stairs.

"We wanted to go home. But Pam has gone and put the kibosh on that!"

"Aren't you going to stay for the week?" I played innocent.

"No! No we are not! I told Pam!" snarled Lew. "I told her!"

Poor Pam.

"Look, we got this cottage so you and Mum could stay. It's got everything you need on the ground floor. You don't have to use the stairs, or anything."

"I don't mind staying," said Mum, chuckling nervously. I wasn't sure if Mum was being contrary or not, but she riled Lew considerably. "Then why did you tell me you wanted to go home? Make up your mind, woman!" he lashed out.

I went into the kitchen and found Pam.

"I told him, Denis, I told him I'm staying the night. I'm not driving back today. I'll take them back tomorrow if that's what they want. I told Uncle Lew, he knows. Don't know why he's now making such a fuss. Give him a night here and he'll probably settle in. I can come back on Thursday, take them home then if he wants."

"Thanks, Pam, but if they want to go home—" I went back out into the living room. "Look Dad, Mum, if you really want to go home now, I'll take you back. If that's what you want."

"I don't want you driving us back! I want Pam to take us home. So we'll go home tomorrow. Finish!"

"Give it a chance, Lew, it's a lovely place, this," said Mary.

Ghrrr.

~

Afternoon tea consisted of the usual fare: buttered bread with sliced ham, cheese, pork pie, pickles, including the piccalilli pickles Lew was so fond of. Nevertheless he declined to join us, determined to sit and sulk in the living room, alone.

"He's not hungry. So he says." Pam rolled her eyes.

"What's up with Dad, Mum?"

"He's not here, is he."

She did not seem bothered. Mum just went on arranging cold cuts and buttered bread on her plate. "Looks nice, all this, doesn't it. I'll eat what I can—"

Lew's rather rude absence from the dinner table robbed no one of their appetite or conversation, and tea proceeded as if nothing untoward was happening. Shortly after the plates were cleared, Aunt Mary's family decided to call it a day. Mary gave me a hug and said a teary good-bye to Lew and Jessie. Kate got big hugs from Maxine and Kevin.

"Coming back over next year, Denis?"

"Hope so," I said, without thinking. I hope so. Frances smiled ever so slightly.

After reading Kate her bedtime story, I came back down and found Jessie and Lew in fine form, regaling Pam and Frances with stories. They'd been a bit gloomy after Mary left, but now the sparkle was back. Even Mum was joining in, just like in the old days.

"Well, they weren't cart horses!" Mum insisted.

"They were big, though, had to be!"

"Talking about some of your winners?" I asked.

"Naaaw, we've been turning back the clock, we have!" Lew said, his grin widening.

"They're fondly remembering horse-drawn funerals." Pam looked bemused.

"Everyone came out to watch," Mum said. "The undertaker wore a top hat with a big, black, silk ribbon all draped and fluffy at the back. He carried a big walking stick. And the horses. Lovely, they were. Four lovely black horses with black feathery plumes on their heads. Pulling the hearse, all shiny black and gleaming. You got a lovely send-off in those days…not like now." Jessie shook her head a bit, then shrugged her shoulders.

After tea, Lew started nagging Jessie to get to bed.

"Think you can get me up out of it, you've got another think coming!"

Ghrrr.

Using his stick to pull himself up, Lew tottered over to Mum's chair and started rocking her back and forth like an ancient seesaw, building momentum for a kind of take-off. No doubt a regular routine, nevertheless a little disturbing to witness. Suddenly Mum was up. Slowly, very slowly, he helped her to the bedroom. Frances and Pam said goodnight and walked upstairs together. Lew returned as I finished putting out a couple of glasses, a bottle of Jack between them. I filled the glasses to the brim.

"You want to go home still?"

"Yes."

"Don't you like this place?"

"I forgot me inhaler."

Of course! Then it all made sense. Although he had quit smoking ten years before, the dark blot had finally seeped across his chest. He told me he now had one lung that worked. I said we could go to a chemist first thing in the morning.

"Might be a good idea." He sniffed his drink. "Couple of puffs. Might help. I only need it every so often, but when I do, I need it something bad."

He seemed to warm to the idea of staying, if I could find an inhaler. I wanted my parents to enjoy the cottage, and I wanted them to stay.

"Alright," he said at last. "We'll stick it out for the week."

"Great!"

We clinked glasses, drained our drinks. I saw Lew to his room. We said goodnight, then I padded up to bed and told Frances I had persuaded Lew to stay.

"Really? Why?" asked Frances. "I thought they really wanted to go home."

I sank into a long sigh of uncertainty. I realized I had badgered them into staying. More days for Mum's forgetfulness to deepen or Lew's smoldering anxiety to flare and burn away my thin veneer of patience. Not a happy prospect. Besides, the countryside bored both my parents to tears. Nothing was nearby. No shops, no sidewalks. No street traffic to look at, no neighbors to talk to, no lampposts or gateposts to lean on. Other than the patio, they would not be able to walk anywhere with any feeling of security and safety. According to Pam, they could barely make it to the bus stop anymore, and I quite believed her. I remembered how slowly my parents had walked the few steps from the car to the cottage, how they had leaned into each other as if pushing against an invisible body of water. Back in Dagenham they could still manage a street or two, but here, with unfamiliar terrain, they would just sit in the cottage all day, stare at the telly, and feel trapped.

"What are you thinking?" asked Frances.

What was I thinking? I was thinking about myself.

"I just didn't want them to be this old, I suppose. They always were old, but this year—"

Frances said not to get mad if Lew changed his mind and wanted to go home in the morning. She was convinced Lew had just told me what I wanted to hear. He wanted to make me happy or, perhaps, get me to stop pestering him. Probably a little of both.

CHAPTER 28

Wickhambreaux and Goodnestone Park

LEW MUST HAVE GOTTEN UP EARLY. Even Kate was still asleep. I smelled the fresh-brewed tea and heard the radio playing softly. I padded downstairs. Lew was making toast, piling on the butter as thick as the bread. He smiled when he saw me.

"Lovely day, son. Sleep alright? We did." He poured out a cup of tea for me. "Now, listen son, I got something to tell you. I've talked it over with your mother, you know what she's like—"

I smiled and, as I sat down, I noticed their little suitcase by the door. It's alright, I told him. And it was.

Pam wanted to have a look around the area before taking my folks home. As usual, Lew and Jessie were more than happy to shoo us out of the cottage. They would read the paper, sit in the garden, maybe study the racing pages—pick a winner! We said we would be back for lunch. Lew told us to take our time, enjoy ourselves, and not be late.

The gravel crackled and sputtered under our tires as we turned down the small lane beside the cottage. Lew and Jessie stood in the gabled doorway and waved and waved until we were out of sight. They were both smiling, and I felt sure they were more than a little relieved to know they would soon be going home.

Instead of turning right towards Woodnesborough, we headed towards Ash. Skirting the village, we glanced at the spire of the twelfth century church of Saint Nicholas, then spotted a garden antique shop. Thick traffic made stopping hazardous, so we pressed on. Pam knew a village, she said, not too far away.

The small side road twisted and carved its way into mellower, more tranquil countryside, and we soon entered the pretty, watercolor village of Wickhambreaux. The expansive village green was right beside a large converted mill on a stream. Great ruffs of grass decorated both banks. The Little Stour River flowed gently past clapboard houses and snug white plaster cottages, some thatched and some with cross-leaded windows. We followed winding streets to unspoiled woodlands before returning to the green. Apart from its odd triangular shape, the village green was a classic, bordered by wooden posts and a looping chain fence. Across the way was the ancient church of St. Andrew, opposite a charming pub, a red-roofed building with gabled windows and turreted chimney stacks. The front of the pub was whitewashed, and window boxes and hanging flower baskets provided wonderful splashes of color along the entire length of the building.

"Don't serve food or coffee, or anyfin' hot, until twelve. Sorry."

It was eleven forty-five. A small dining area had been set for lunch. Wait staff were waiting. We asked for something uncooked, perhaps a slice of pie. We might just as well have asked for a carpaccio of lark's tongue with a puree of roasted plankton. Stares. Again, the answer was no. The bartender obviously had no idea what it was like to travel with a small child or, come to that, how to cater to visitors anxious to spend money. Oh, well.

Upon our return, Jessie and Lew were sitting in front of the cottage, on the low wall beside the gabled door, basking in the sun like a pair of happy old lizards. Smiling, we went inside and fixed a salad lunch with sliced ham and boiled eggs.

"Seen all you wanted to see then, my son?" Lew asked, as always.

Hackle. Hackle. Hackle.

He laughed at me, the way he used to. Everything seemed back to normal. But things weren't quite the same. That afternoon, after our festive lunch, Lew and Jessie went home with Pam. I checked their bedroom to make sure they had left nothing behind. I found the bed made, the pillows fluffed, a bedside lamp placed back as it had been, as if my folks had never been there. After they left, the cottage seemed a bit empty. Silent. I felt a nip of regret, wishing things had been different. A fizzy sort of sadness bubbled at the back of my throat. Time to get some air.

We decided to go out and toodle around the local village of Woodnesborough. We parked near The Charity Inn, and Frances led the way. Beyond the main road we wound our way along a quiet village street, up a slight incline towards the parish church of St. Mary's and Woden Hill. Apparently, the village was named for a Viking god. And, we learned, burial sites had been found predating the many Roman roads that once crisscrossed this ancient settlement. Woodnesborough was a community that continued to thrive today as it had done long before the Danes and Saxons, long before the time of Christ.

~

The sun rained upon our cottage, shimmering off the white walls, filling the red barreled tiles on the roof with the warmth of early morning. The prospect of another glorious day lay ahead. We were not exactly in a big touring mode, quite happy just getting to know our neck of woods, which happened to include an old baronial estate called Goodnestone Park.

After we gained admission, Frances strode back to the ticket booth, a small wooden shed with a counter and a windowless opening. Inside the little hut sat an elderly man with a silver-gray, balding head, a suntanned, relaxed face, and a faraway look in his eye. Well-dressed in the country style, he wore a checked green shirt, a woodland-green woolen tie, and a hay-colored corduroy jacket with leather patches.

"Excuse me?" asked Frances, with a take-charge smile on her face. "We just bought two adults and a child ticket for ten pounds?"

A question mark ended her statement, denoting something not quite right. The old ticket seller seemed quite oblivious.

"Yes, do enjoy your visit!" he said in melodious tones.

"But in your brochure, it says, here," Frances flurried the pamphlet we had gotten with the tickets, "a family ticket is seven pounds."

"Yes," the old chap said slowly, looking a bit perplexed.

"Can we have the seven pound ticket instead of the ones we got?" Frances asked.

"Ah, no, you see, the seven pound ticket is a family pass. And a family pass is for two parents or guardians and two children. Under ten."

"But that makes no sense. We are a family. Why can't we have a family pass?"

The old chap stood there for a moment, thinking it all through. Then he studied the park brochure. He looked up and blinked. "I think they'll have to change the wording here."

"Ask the powers that be," I suggested.

A glimmer of a smile appeared on the old fellow's face as he handed Frances her three pounds. She thanked him and said she would spend it on a guide book or something.

"How about some ice cream! That would be frightfully nice, wouldn't it?" He leaned across his counter and pointed towards Kate, who perked up instantly. "Ice cream! Don't you think so?"

Kate grinned back up at him.

We ambled along the terrace towards well-tended grounds surrounding a stately mansion, built at the beginning of the eighteenth century. Originally, the gardens were rather French and formal. By the middle of the eighteenth century the more informal, naturalistic style of Capability Brown held sway and a softer meadow look was ploughed into the land. The house we saw overlooked a vast, grass-stepped terrace leading to a park setting with created meadows, artfully placed trees, and commanding views of the North Kent Downs. Visitors were not allowed inside the mansion. In a way, not having to see more baronial oil paintings, crests of arms, and suits of armor, especially on such a splendidly sunny day, was a bit of a relief.

We walked past two rather tall, well-dressed ladies of a certain age. One bade us good morning in a fruity yet commanding voice, then went on with her conversation. Frances took the lead and headed for a copse and away from the parterre, the last remaining formal garden.

"You're going the wrong way!" the fruity-voiced lady called out to us.

Frances muttered something about busybodies as she pushed Kate down the nearest path, blithely ignoring the woman now barreling down on us.

"Excuse me! I say!"

We stopped and turned. Up close, the woman appeared to have frozen smile lines drawn into a face coated with talcum powder.

"Did we do something wrong?" asked Frances, sounding just a tad sarcastic.

"Oh, no! But you see, if you go that way, you'll miss the tree, it's only just over there! Follow the little arrows." The lady's fruity voice sounded a little bruised. "Shame to miss it."

"What tree?" Frances turned back.

"That tree! D'you see it? Planted during the reign of Charles the Second. Makes the tree older than the house. Quite splendid." The lady sounded sweetly intimidating and her wide oval smile held us like a lasso until we went to look at the ancient tree. On closer inspection, the tree looked like a giant bush, gnarled, wind-blown, and mangled.

"Now carry on, that's it, carry on," Fruity Voice, who had been watching our progress, called out to us. "And do enjoy the rest of your visit!"

"This tree is boring!" said Kate.

She got out of her stroller and led the way to the back of the house, into the woodland area. In an almost black-green setting, powerful bursts of color were supplied by ancient rhododendrons, giant foxglove, and vast plantings of wildflowers. We wended our way around little pathways that opened on grassy areas with a spectacular array of roses and hydrangea. Beyond the house, we followed more paths with borders thick with flowering perennials, moss-covered statuary, and stone urns haphazardly flopped with weeds and clumps of woodruff.

Kate squealed as she discovered a large toad in the bottom of an ornamental well. The toad croaked quite loudly but stood his ground and stared back at Kate, not showing the least bit of concern. Beyond the toad in his hole, we came upon a disused tennis court. Interwoven with weeds, the net sagged, ill-kept and forlorn-looking. Perhaps the estate was owned by a noble family fallen on hard times. Who were they; who lived there? The fact that visitors were not allowed inside now added to the mansion's allure.

Jane Austen visited Goodnestone on many occasions, for dinners and extended dancing parties. After one such protracted and apparently inspiring visit, she had plotted her masterpiece, *Pride and Prejudice*. Of course, that snippet of literary trivia piqued my interest even more. We speculated. Romanticized. Imagined. If they had dancing, there must be a ballroom! Frances, even Kate, wanted a look inside. We walked over to the back of the enormous house shrouded in shadow and mystery. As discretely as we could, we crept up to a large window. Like kids staring into a sweet shop that has just closed, we peered in, faces pressed against the glass. Not much light inside, but we could see a large living room with a massive fireplace. Above the mantle hung a large oil painting of a man in stately robes. As our eyes grew accustomed to the interior light, we recognized the man staring out from the gilt frame. It was the old duffer selling tickets in the little wooden booth!

"Do you think he's the lord of the manor?" I asked, surprised.

"Must be! Doubt if they'd have an oil painting of the ticket collector," Frances answered.

I nodded and smiled as we walked back to the path from which we should not have strayed. But what fun to peek!

On the way out we saw his lordship taking the air outside his ticket booth. He looked pleased to see us again, delighted to learn we enjoyed the gardens, and took an exaggerated interest in Kate's discovery of a toad. He was either a children's entertainer or had several grandchildren, for he pulled off the kindly old cove act with great ease and aplomb.

"Do come back. You don't have to take the tour, but come back, have a picnic. Stroll about the park. It's quite a lovely place to see. Come anytime." He smiled genially. "We're always here."

Then his wife, the fruity-voiced woman we had met earlier, came over. Her ladyship told us they were about to address the jungle at the back; they hoped to restore the entire garden to its former glory. And we must come back and see it then. We said we would be delighted to return. And don't forget that picnic! said his lordship, quite definitely. The talk of food made us think of lunch. The old chap suggested the pub just outside the main gate, across the street from the estate church of the Holy Cross. Worth a visit, he told us.

Although the pub seemed pleasantly rustic, the bill of fare was rather meager, so we set off for a village within vigorous strolling distance of our cottage in Hammill. Chillenden was quite small, just a few fair-sized houses behind high boxwood borders. The village pub, The Spread Eagle, was a tiny little place, but we could tell people came here to eat as well as to drink. The menu was varied and adventurous—including a number of champagnes by the glass! Times change.

Frances and I shared a large prawn salad with an Asian dip and a plate of roast beef, and Kate had a sausage sandwich. Though we declined the champagne, the food was first-rate. I wished we had brought my family here on Sunday, but Frances said they would not have enjoyed it as much as the other pub's rough and tumble charm. She was probably right.

~

The rest of the day passed with languid ease. While Frances and Kate napped, I decided to visit a local vineyard. I followed the familiar grape emblem down a narrow track, past regimented rows of vines strung out with great austerity on bands of wire as thick as coat hangers. I parked in front of a hut that looked like a giant tin can sliced through from top to bottom. Sitting outside was a man in late middle years, with straggly gray hair and large gray eyebrows. His eyes were closed and he was lying back in his chair, catching rays along with forty winks. He breathed and exhaled with faint flapping snores. The collar and the front of his shirt had been rolled down as much as possible to expose more of his neck and chest to the sun. I said hello, carefully, not wanting to startle him. The sleeping figure jolted awake. He blinked and smiled, showing teeth as misshapen and haphazardly arranged as the tombstones on Boot Hill. Another victim of National Health dentistry.

"Come for a tasting, have you?" he asked hopefully.

Just inside the doorway was a trellis table. I saw large metal tanks and plastic tubing reminiscent of plumbing, and something that looked like an unearthed septic tank.

"What kind of wine do you make here?"

"White," he said. "White wine."

Wine basket pressed? Steel- or oak-barreled? How long was the wine cellared? I asked no questions. And thankfully received no sermon on the style of wine used, no discourse on the varietals used in the blending process. He was as clueless as I was. White wine, he said, and white wine it was. He opened the fridge and took out a couple of long, thin bottles.

"Fur-go. He uses Fur-go. I think that's how the winemaker pronounces it."

"Thurgau?" I said helpfully. "German-style wine?"

"Yes, yes, that sounds about right. And yes, it is German. I'm not up on the ins and outs of it, but you can't grow the French stuff here. We have too much rain, not enough sun, and the French grapes, well, you know, French—"

He spoke disdainfully, implying that Gallic varietals lacked the necessary vim and vigor to stand up to the vagaries of English weather. He poured a small quantity from the first bottle into a tiny plastic tumbler, not much bigger than a thimble. It tasted like a very good quality vinegar.

"It's cold!" I said, using my tongue to push out bits of cheek the wine had shriveled.

"Yes, I know, it is a bit, isn't it," he said, somewhat apologetically. "I'm not the winemaker. I'm a partner, but on the business side. Like to try another one?"

"Well, I'm driving and, you know..." I smiled. I shrugged.

"This one's better. I'll join you. Hate to see a man drink alone," he said brightly, as he poured each of us a small plastic cupful. "Tastes of raisins. Sultanas, more like. Intense."

The heavy wine was indeed shot through with raisins and tasted like spotted dick. I liked it.

"Better, yeah?"

"Better!" I said, with some relief.

"Best one by far. Now don't let's bother with these thimbles." He waved a dismissive paw at the tiny plastic cups, then found two real wine glasses in a filing cabinet. He grabbed the bottle and ushered me out of the tin shed, back into the sunshine. We sat and drank the wine.

"I used to work on the boats. Shuffled paper. Made money. Put the dosh in this place. We've only just started really." He picked up the bottle and turned it slowly in his hand, as if examining it for the first time, then he looked at me. "I think we should kill it, don't you?" Without waiting for a reply, he poured again and, between us, we finished the bottle. Half an hour later, armed with Kentish Thurgau in bright, copper-colored bottles, I drove back to the cottage. Very carefully.

Later that evening Kate saw the first half of *Calamity Jane* before going up the wooden hill to Bedfordshire. After she went up, we ambled onto the patio to enjoy the remains of the evening. There was a rustle in the bushes, then a cat bounded across the patio, heralding a brief and sudden breeze that raked a few remaining leaves that swirled and fell. The cat and the breeze vanished as magically as they had appeared. And all was still.

"I wish we had found this place earlier," I said.

"I'm glad we didn't. I wouldn't have gotten you to go anywhere else if we had."

Frances smiled, I nodded. She was probably right.

~

We'd been looking forward to returning to Sandwich, ancient and layered with history as rich as a trifle, and virtually undiscovered. The following day, we found new sights without even looking. The Butts were sequestered right on the edge of town. Why the area was called The Butts, no one knew for sure. The ancient earthworks partly followed the river Stour as it swept around the outskirts of the town. All that remained of the old city walls originally built to keep out the Saxons, the Danes, and the ever-persistent French, the Butts now provided a leafy walkway by the river. We followed a family of ducks as they waddled through a green-gold pavilion of weeping willows arching across the grassy battlements. Then, quite abruptly, the tree line ended, the grass verge turned to tarmac and the river seemed to disappear beneath the local co-op.

Back on Strand Street, beautifully preserved yet still very much in use, we saw a house with a smugglers' hidey hole from the sixteenth century, also a wine shop in business since the twelfth century. The corner pub, The Admiral Owen, still had original beams dating back some eight hundred years. We walked around until we found the little teashop we had discovered the year before. We sat down, got Kate settled, then started looking at the menu.

Frances noticed him first.

He had followed us in. And now he stood beside our table, looking at us. I glanced up with a thin nervous smile. His hair was long and straight and hung in rigid strands almost to his shoulders. He looked about forty, tall and lanky, with a very thin face. His eyes looked milky and his cheeks appeared to be ruddy, though they were actually crisscrossed with spidery red veins. His nose was red, too, and slightly puffed. There he stood, arms at his side, fingers shaking ever so slightly, a very serious drinker reporting for duty. We studied our menus with more than the usual interest, hoping he would just go away. Was he the local nutter or did he just want money? I couldn't tell.

"It's all good," he said suddenly.

I thought he was referring to life, or his overall well-being. We looked up, nodding agreement, then continued staring at the menu, gripping the edges with renewed intensity. Frances leaned over, looking very anxious. She started to whisper urgently.

"You need a few more minutes or you ready to order? It's fine with me." The man smiled at us, a little pad now in hand. Our waiter.

"Saw you come in. I'd just popped out for a ciggy." His words were not slurred, but his speech sounded a little soggy about the edges. After placing our order at the back of the shop, our waiter came back, smiled and waved at Kate, and sat down at the next table, facing us.

"We had no idea you worked here," I said, trying to be casual.

"I own this place, actually. Me and the wife. We just re-opened last week."

"Really!" I said, with some relief, adding with complete honesty, "Who knew?"

"We discovered it last year," said Frances, still a tad nervous.

"There was a nice old lady. Silver-haired. Charming. She was here then," I said.

"Of course she was! That's my old mum, that is! 'Ere, Mum! Mum!" he shouted through to the back. "People over from the States. Here last year!"

Dressed in waitress-black with a frilly white apron, looking just the same, the friendly silver-haired lady we'd met the previous year popped her head out from the tiny kitchen. She smiled and waved, pleased we had returned. We were somewhat reassured.

"Good timing. If you'd come a month ago—" He inhaled on an imaginary cigarette, then continued with his slightly soggy syllables, "We got this bloke in to run the place. Was getting a bit too much for Mum. But he was useless." He leaned closer, giving me a hint of stale hops and cigarettes, and gripped the side of the table. "Naused it, he did." He stretched the word "naused" like elastic, then went on, "Completely naused it up. So we took it back. Me and the wife, you know—got things back on course. Shipshape. Ah, look! Here's your order!"

He stood up as his mum appeared with a trayful of scones, jam, clotted cream, and a pot of tea. With no other tables to serve, our newfound friend sat down again and stared down at his feet with one elbow on the table.

We tried to ignore him, started serving ourselves, but he wouldn't go away. He introduced himself. We did likewise. It seemed churlish not to. Our new best friend was called Gavin. As we poured tea, Gavin explained how he and his wife planned to revitalize the little teashop by transforming it into a French cafe at night, with bistro food, checkered tablecloths, candles, Piaf in the background. Sounded like a good idea, I said. Gavin and his wife had no children, but they did have a couple of dogs, and they sailed. And would I like to see some pictures of their boat?

"It's a real beauty. All wood." He took out an old battered wallet and went on forcefully but quietly, "No plastic crap. No plastic anywhere. All brass fixtures. Proper, this. Proper!"

While Frances and Kate ambled over to "Mum" for a chat, Gavin showed me photos of his all-wood sailboat, varnished and polished. The craft looked like a very large piece of indoor furniture, beautifully finished and half-submerged in water. He spoke lovingly of his boat, said he and his wife planned to sail her across the ocean blue and thread the islands in the Caribbean.

"Her name's Sandy," Gavin said, softly.

"It's your baby," I said.

He looked at me as if a penny had dropped.

"You're right. Our baby. Yeah. Yeah, it is, she's like our child." Carefully, he tucked the pictures back into his wallet. Then, thoughtfully, "Yeah, she is—"

Gavin appeared momentarily despondent, then he brightened up when a woman with a couple of dogs waved to him from the street. Suddenly eager tails were thudding against legs and door frames, as the woman entered the tearoom with two rambunctious fur balls.

"You still here. Glad I caught you," she said, puffing on a cigarette.

"Just coming, just coming! It's the wife!" Gavin introduced us all to his missus. "Right, I'm off then," he said hurriedly. "Give the dogs a run out. Don't forget to come back! Bye, Katie, tell your mum and dad—beef bourguignon. On tonight!"

Gavin hauled himself to his feet, waved good-bye, grabbed the leashes, and was dragged out of the teashop-cum-cafe like a scrawny kite on a couple of strings, pulled this way and that. I could only hope he had a better grip on his yacht rigging than he had on his dogs.

We saw our new friend about half an hour later as we drove out of town. He was standing outside the Admiral Owen, quite alone, drinking a pint of beer, a cigarette cupped within his fingers. We waved and yelled out to him as we drove past. He looked up, stared right at us, and had no idea who we were.

∼

The week had slipped by with the deceptive speed of a leaf on a stream. Suddenly it was Friday. We had not traveled far afield, more than happy to retrace our footfalls and rediscover some of the delightful villages, cafes, and pubs we had come to love in that green and pleasant corner of England. We returned to Broadstairs. Right on time for the Dickens Festival!

The town was filled with bustled and bonneted ladies accompanied by top-hatted, bewhiskered gentlemen who appeared to have stepped out of a Dickensian Christmas card. Down on the beach, people clambered out of ancient bathing machines, in actual striped bathing costumes. Kate and I followed the faux Victorians into the briny sea.

We splashed about in the clear, clean harbor while Frances read a book on the beach, wrapped in a sweater. Kate and I played for an hour or so before wading over towards the curving pier, bedecked with floats and drying nets hung against the mossy green harbor wall. Frances was waiting for us with towels. I was hungry for fish. I tried to interest my family in some winkles at the end of the harbor, but they had other fish to fry, or at least fried fish to eat. We ambled back to the fish shop we had found with Lew, in the curve of Harbor Street, for a lovely lunch of cod and chips.

And then it was Saturday, time to leave. Our week at Madrigal Cottage had been all too short. We drove away slowly, reluctantly. After so many years, I had found the England I had imagined. The spirit of the place, I knew, would stay with me for some time. Suddenly I knew why Madrigal Cottage had felt so familiar to me. I had felt at home.

CHAPTER 29

Back to Dagenham

"You're late! Where did you get to?"

When we arrived in Dagenham, Lew was at the door, angry. Then, just as quickly, he appeared relieved to see us.

"We were getting lunch stuff, Dad!"

"I told him that's what you were doing, but he wouldn't listen." Pam sounded a little exasperated. "How are you, Denis, alright? Hello, Katie."

My cousin had arrived in Dagenham an hour earlier, around noon. Although we were coming from different places, Lew had somehow expected us to arrive together and when we had not, he had become anxious. Fortunately he calmed down and kept himself busy putting out cold meats and cheeses and sausage rolls onto plates. We sat down for lunch within ten minutes.

"Had a good time, then? You and Frances and Katie? In that little cottage of yours? Saw what you wanted to see"

"We did, Dad." I smiled, remembering "I love coming back here now, Dad, I really do."

"Well, that's how it should be!" said Lew, quite definitely.

While we ate, I said I had tried to get Frances and Kate to eat cockles and winkles on the harbor wall at Broadstairs. Frances groaned, and Kate made oooh-yuk sounds. I changed tack.

"Remember the cockle teas we had on Sundays, Mum?"

"No, I can't say I do," said Jessie, tearing at a slice of bread.

"Of course you do," scolded Lew. He went on to explain, mainly for Frances' benefit but also, perhaps, to remind Mum, what Sunday teas were like.

"The fish man showed up, on Sunday afternoon. Sold prawns and winkles and cockles, whelks and shrimps. Never much liked

304

whelks. Jessie got the prawns, I got the winkles, and Denis had the cockles. Lots of vinegar and pepper and bread and butter. Lovely."

"I rather like shrimps," said Pam, quietly. "We enjoyed that sort of seafood tea, ourselves."

Lew grinned at the shared memories. Seafood, an occasional Sunday afternoon treat, was sold from the back of a van that dripped with briny ice water. A few honks of the horn were enough to attract regular customers. The crustaceans were never weighed out, just scooped up in pint and half-pint tin mugs. Mum always wanted big, pinky-red prawns, the most expensive crustacean he sold. "Knock 'em down," Lew would say, and the fishmonger would reluctantly bash the mug on his makeshift counter, bending a sea whisker or two but allowing for a few more pricey prawns. The cockles were like very tiny clams, and they were my favorite, along with winkles, but eating them required patience and a little skill. Needles or hat pins would be distributed along with saucers filled with vinegar and pepper. Using a needle, I would flip off the winkle cap, then twist inside the shell and pull out the tiny crustacean. Rather than eat one at a time, I preferred "winkling" out a whole bunch and making a sandwich.

"We didn't always get prawns," said Jessie, half remembering.

"No, *we* didn't." Lew cast a knowing smile in my direction. "You're right there, gel!"

After the table was cleared, I popped upstairs as I always did, to have a look at my old room. Lew's room now. And there it was. The inhaler he had forgotten to bring to the cottage. It was a big, old-fashioned looking thing. I went back downstairs.

"Do you want a drink?" asked Mum.

"No darling, we've got a bit of a drive after we leave you."

"Where you going then?"

"We're staying close to the airport, Mum, before we go home."

"Home? Where's that then?" asked Mum.

"You know, Mum," I said with a slight smile.

"America!" said Lew testily.

"You live all the way over there!" Mum sounded surprised, as she always did. "You sure you don't want a drink?"

We had reached that part of the afternoon when food had been eaten, plates cleared, and all the remaining bits of conversation had been teased out until no words were left. We all hugged and kissed good-bye. Mum plonked back down in her chair, teary-eyed, as the rest of us went outside.

"You'll call us, then, before you go." Lew said it like an order.

"As always. And when we get home, I'll call then." I said.

"You do that," growled Lew. "Wait there. I'll get your mother—"

Lew went back inside the house. Pam gave me a hug.

"He seems so sad," I said.

"I know. He doesn't think he's ever going to see you again."

"Oh, that!" I smiled with some relief. "He's been saying that for the past ten years."

"I know," Pam said softly, as if she knew something I did not.

Lew helped Mum out to the front porch. And there they stood. Mum seemed happy again, pleased to see me. Lew's face remained stoic, grim, willing the tears to stay in place. I had a grin fixed onto my face, a mask covering what I felt but could not show.

"Well, Dad, next year then. We'll find somewhere else! A bit closer." I tried to be optimistic.

"No, son, we can't… We won't be able to manage it." He sounded firm.

"We'll do something else then. Day trips. We'll stay in London, then come down. We'll see you both here, in Dagenham. I'll still bring the Jack!"

"That'll be handy!" At that, Lew's face crinkled into a bit of smile. The tears held. "I'll always be with you, son," he said quietly. "I'll always be with you."

After leaving my parents' home, my old home, we drove around the corner to Campbell Infant School. Kate wanted to see my old school.

We pulled up at the infant school and got out for a better look. A long, single-story building with a high fence and big, wrought-iron gate. I remembered an assembly hall in the center of the building, with classrooms ranging out on either side like slightly curved horns. At both ends were outdoor toilet facilities, one for girls, one for boys. Between the slight curve of the school was a playground with a sandbox, usually covered because the sand was invariably wet.

"Is this where you were naughty?" Kate grinned, wanting to know more.

"Well, I was a little bit naughty in this school—"

Kate insisted I tell her what I'd done. I was happy to do so, happy for the distraction. Our school day always began with a religious assembly. We sang a couple of hymns, then enjoyed an uplifting reading or an encouraging chat from the headmistress. At the end of the assembly, the Lord's Prayer was intoned by the entire school, our heads bowed, eyes closed. It was during this plea for forgiveness I got into trouble. For some long-forgotten reason, I started fighting with the boy next to me. It began with nudging. Then pushing. I kicked him. He kicked back. Then we really got into it. Our heads were still bowed in prayer, eyes tightly shut, so we had no idea the entire school was watching. "The power and the glory for—" Suddenly, shockingly, we were pulled apart. Eyes shot open. Surrounded by staring kids. Lots of open mouths. Amen. Grabbed by our jacket collars, we were hauled up before the headmistress and soundly admonished. Quite right, too. It's one thing to intone the Lord's Prayer before a battle, quite another to start one during it. We were told to remain on the stage and face the wall, heads bowed. Alas, that was not the end of it. I started to mumble and grumble to myself, something I apparently still do. I must have mumbled too loudly. Once again I was facing the headmistress. Plump wattle shook with rage. I was spun around and smacked several times on the back of my legs, behind the knees. It stung painfully because I was wearing short trousers. When I got home that afternoon, I still had the white mark of the headmistress' thin and bony fingers across the back of my legs.

"What did nanny say?" asked Kate, giggling. "Was she mad they hit you?"

"Not really. It was the way it was then," I said. "So, what do you think of my infant school?"

Kate looked through the railings and asked if she could play in the sandpit. I took the hint. We got back in the car and drove slowly along Langley Crescent, one last look toward Romsey Road. I was moments from my old home. I wondered if Mum and Dad were still standing outside. What a daft thought! I realized they would be back indoors tucked up around the gas fire, watching the telly, Pam serving tea and making an inordinate fuss of them. I felt good about that. I drove past Castle Green, then onto the highway towards the Orbital.

The roads from Dagenham to Dartford had been widened, streamlined with curvy fly-overs, smooth, steel crash barriers, and pencil-thin highway lights. An elongated black sculpture on a rain-stained foundation of gray. The journey would take no time at all.

Ford's, Saturday morning pictures at the Grange, Becontree Station, the fish shop, the Fanshaw, the mobile eel and pie shop, dog shit on the sidewalks, Checquers Corner, the endless stream of traffic, the German bakery, the Dandy and Topper comics Lew brought home on Fridays, the tiny joke shop near the Briggs Factory, my brother's violin playing, my dog Rex, the sludgy ditch-like stream through Gorsebrook Park, the scouts on Fridays, Knock-down Ginger blocks away, St. George's Day Parade, Sunday School, Harvest Festival, the allotments dirt-packed with vegetables, horses running at Wincanton, the billiard hall below the shops on the railway hill, the gothic drabness of St. Albans, the grit that swirled up from unwashed streets into my eyes, the remnants of the old Thames marsh, the ships hooting on New Year's Eve, my parents home on a Saturday night with bingo winnings, the smell of talc and drink and cold, the sound of their laughter. All of it was swept beneath an elevated highway that threw a permanent shadow across Dagenham, across my past. The journey only took fifteen minutes. No time at all.

Epilogue

TIME PASSES INTO HISTORY, and the people we love pass into memory.

Jessie and Lew may not have shared our subsequent adventures in England, but neither were they far away. Wherever we gadded about, whatever sight we saw, there was always a cafe or a pub close by. Quite easy to imagine my folks nestled into a little alcove of an old saloon bar or in the bay window seat of a teashop, having just shooed us off on another sightseeing jaunt. Just as easy to imagine what they might have been saying.

"Buggered if I know what they want to see. There's nothing there! Just ruins." Lew growled as he stirred his tea while scrunching down on a piece of hot buttered toast.

"I wouldn't have minded seeing it, meself."

"What you talking about, woman! You wouldn't want to go traipsing after them!"

"Don't tell me what I can and can't do. Hell next!"

Ghrrr.

Ignoring him, Jessie peered out of the window into the narrowing street, watching as we turned a corner and disappeared from view. Lew would be watching as well, shaking his head, smiling gently.

"Now come on, Jessie, gel! Drink your tea before it gets cold. They'll be back."

So Mum would get on with her tea, and both of them would be quite content to sit in the warmth until we returned. Then Jessie would beam her widest smile, and Lew would stagger to his feet to greet us, ramrod straight, eager to know if we had seen all we wanted to see. Not quite, Dad, not quite.

AUTHOR'S NOTE

I AM BLESSED, or cursed, with a memory that snags trifles, incidents, and gobs of conversation quite accurately. Notes and photos also helped trigger memories and brought images flooding back, like scenes from a favorite movie.

Even so, there were gaps my wife, Frances Erlebacher, helped me bridge. Her invaluable insights and recollections enabled me to recall in greater detail many of our experiences. And it was Frances who convinced me to take a break from plays and write up our travels and adventures. I wrote a few chapters, got the thumbs up, and ploughed on, never knowing where it would lead and how it would turn out. Never realizing how much I would learn about my family, my country, and myself. Frances edited as I wrote, offering encouragement, suggestions, and sage advice along the way and never losing heart in the project.

So you can blame Frances. It's her fault I was yanked back to England and became a tourist in my old country and the reluctant (at first) writer of this book. And for that, I am eternally grateful. I would also like to thank a few others who were in my corner throughout the Prodigal Years. Heather Hoerle, my one-woman cheering section. Bob Kaylor, who couldn't wait to read more about my funny old folks. Dan Snodderly, who edited and proofed and advised throughout. Jim Grove for our lovely website and endless technical advice. And the stalwart Andy Zvara, who always believed it would happen. Last but not least, I want to thank Jessie and Lew for always letting me follow my own path, and Kate for bringing a twinkle to aging eyes.

ABOUT THE BOOK

YEAR ONE, DAGENHAM, is in fact three annual visits telescoped into one. The following years happened pretty much as I have described them. At least that's how I remember it. I've changed details of some of our rental accommodations for reasons that will become apparent. Names of family members remain the same, but for privacy I've changed the names of friends and folks we met on our travels—with the exception of Kate at Walmer Castle.

The sites, towns, and villages featured in the book are all within a half-day trip from London. I hope you will discover and enjoy them as much as I did. You'll find links to many of the places we visited in the "our travels" section of our website, ayankbacktoengland.com.